Dictatorship and Development

Rafael Leonidas Trujillo, Dictator of the Dominican Republic (1960 picture).

DICTATORSHIP and DEVELOPMENT
The Methods of Control in
Trujillo's Dominican Republic

HOWARD J. WIARDA

UNIVERSITY OF FLORIDA PRESS

GAINESVILLE / 1968

R. W. BRADBURY
Professor of Economics

EDMUND E. HEGEN
Assistant Professor
of Geography

T. LYNN SMITH
Graduate Research Professor
of Sociology

FELICITY TRUEBLOOD
Assistant Professor
of Comprehensive English

A University of Florida Press Publication

SPONSORED BY THE
CENTER FOR LATIN AMERICAN STUDIES

PRINTED BY STORTER PRINTING COMPANY
GAINESVILLE, FLORIDA

TO

Iêda Siqueira Wiarda

Preface

THE WEAKNESS of political institutions and the dysfunctional aspects of the political process in the post-Trujillo Dominican Republic were most clearly demonstrated in 1965 by the breakdown of the system into revolution and civil war. Though some of the problems which the revolution unmistakably brought to the surface were products of the immediately preceding years, other perhaps more basic problems were of an earlier vintage, going back to the lengthy 1930-61 dictatorship of Trujillo. Trujillo's rule marked a turning point in Dominican history, and the more recent difficulties of the country served to demonstrate how pervasive was the legacy of his regime.

Not only is an understanding of the Trujillo dictatorship necessary in order to better comprehend present-day Dominican politics, but the regime is also important and worthy of study in its own right. For Trujillo's system of control was unique in Latin America—a curious, complex, colorful, and most interesting kind of dictatorship which had few precedents in hemispheric traditions. This analysis thus focuses on the methods and nature of Trujillo's dictatorial control and seeks to offer some conclusions concerning the legacy bequeathed the Dominican Republic by his rule. It is neither a complete history of the "Era of Trujillo" nor a biography of the Generalissimo, though the highly personal nature of his rule makes some consideration of Trujillo's life and personality necessary. Rather, it looks at his dictatorship in historical and comparative perspective, presents some hypotheses concerning theories of dictatorship and of socioeconomic-political development, and suggests the place of the Trujillo regime within these frameworks.

Materials for this study and for a planned subsequent volume dealing with the post-Trujillo period were gathered through interviews and in libraries and archives in both the United States and the Dominican Republic. Research in the Dominican Republic, conducted on six different occasions for periods ranging from a few days to ten months, was aided by grants from the Caribbean Research Institute of the University of Florida, the Fulbright-Hays program, and the Faculty Research Council of the University of Massachusetts. A debt of gratitude is owed to these sponsoring organizations.

The author also wishes to thank a number of others who have contributed in a major way to this study: Professors Harry Kantor, Manning J. Dauer, and L. N. McAlister of the University of Florida; Professor Donald C. Worcester of Texas Christian University; Ing. Luis Crouch of Santiago de los Caballeros, Dominican Republic; Mr. Abraham F. Lowenthal of Harvard University—all of whom have read and commented upon an earlier draft of this study; Vetilio J. Alfau Durán, Julio J. Julia, and their staff at the Archivo Nacional; the staff at the library of the Universidad Autónoma de Santo Domingo; the hundreds of Dominicans who submitted to interviews; and Iêda Siqueira Wiarda, herself a political scientist, whose comments on this and other manuscripts have always been most helpful. None of these organizations or people are responsible for whatever errors of fact or interpretation may appear in the book; the mistakes are solely the author's.

HOWARD J. WIARDA

University of Massachusetts, Amherst

Contents

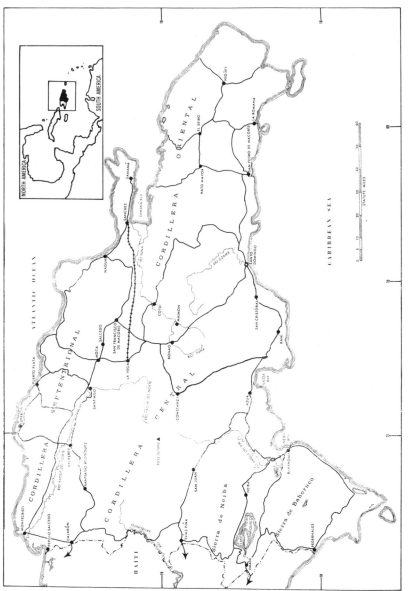

The Dominican Republic

I. Introduction

THE DICTATORSHIP of Generalissimo Rafael Leonidas Trujillo Molina in the Dominican Republic was perhaps more absolute than any previous dictatorial system in Latin American history. For thirty-one years, from his takeover of the presidency in 1930 until his assassination in 1961, Trujillo ruled his nation with an iron hand. He was considered to be, and indeed took great personal pride in being, the dean of the strong men of the Western world: he ruled longer than any other leader in Latin America in the twentieth century and, at the time of his death, had been in power longer than any living dictator in the world.[1]

This study explores the mechanisms and techniques, the nature and functioning, the legacy and implications, of the Trujillo regime. It is concerned with the political dynamics of what was possibly the tightest and most personal dictatorship in the world, and attempts to place the Dominican regime within a framework of comparative political systems. In order to understand more fully the workings of the Trujillo dictatorship, it is thus necessary to

1. Trujillo's only rival to this last claim is Antonio de Oliveira Salazar of Portugal. Both Trujillo and Salazar held positions of power in the 1920's; but while Trujillo took over the presidency in 1930, Salazar did not become premier until 1932. Trujillo's death in 1961, however, enabled Salazar to surpass him in longevity of rule.

examine and consider both the physical and theoretical settings of his regime.

The Physical Setting

The Dominican Republic is located midway in the long chain of Antillean islands that stretches across the Caribbean from Florida to Venezuela. Occupying the eastern two-thirds of the island traditionally known as Hispaniola, it has 19,000 square miles of territory (about equal to that of Vermont and New Hampshire combined).

Though the Dominican Republic shares Hispaniola with Haiti, the two countries have little else in common. Haiti has one-third of the island's area but two-thirds of its people: five million as opposed to a population of around three and a half million in the Dominican Republic. The eastern end of the island is culturally Latin and Spanish-speaking while the western end is French- or patois-speaking and in many ways culturally African. Both countries, however, have traditionally shared the problems of grinding poverty, tempestuous and divisive political histories, the almost complete absence of democratic or constitutional traditions, and enormous social and economic gaps between rich and poor.[2]

It has been estimated that about 10 per cent of the Dominican Republic's population is white, another 20 per cent Negro, and the remaining 70 per cent mulatto in varying degrees.[3] There are isolated pockets of Chinese, Japanese, and West Indian peoples scattered around the country; but very few strains of the area's indigenous Indian population remain. Prejudice is more social and economic than racial, though it is notable that the traditional ruling elite is almost exclusively white and that in some areas the lines between the several shades of mulatto are sharply drawn.

The Dominican Republic is officially described as being 98.2 per cent Roman Catholic, 1.4 per cent Protestant, and 0.4 per cent other. Though Catholicism has traditionally been the state religion,

2. Raymond E. Crist, "Cultural Dichotomy on the Island of Hispaniola." Short citations are used in the notes; for complete information see the alphabetical listings in the Bibliography.
3. William S. Stokes, Latin American Politics, p. 17. These estimates are probably more accurate than the official figures of 28.1 per cent white, 11.5 per cent Negro, and 60.4 per cent mixed. Donald S. Castro et al. (eds.), Statistical Abstract of Latin America, p. 23.

religious freedom exists; and though the country is overwhelmingly Catholic, Catholicism does not seem to be as strong a force as it is in several Latin American countries.[4]

Most Dominicans are rural. Only 35 per cent of the population live in towns of 1,000 persons or more, and the remaining 65 per cent are considered rural. Of those classified as urban, 37 per cent live in the capital city of Santo Domingo, whose population is approaching 350,000, and the second largest city, Santiago de los Caballeros, has close to 100,000 inhabitants. There are no other major cities in the country, but a number of towns have populations ranging from 10,000 to 30,000. While Santo Domingo on the southern coast is by far the largest city in the country, the primary nucleus of population concentration is in the northern Cibao Valley, the center of the landed "first families" of the Dominican Republic. The overall population density is 140 people per square mile, a low figure for the West Indies but high in comparison with the rest of Latin America.[5]

Because its landforms are the most complex in the Antilles, the Dominican Republic has a wide variety of climatic patterns. It is a tropical country, but the conditions stemming from its location are moderated by high elevations, the trade winds, and insularity. The four principal mountain ranges which cross the country have historically made transportation and communications between different areas difficult and hindered national integration.[6]

The Dominican Republic also has a wide variety of largely unexplored and untapped mineral resources. The known minerals include gold, petroleum, iron, bauxite, marble, nickel, sulphur, copper, and rock salt. Few of these minerals are being fully exploited, though it is doubtful whether the deposits of most of them are extensive.

The outstanding resource of the country, however, is an abundance of good agricultural land. Between the mountain ranges lie some of the most fertile valleys to be found in the Americas. Chief of these are the northern Vega Real and the Cibao, whose coal

4. Castro, p. 22; and J. Lloyd Mecham, *Church and State in Latin America,* p. 354.

5. Dirección General de Estadística y Censos, *República Dominicana en Cifras,* Cuadro 2; and Donald R. Dyer, "Distribution of Population on Hispaniola."

6. See the appendix entitled "Quisqueya: A Physical Description" in Selden Rodman, *Quisqueya,* pp. 175-76.

black soils make it the agricultural heartland of the nation. Throughout the island are many smaller, but not less fertile, oases of rich land. Estimates in 1960 indicated that 23 per cent of the country's total area was being cultivated and that another 12 per cent was in pasture.[7]

In the midst of this natural wealth, the vast majority of the population remains extremely poor. As compared with a per capita income for all of Latin America of $325 per year, that of the Dominican Republic is variously estimated at between $189 and $235 annually.[8] The statistics do not tell the full story, for most of this wealth has traditionally been concentrated in a very few hands. The rest of the population lives in abysmal poverty, as close to the subsistence level as anywhere in Latin America. The majority of Dominicans are without adequate food, water, and housing, have no medical or health facilities, no educational or recreational opportunities, no electricity, insufficient land, and above all, no hope. The results of the grinding poverty may be seen in the bloated bellies of the children and the deformed bodies of many adults.

The cornerstone of the cash economy is sugar cane. Sugar, by value, supplies more than half of the country's exports, while cacao, coffee, rice, tobacco, bananas, a few other crops, and beef have also been produced for the world market. The Dominican economy is thus tied intimately to the world price for her products, and fluctuations in the international market, primarily in the price of sugar, have made and unmade Dominican governments for half a century. Wages in the agricultural concerns have frequently been less than $1.00 per day, and the seasonal nature of the work means that unemployment rates fluctuate between 30 and 50 per cent.

The nation's poverty is also manifested in its educational system. Though the official figures place the illiteracy rate at 60 per cent, it may run as high as 80-90 per cent in the countryside. From the primary level to the national University the schools have inadequate and poorly trained teachers and few books and teaching aids. Little in the way of practical vocational training is available. Though the Dominican Republic remains primarily an agricul-

7. John P. Augelli, "The Dominican Republic," p. 4.
8. *United Nations Monthly Bulletin of Statistics,* XVII (June, 1963), Table 53. See also "Report on the Dominican Republic," *Latin American Report,* p. 7. The entire issue of the *Report* is devoted to the Dominican Republic.

tural nation, manufacturing and industry developed rapidly during the Trujillo era. Initially, industrialization was confined to the processing of the country's agricultural products, primarily sugar cane, but a number of manufacturing plants were soon established as well. To facilitate economic development, transportation and communications facilities were greatly improved. Three major highways were built which fan out from Santo Domingo to the east, west, and north, connecting all the major cities with the capital; paved secondary roads then feed into these highways, thus creating an effective web over most of the country. These facilities helped Trujillo to unite his diverse, regionally oriented, and fragmented land and to exploit much of its previously unused natural wealth.[9]

While in many respects nature has been bountiful to Hispaniola, history has been considerably less kind. This was well stated by the distinguished United States writer, Washington Irving, who in 1828 wrote that this was "one of the most beautiful islands in the world and doomed to be one of the most unfortunate."[10]

Hispaniola has had many firsts. The island was discovered by Columbus on his first voyage. Santo Domingo, the oldest permanent European city in the New World, was founded on the southern coast. The earliest experiments in Spanish colonial government were conducted here. In Santo Domingo the first vice-regal court and *audiencia* were established and the first university chartered. The colony was also the scene of Latin America's first palace revolution, and the pattern of revolution and upheaval has persisted into modern Dominican history.[11]

From the beginning a rigid, hierarchical social structure was established. Patterning the colony on the model of the Spanish court and society, Columbus' brother Bartolomé and son Diego established themselves and a few others as the nobility, artisans and soldiers as the small middle class, and the natives as servants and slaves. This pattern also persisted into the modern era with the only change being the substitution of African slaves for the native Indians. Class lines were tightly drawn, and few moved from one socioeconomic level to another. The political and social systems were early organized along corporative lines. Juan Bosch persuasively argues that the rigid stratification provided the psy-

9. Augelli, pp. 1-6.
10. Quoted in H. P. Davis, *Black Democracy*, p. 7.
11. Lewis Hanke, *The First Social Experiments in America*.

chological foundations for the rise to power of Trujillo, who was born in the middle sector and aspired above all else to achieve a higher rank.[12]

During the first half-century of Spanish rule Hispaniola flourished, for it served as a base for the expeditions of Pizarro, Balboa, Córtez, and other conquistadores to other islands and the mainland. The more lucrative conquests of Mexico and Peru soon turned the island into a poor way station, however. The indigenous population had all but been exterminated by the diseases the Spaniards carried,[13] and the Europeans had emigrated to the more attractive mainland. By 1550 Hispaniola had been almost abandoned; there was little readily accessible gold or silver, hence the colony was of little value to the crown. Though it experienced a resurgence of prosperity in the eighteenth century, Hispaniola remained the neglected, poverty-ridden tail end of the vast Spanish empire for the better part of three centuries of colonial rule.

The colonial institutions which Spain brought to Hispaniola did not differ markedly from those established in other areas of Latin America. The political structure was one of absolutism, of a hierarchy of despotisms from king to captain general to largely autonomous *hacendado*, all of whom exercised autocratic power within their respective spheres. The system provided no training in self-government or democracy. The Church served as an arm of the government and was characterized by an authoritarianism that paralleled and at times rivaled the State concept. The economy was one of exploitation and of agrarian feudalism, and the considerable natural wealth of the island was siphoned off rather than being used for internal development. Indeed, Spanish Hispaniola throughout its colonial period provided a vivid illustration of the way in which an exploitive colonial government can be an instrument of ruin. The history of continuous spoliation and destruction of human life and wasting of material resources left the country, after the dissolution of the colonial system in the early nineteenth century, with few native traditions or institutions which could have smoothed its transition to independence. The colonial era bequeathed a legacy which the Dominican Republic is still attempting to overcome.

Throughout Hispaniola's history her geographic location at a

12. Juan Bosch, *Trujillo*, p. 21.
13. Santo Domingo provided Hans Zinsser with a major example to prove his thesis in *Rats, Lice, and History*.

strategic point overlooking the entire Caribbean and Central American area has caused the island to be subjected to successive changes of ownership, outside influences, and foreign occupations. Its government has often been determined by the interplay of the great powers, and the covetousness with which these powers have looked upon the island has been symbolized in the title of Sumner Welles' classic history of the Dominican Republic, *Naboth's Vineyard*. French buccaneers settled in the western end of the island in the sixteenth century, and British swashbucklers and pirates invaded the colony in 1586 and 1655. (A cannonball from one of Sir Francis Drake's ships is said to be still lodged in the roof of the Cathedral.) Dutch pirates also sought a conquest, and by the Treaty of Ryswick in 1695 French claims to the western one-third of the island were formally recognized.

After three centuries of Spanish rule, the eastern two-thirds of the island was also ceded to France in 1795. Due to the more pressing needs of her European wars France was not able to effectively occupy the island, and under Toussaint L'Ouverture and Jean Jacques Dessalines the French slave colony successfully revolted against Napoleon's rule and declared its independence. In 1805 Dessalines, Henri Christophe, and their black army invaded the Spanish-speaking end of the island, instilling terror in the white ruling class. With the aid of the English fleet, however, the Haitians were driven out and in 1809 the colony was reunited with Spain.[14]

In 1821 the Spanish colony declared its independence from the mother country. But before help could be secured from Simón Bolívar's Gran Colombia, Haitian columns under Jean Pierre Boyer again overran the island. Haitian occupation from 1822 to 1844 was cruel and barbarous. Indeed, it is the opinion of Welles that the basic cause of the anarchy, unrest, chaos, and dictatorship which characterized Dominican independent history should be attributed to the economic ruin and obliteration of European civilization which occurred during the twenty-two-year Haitian domination.[15]

The Dominican Republic's struggle for independence lasted for half a century; when independence eventually came, Dominicans were ill-prepared for it. Juan Pablo Duarte, the great national independence hero of the Dominican Republic, organized a secret resistance movement, La Trinitaria, which led the struggle, and

14. Rodman, p. 44.
15. Welles, *Naboth's Vineyard*, pp. 900-901.

finally, in 1844 the Haitians were driven out. From that date until 1899 three dictators—Pedro Santana, Buenaventura Báez, and Ulises Heureaux—dominated Dominican history. The Latin American historian Hubert Herring calls all three "brazen opportunists, ready to betray their country for their own ends" and states that "nowhere else has *personalismo*—the rule of the boss—been more persistent than in this weak nation."[16]

Santana and Báez emerged as the two most prominent leaders in the new republic, alternating in power for many years and in the process almost destroying the infant country. Santana became convinced that the nation could no longer defend itself against Haiti's continuous assaults and in 1861 the Dominican Republic was placed under the control of Spain, Santana being named governor-general. Spanish rule proved inept and unprofitable, and in 1865 Isabella II, with a timely push from Dominican forces, withdrew her troops. The idea of a protectorate remained, however, and Báez approached the United States with a plan, but the questionable involvement in the matter of a United States land-speculating company came out and the Senate failed to ratify the treaty.[17]

During the 1870's the country passed through a period of instability which included the return of Báez to the presidency for the fifth time and the coming to power of the country's first, but short-lived, democratic government. The chaos culminated in the emergence of another strong man, Heureaux, in 1882. He ruled the country as dictator for seventeen years, a period described as "perhaps the most pitiless tyranny in the history of Latin America."[18] In his history of the Dominican Republic, *Quisqueya*, Selden Rodman writes that "only by looking ahead to the equally ruthless and 'successful' career of Rafael Leonidas Trujillo Molina in our time can any accurate comparisons be found for the method and madness of Ulises Heureaux." He bought off most of his rivals and subjected the rest to villification, exile, or murder; he employed an army of spies, sent assassins abroad, and enriched himself, his friends, and his relatives at the expense of the people. Rodman concludes: "Only in respect to the techniques of the modern totalitarian state, still to be invented by Hitler and Stalin— the single party, the mass rallies, the propaganda mills, the re-

16. *A History of Latin America*, pp. 425-26.
17. See Dexter Perkins, *La Cuestión de Santo Domingo*.
18. Herring, *A History of Latin America*, p. 426.

writing of history, the indoctrination of children, the racial persecution, the military juggernaut—did Ulises Heureaux yield anything in refinements of despotism to his infamous successor" (page 92).

Following Heureaux's death in 1899, the country returned to the same kind of chaos which had gone before. Four revolutions took place and five presidents gained office in six years. Heureaux' and his successors' policy of raising finances by simply printing more money and floating ruinous foreign loans brought the country to the verge of bankruptcy. As a result the foreign creditors began threatening to use force to collect. In 1905 the United States took over the administration of the customs receivership in the hope of averting European intervention, but this did not prevent the political situation from deteriorating still further. After years of continuous upheaval, which included the ascension of the archbishop to the presidency, President Wilson in 1916 authorized the United States Marines already in the country to take control.[19]

During the United States occupation, 1916-24, the Dominican Congress was suspended, the Supreme Court stripped of its authority, and the military governor granted power to rule by decree. Roads were built and sanitation, communications, and education improved, but the Marines frequently assumed arbitrary power and often abused their authority. Perhaps the major historical effect was the creation of a modern, unified constabulary, for it was through this body that Trujillo rose to power and took over the country. Noel Henríquez called him "the bastard son of the occupation forces," and it is for this reason that the United States is often held accountable by Dominicans for the entire Trujillo era.[20]

A new constitution was promulgated in 1924 and Horacio Vásquez was elected president. During his term of office a combination of relative freedom and order existed for the first time in two decades. But Vásquez alienated his friends and enemies alike by filling many government posts with his relatives and by extending his tenure from four to six years. He became ill in 1929, the same year in which the Dominican economy was critically hurt by the world depression. The following year a revolution led by Rafael Estrella Ureña was launched against the tottering government. The

19. See Enrique Apolinar Henríquez, *Episodios Imperialistas*, pp. 270-90.
20. *La verdad sobre Trujillo*, pp. 92-93.

National Army, by this time under the firm control of Trujillo, failed to defend the regime and it quickly fell. In 1930 Trujillo gained the presidency and his thirty-one-year reign began.

Prior to 1930, then, the Dominican Republic remained primarily a traditional, pre-industrial, agrarian society. There were few organized groups within the country, and political power was largely determined by the interplay of "first family" relationships. Rival caudillos jockeyed to gain the favor of rag-tag, unprofessional armed bands. The political system was still essentially unintegrated, diffused, undifferentiated, unstructured and unorganized, particularistic, and traditionalistic. If it were not for the fact that its principal crop was sugar, the Dominican Republic in 1930 might have resembled the stereotype of a sleepy, poverty-ridden "banana republic."

The history of the Dominican Republic had been characterized by successive dictatorships and revolutions, anarchy and civil wars, foreign interventions that drained its wealth, and economic and social problems that appeared unsolvable. The Dominican pattern had been one of recurrent periods of utter chaos and of absolute despotisms; its leadership seemed to have correspondingly alternated between ineffectual poets and bloodthirsty tyrants. It was a poor and underdeveloped, semifeudal country. The lines of cleavage in the political society were deep. During its independent history, between 1844 and 1930, the presidency had changed hands fifty times (an average of once every 1.7 years) and there had been thirty revolutions (an average of one every 2.9 years). It was second in the world only to Venezuela in the number of constitutions which had been enacted. This spectacle caused Miguel Angel Monclús in his *El Caudillismo en la República Dominicana* to cry out, "Where will it stop?" (page 157). It stopped, at least temporarily, with the establishment of the Trujillo dictatorship.

The Theoretical Framework

The Trujillo regime, as we shall see, was clearly a very severe kind of dictatorship, but beyond this, was it a dictatorship of any particular genre? Was Trujillo another in the long line of Dominican caudillos or men on horseback, or was his regime somehow different? If his dictatorship, as some have claimed, was tending more towards totalitarianism, how could such a complex, "modern" kind of dictatorship arise in such a traditional, underdeveloped society? And are there any implications which a study of his regime may yield concerning comparable systems? In order to provide answers to these questions, a consideration of patterns of dictatorship and of the process of national social change and political development is required.

Particularly in the post-World-War-II period, dictatorship in its many forms has become an increasingly important subject of concern for many students of comparative politics. This is not to say that dictatorship has not fascinated political analysts in the past. From the founding of political science by Plato and Aristotle to the present, much has been written concerning tyrannies, dictatorships, despotisms, autocracies, absolutism, Caesarism, Bonapartism, caudilloism, authoritarianism, and totalitarianism. The analysis of dictatorship, however, has been especially stimulated in the twentieth century, first, by the rise of totalitarianism in the Soviet Union, Nazi Germany, and possibly other countries, and, second, by the trend toward authoritarianism in many of the new or developing nations.

The synonymous use of a large number of terms (dictatorship, authoritarianism, and the like) to describe a wide variety of political systems and practices has led to a good deal of unclear thinking and writing and makes a number of definitions and classifications concerning different kinds of dictatorship desirable. Most of the commonly used terms, in addition, have acquired emotive meanings which have further impaired their usefulness. Not only are terms like "tyranny" or "totalitarian" used for labeling policies or governments of which one may disapprove, but they may also tend to obscure the realities of political systems in nationalistic arguments. In Latin American politics, for example, exiles from Trujillo's Dominican Republic, Alfredo Stroessner's Paraguay, and other dictatorships have on occasion argued at length over which system was the most "totalitarian," as though the degree of totalitarianism were almost a matter of national pride. Though the examples could easily be extended, it seems clear that greater care and precision in the use of these terms would be helpful.

Those scholars, however, who have attempted more technical definitions and more precise formulations of categories of dictatorships have tended to use rather static models. The most commonly accepted distinction is made between traditional dictatorship or authoritarianism and modern dictatorship or totalitarianism. While this distinction is in some respects quite useful, it tends to ignore the more dynamic transitional factors involved in social and political change. Further, it tends to lead to dichotomous, either/or thinking and generally fails to take into account that even in the most totalitarian systems the controls of the dictatorship have not been "total" and that the lines between authoritarianism and totalitarianism may be matters of degree and not necessarily of kind. It may be (and, indeed, is the argument of this study) that a conceptual framework which relates typologies of dictatorships to theories of political development and modernization, and which thus allows for numerous transitional kinds of regimes, would be a more useful theoretical tool than those which have been most commonly employed in the past. While the distinction between traditional dictatorship and modern totalitarianism is thus of limited utility, it does provide a convenient starting point for discussing some of the relevant literature.

Traditional dictatorship.—Historically, there have been many kinds of dictatorships. Though varying in a great number of aspects, these traditional dictatorships have exhibited a number of important common features. The most basic similarities between them also help us arrive at a rough, working definition of dictatorship: a system in which the ruler(s) is not responsible to other elements in the society for what he does. Dictatorship may be looked at as a system of one-way controls in which there are no effective checks and balances on the ruler(s). If one prefers to use the term autocracy, then the ruler is the *autos* who alone wields power, making decisions without the consent of others in the political system. The autocrat is able to "dictate" to the political community without allowing it to effectively participate and share in decision-making. The term authoritarian also denotes a system in which the dictator, king, *junta*, committee, or party attempts to monopolize power and refuses to share it. Concentrated authority exercised arbitrarily, which may exist in a wide variety of forms, seems to be the most common characteristic of dictatorship.[21]

In traditional dictatorships, ordinarily, the rule which the dictator exercises is of necessity limited to military and political controls.

21. The opposite of autocracy or concentrated power would be heterocracy, a system in which authority is shared, again in a number of variations. A more common way of referring to heterocracy would be to call it "pluralistic democracy." See Carl J. Friedrich and Zbigniew Brzezinski, *Totalitarian Dictatorship and Autocracy*, pp. 3-4; and Karl Loewenstein, *Political Power and the Governmental Process*, pp. 55-56.

While the traditional dictator may thus monopolize arms and control the military apparatus, the structure of the government, and the machinery of the state, he will not normally seek to monopolize such nonmilitary and nonpolitical areas of life as the family, education, or thought processes. As a rule, authoritarian regimes will not seek to control all socioeconomic relationships. The level of technology in the system simply makes such "total" dictatorship nearly impossible.

While the similarities among different kinds of traditional dictatorships are quite striking, some old-style dictatorships introduced new techniques which gave them a superficial resemblance to modern totalitarianism. Thus Caesarism and Bonapartism, both based primarily on military and political controls, added a personal appeal to and the corresponding support of the masses. Pharaonic Egypt operated under a state-planned economy and deified its rulers. Some theocratic city-states have also been cited as the precursors of totalitarian systems. None of these earlier regimes, however, had the complete syndrome of controls characteristic of modern totalitarianism—totalitarianism seems to be a much more complex kind of dictatorship than were any of these traditional regimes.[22]

Caudilloism is the peculiarly Hispanic kind of traditional dictatorship.[23] Present in the histories of both Spain and Portugal, it seems to be particularly prevalent in the Spanish colonies in Latin America. Caudilloism therefore merits special attention because the Trujillo regime is often considered to be a caudillo-like dictatorship.

The caudillo (roughly translated, "strong man" or "man on horseback") was perhaps the most characteristic form of political leadership in independent Latin America until the present century. Caudillos galloped in and out of the presidential palace with frequent regularity. For many of the Latin American nations, caudillo rule alternated with periods of disorder, and the assumption

22. For a discussion of some of the variations among the traditional dictatorships see especially William Ebenstein, *Totalitarianism;* Karl Wittfogel, *Oriental Despotism;* and Barrington Moore, Jr., "Totalitarian Elements in Pre-Industrial Societies."
23. For an excellent collection of readings on caudilloism, see Hugh M. Hamill, Jr. (ed.), *Dictatorship in Spanish America.* The literature on the subject is vast. Especially useful for comparative purposes are Samuel E. Finer, *The Man on Horseback;* J. Fred Rippy, "Dictatorship in Spanish America"; R. A. Humphreys, "Latin America"; and Magnus Mörner, "Caudillos y Militares en la evolución hispanoamericana."

of power by these strong men was often the only alternative to chaotic factional strife or even civil war. The history of much of Latin America during the first hundred years or so of independent countries often reads very much like an endless listing of successive caudillos.[24]

A highly personal concept of leadership evolved in most of Latin America, but caudilloism implies more than merely charismatic authority. Caudillo rule was more prevalent, significantly, in the nineteenth century semifeudal Latin America before the onset of modern industrialization and its accompanying sociopolitical effects. The country ruled by a caudillo usually resembles a large hacienda and its leader plays the role of national *patrón*. The *patrón* often possesses large landholdings and controls many businesses and commerce. Nepotism is prevalent, and the family of the caudillo frequently shares the wealth and spoils that accrue with the acquisition of the presidency. Political power may be thought of as a concession, and the concessionaire tends to use his office for self-advantage and enrichment. The caudillo is usually viewed as a great national father who must take care of his humble children and who must exercise tutelage over his ignorant people.[25]

The means by which the caudillo maintains himself in power are typically (1) control over the armed forces, and (2) control over the apparatus of government. As one student of caudilloism has stated, "one normally thinks of a caudillo as a military man, almost literally a man on horseback, who is at the same time the political boss and absolute ruler of his country."[26] The military thus usually provides the ultimate backbone of a caudillo dictatorship, though the regime need not necessarily be overly oppressive; and the caudillo usually remains in office by extending his term beyond the constitutional limitations or by working through puppet presidents.

The military or para-military caudillos were often closely aligned with the traditional, semifeudal socioeconomic order. The Church, the landed elite, and the armed forces frequently saw that they had a common interest in preserving the status quo of the old

---

24. For attempts to explain caudilloism within a conceptual framework of comparative political development, see Fred R. von der Mehden, *Politics of the Developing Nations*, Chapter 3; and Bernard E. Brown, *New Directions in Comparative Politics, passim.*
25. R. A. Gómez, *Government and Politics in Latin America*, pp. 97-99.
26. Charles E. Chapman, "The Age of the Caudillos."

order. In most of the Latin American countries, traditional society was thus perpetuated into the twentieth century.[27]

Caudilloism in Latin America was not unlike the other kinds of traditional dictatorships previously discussed. In writing of caudillo regimes William W. Pierson and Federico G. Gil were reminded of such classic dictators of history as Dionysius, Caesar, and Napoleon, and concluded, "One would find in a study of each of these men as ruler an imperative demand for order; an effort to secure better administrative service, as in the collection of taxes; a reliance on military support; a building program—roadways, buildings, monuments, and public works; a foreign policy calculated to arouse patriotism; and some one specially favored policy, such as the grant of opportunities to an oppressed class, the encouragement of prosperity, or the extension of the national domain. These famous dictators were intolerant of criticism and inclined to limit popular participation in public affairs."[28]

Viewed in this framework classic Latin American caudilloism of the nineteenth and early twentieth centuries does not differ altogether from the authoritarianism which has become prevalent in the new states. While beginning their independent life in the post-World-War-II period at least formally as constitutional democracies, many of these new nations have evolved toward strongman or dictatorial rule. The authoritarian systems which have been established in many African, Middle Eastern, and Southeast Asian states represent other variations in the general category of more-or-less traditional dictatorships.[29]

It should remain clear that all of the various types of traditional dictatorships changed over time and that the basic similarities among them should not be overstated. What they had in common, nevertheless, may be emphasized: no matter how dictatorial in certain areas of control—primarily the military and the political—they seldom exercised complete dominance over all aspects of human existence and were hence not "total." However absolute in

27. See Roger M. Haigh, "The Creation and Control of a Caudillo," for an interesting case study of the relations between a caudillo and his society's dominant kinship elite.

28. *Governments of Latin America*, p. 139.

29. The literature on authoritarianism in the new states is becoming extensive. See, for example, Martin L. Kilson, "Authoritarian and Single Party Tendencies in African Politics"; Rupert Emerson, *From Empire to Nation*, pp. 271-92; Zbigniew Brzezinski, "The Politics of Underdevelopment"; and St. Clair Drake, "Traditional Authority and Social Action in Former British West Africa."

some aspects of human existence, the traditional dictatorships were still limited—limited by such factors as feeble lines of communications and frequently by the mutual contractual obligations on the part of both ruled and rulers. Total control (totalitarianism) did not become effectively possible until the present century.

Modern totalitarianism.—It has often been argued that totalitarianism is *sui generis*, an historically unique form of dictatorship peculiar to this age of advanced technology and mass society. By its very name, the controls which the totalitarian dictator exercises over his people are not limited but total; no facet of existence in a totalitarian dictatorship can be permitted to remain free from control by the regime. As Benito Mussolini once wrote, "The Fascist concept of the state is all-embracing; outside of it no human or spiritual values may exist, much less have any value. Thus understood, Fascism is totalitarianism and the Fascist State, as a synthesis and a unit which includes all values, interprets, develops, and lends additional power to the whole life of a people."[30]

It is in this matter of "total" control over all aspects of life that totalitarianism is said to be sharply differentiated from the various traditional kinds of dictatorship. The control which the traditional dictatorships exercised, as has been emphasized here, was usually limited to the political and military realms. Other areas of existence, however, such as the family, religion, education, thought processes, and so forth, were often independent of official direction. Like the political-military authoritarianism of history, modern totalitarianism controls the political and military structures; but it goes far beyond politics and seeks to control man's whole being, his thinking as well as his institutions. This kind of total control has become possible only in modern times since it depends on the modern technology of communications, modern forms of organization, and the modern technology of terror. The historic kinds of dictatorship may have sought this type of total domination but the effectiveness of their means was limited. Caesar and Napoleon, oriental despots, and Latin American caudillos issued commands or decrees governing many areas of life, but they could not fully suppress criticism by invading privacy, exact universal obedience through a technologically efficient terror, nor

---

30. Quoted in Robert C. Tucker, "Towards a Comparative Politics of Movement Regimes," p. 281.

impose thought control through an official ideology.[31] All this stands in marked contrast to those totalitarian systems which emerged in the post-World-War-I years. The wedding of twentieth century science and technology has meant that present-day dictators now have unprecedented means of effective control and oppression, and some have not hesitated to employ them.

It matters little, then, in the actual functioning and practice of totalitarian regimes whether they are of the Left or Right, whether Communist or Fascist. Mussolini's Italy, Hitler's Germany, and Stalin's Soviet Union were obviously not wholly alike, differing in their ideological underpinnings, historical antecedents, and so forth;[32] yet they were sufficiently alike in their methods of control to enable students to compare and contrast them in a way which yielded significant and meaningful relationships, both theoretically and practically. This study proceeds on the assumption that such comparative methods and techniques are useful.

While it is generally agreed that totalitarianism in any one of a number of forms and "isms" is related to modern, technological and industrial society, scholars have differed concerning its essence. Thus Hannah Arendt saw "atomization"—the destruction of all personal allegiances, groupings, or solidarity at any point in the political system and the corresponding isolation of separate individuals—as the key to comprehending totalitarianism.[33] William Kornhauser and others have stressed the importance of modern mass society which, with few independent intermediate organizations standing between man and the state such as exist in pluralistic societies, tends to be vulnerable to totalitarian movements.[34] Psychologists have frequently emphasized the importance of authoritarian personality traits in societies which came under totalitarian rule,[35] while political sociologists have tended to accent the class makeup of totalitarian movements.[36] Others have stressed

31. Sidney Hook, "The Hero in History," p. 52. For an early attempt to put totalitarianism in comparative perspective, see Gabriel A. Almond, "Comparative Political Systems," p. 403.
32. See Alexander J. Growth, "The 'Isms' in Totalitarianism."
33. *The Origins of Totalitarianism*, p. 389.
34. *The Politics of Mass Society*, pp. 74-76. See also the works of José Ortega y Gassett, Daniel Bell, Reinhard Bendix, Erich Fromm, and David Riesman.
35. T. W. Adorno *et al.*, *The Authoritarian Personality*, is a pioneering study in this area. See also Zevedei Barbu, *Democracy and Dictatorship*.
36. Seymour M. Lipset, *Political Man*, stresses the middle-class basis of fascism, for example. An excellent critique is Joseph Nyomarkay, "Classes and

such factors as racial persecution, ideology, or the concepts of total power,[37] expansionist and isolationist tendencies,[38] the "permanent revolution,"[39] and a number of other contributing elements in seeking to arrive at a complete understanding of totalitarian systems.[40]

No one of these explanations, as most of their formulators would agree, seems sufficient to fully explain totalitarianism. By the same token, many of the concepts discussed above do contribute in varying degrees to an understanding of this uniquely modern kind of dictatorship. What seems to be required, then, particularly in keeping with the organic nature of totalitarian systems, is a model which combines the most useful of the various approaches and which thereby better accounts for the complexities of totalitarian rule. Carl J. Friedrich and Zbigniew Brzezinski in their *Totalitarian Dictatorship and Autocracy* present such a model which defines totalitarianism in terms of a syndrome of traits, a cluster of six interrelated characteristics which are mutually dependent:

1. an official ideology, consisting of an official body of doctrine covering all vital aspects of man's existence to which everyone living in that society is supposed to adhere, at least passively; this ideology is characteristically focused and projected toward a perfect final state of mankind, that is to say, it contains a chiliastic claim, based upon a radical rejection of existing society and conquest of the world for the new one;

2. a single mass party led typically by one man, the "dictator," and consisting of a relatively small percentage of the total population (up to 10 per cent) of men and women, a hard core of them passionately and unquestioningly dedicated to the ideology and prepared to assist in every way in promoting its general acceptance, such a party being hierarchically organized, and typically either superior to, or completely intertwined with the bureaucratic government organization;

3. a system of terroristic police control, supporting but also supervising the party for its leaders, and characteristically di-

---

Totalitarian Movements" (unpublished), in which it is pointed out (p. 28) that a totalitarian regime cannot by definition be limited to a single class.

37. See Bertram D. Wolfe, "The Durability of Soviet Despotism."

38. Ivo K. Fererabend, "Expansionist and Isolationist Tendencies of Totalitarian Political Systems."

39. Sigmund Neumann, *Permanent Revolution.*

40. This paragraph hardly does justice to the wide range of interpretations, explanations, and analyses of totalitarianism. See also William Ebenstein, "The Study of Totalitarianism," and Daniel Bell, "Ten Theories in Search of Reality."

rected not only against demonstrable "enemies" of the regime, but against arbitrarily selected classes of the population; the terror of the secret police systematically exploiting modern science, and more especially modern psychology;

4. a technologically conditioned near-complete monopoly of control, in the hands of the party and its subservient cadres, of all means of effective mass communication, such as the press, radio, motion pictures;

5. a similarly technologically conditioned near-complete monopoly of control (in the same hands) of all means of effective armed combat;

6. a central control and direction of the entire economy through the bureaucratic coordination of its formerly independent corporate entities, typically including most other associations and group activities.[41]

Robert C. Tucker has more recently suggested that another vital aspect of totalitarian systems, the totalitarian dictator himself, should be added to this list;[42] and, given the highly personal nature of the Trujillo dictatorship, it does seem useful to include this characteristic within the Friedrich and Brzezinski syndrome of traits.

This cluster of characteristics, closely interrelated and existing in combination, provides a better analytical tool for the study of totalitarianism than any one of the "single cause" explanations. The combination of these seven mutually dependent traits also enables us to better distinguish traditional dictatorships from modern totalitarian systems. While certain of the traditional dictatorships may thus have had two or three or possibly even four of these totalitarian aspects, none of them had all. All of these features must be present for a regime to be considered fully totalitarian.

The transitional problem.—Most of those who have drawn the distinction between traditional dictatorship and modern totalitarianism have, perhaps inadvertently, made the contrasts nearly absolute. Thus a dictatorship is classified as either one or the other with no categories in between. There have been almost no attempts to formulate a more complex model for transitional systems. Where does Nasser's Egypt, Castro's Cuba, Sukarno's Indonesia, Nkrumah's Ghana, or Perón's Argentina, to name only a few of the more prominent recent examples, fit into the traditional

41. Pages 9-10. For a good discussion of this model see Fererabend.
42. "The Dictator and Totalitarianism."

dictatorship or modern totalitarianism classification? The literature on dictatorship has thus far failed to adequately answer this question.[43]

This failure has often been reinforced by the orientation of the scholars most concerned with the subject of totalitarianism. It is significant that the foremost students of totalitarian theory and practice, such as Arendt, Ebenstein, Friedrich, and Brzezinski, are European specialists who have thus dealt primarily with relatively "developed" political systems but who are not equally comfortable or "at home" in dealing with other areas which may have less developed systems. There has also been a certain prejudice in totalitarian analysis in favor of the Northern European countries of Germany and the Soviet Union. While Mussolini's Italy and Franco's Spain were probably less totalitarian than these others, to dismiss them cavalierly, as a few writers have done, with the sentiment that "the Latins aren't up to it" represents both narrow thinking and bad scholarship. Finally, it is only in the past few years, after totalitarianism had been thoroughly analyzed, that a revived or increased emphasis on the developing countries of Latin America, Africa, the Middle East, and South and Southeast Asia has come; and there have been only limited attempts to link the concepts provided in the expanding body of literature on social change and political development with the earlier discussions of types of dictatorship.

Some of the attempts to discuss the transitional problem, in addition, have concentrated on what seems to be peripheral problems. Ernst Nolte, for example, appears to see fascism as consisting of anti-Marxist movements of different historical types: (1) traditional "pre-Fascist" regimes such as those of Horthy, Pilsudski, or Salazar; (2) less traditionalist "early-Fascist" regimes such as that of Franco; (3) non-traditionalist "normal-Fascist" regimes such as that of Mussolini; and (4) anti-traditionalist "radical-Fascist" regimes such as that of Hitler.[44] But the approach seems to ignore the broader syndrome of totalitarianism, does not

43. For a critique of the static totalitarian model with regard to changes in the Communist systems, see H. Gordon Skilling, "Interest Groups and Communist Politics." An excellent attempt using the Franco regime as example and point of departure to formulate a model for transitional systems is Juan J. Linz, "An Authoritarian Regime." Linz' formulations are given more attention in succeeding pages.

44. Klaus Epstein, "A New Study of Fascism." This is a review article which analyzes Ernst Nolte, Der Faschismus in seiner Epoche. The Nolte volume has more recently been published in English as Three Faces of Fascism.

adequately treat the subject of transition from one type to another, and leaves a host of definitional and philosophical problems. Latin American scholars, on the other hand, have usually concentrated on the juridical aspects of the political system and have often sought to limit the possibilities for dictatorship by constitutional engineering. Friedrich and Brzezinski conclude their path-breaking work with an ambitiously entitled chapter, "The Stages of Development and the Future of Totalitarian Dictatorship" (pages 293-303), in which they discuss the development of totalitarianism in Communist China and the Eastern European countries, but fail to treat totalitarian developments in the rest of the world with anything more than a passing reference. The authors do not adequately fit what they themselves consider the key variable—technology, economic development, or industrialization—into the discussion. The list of examples could easily be multiplied.

Totalitarianism, as we have stressed, is a relatively new historical phenomenon which is tied closely to the industrial and technical developments of the twentieth century.[45] Industrialization and modern technology have not only created the means by which totalitarianism becomes possible, such as terror techniques, new forms of organizations, communication, and so forth, but they have also created the need for totalitarianism. The various kinds of traditional dictatorships had little need to impose totalitarian controls since the people they dominated were still largely unorganized, atomized, isolated, inarticulate, and outside of effective participation in politics. Slaves or peasants posed little threat to these regimes and were usually easily crushed when an uprising did occur. In pre-industrial, agrarian societies, the traditional dictators found it not only technically impossible but also unnecessary to impose the vast web of controls which characterizes a totalitarian system.

Industrialization and large-scale economic development help create both the means and the need for totalitarianism. These processes tend to draw the previously isolated sectors of the society into politics. Industrialization usually gives rise to trade unions and business associations and is ordinarily accompanied by the growth of civil services and the organization of political parties. The rise of these and other voluntary associations, which become

45. This section draws heavily on the excellent analysis by John H. Kautsky, "An Essay in the Politics of Development."

increasingly conscious of their own different interests and of their organized strengths, tends to break up the monolithic structure of traditional society and to produce the beginnings of more pluralistic, competitive system. As Kautsky states, totalitarianism in the developing countries may thus grow out of "the attempt to make the maintenance or even the acceleration of industrialization compatible with the prevention of the growth of such organizations, or their suppression where they have already grown" (page 93).

There remains a great difference between traditional dictatorship, which occurs frequently in traditional, underdeveloped societies, and modern totalitarianism, which has arisen in somewhat more developed and less traditionalistic societies. In those developing countries which are earnestly seeking rapid economic development and industrialization, however, questions of religion, the family, belief systems, and the like all acquire a political meaning, and totalitarian techniques may be used in an effort to change the traditional patterns and achieve modernization. The totalitarianism of these systems may be inhibited by technological underdevelopment, but the technologies of these nations are rapidly modernizing. Roads are being built, radios acquired, and overall transportation and communications improved. At the same time the previously isolated elements are uprooted, mobilized, organized, and infused with all-encompassing, new, and conflicting systems of ideologies and values. While this is the essence of the political development or modernization process, it also provides the necessary ingredients for the growth of more fully "developed" kinds of dictatorship.[46]

A certain amount of coercion seems to be a necessary ingredient in the developmental process. The extent of this coercion may, however, vary significantly from one political system to another. In order to speed the economic and industrial development of the Soviet Union, for example, Stalin employed extremely coercive techniques which have been commonly called totalitarian. Other post-World-War-II leaders, particularly in the emerging nations, have also sought to accelerate development by employing varying degrees of coercion. The borderline between the amount of coercion required to lift a society out of its traditional pattern into the

---

46. The literature on political development is now vast. A recent, sophisticated statement is Lucian W. Pye, *Aspects of Political Development*. For the link between the developmental process and totalitarianism see the introductory essay by the editors, Harry Eckstein and David E. Apter, *Comparative Politics*, pp. 433-40.

modern world (generally considered to be a "good thing") and the amount of coercion which may make the system totalitarian (a "bad thing") is not always clear-cut.[47]

It would thus be possible to find a country in the transitional phase, neither wholly traditional nor fully modern, in which all the seven traits of totalitarianism—official ideology, single party, terroristic police, communications monopoly, weapons monopoly, centrally directed economy, and totalitarian dictator—may be operative. Would such a society then be totalitarian? The answer is that it depends: not merely on the presence of the seven characteristics of totalitarianism, but also on the degree to which they are applied and effective, given the technological level and social and political basis of the system. The differences between totalitarianism and more traditional kinds of dictatorship, therefore, may be more of degree than of kind, and it may be possible by combining models of dictatorships with models of development to devise indices to measure these degrees more accurately than in the past.

The formulations of Juan J. Linz provide an excellent example of an attempt to devise a model appropriate for dictatorships of a transitional sort. Describing Franco's Spain as an "authoritarian regime" which corresponds neither to the model of the totalitarian nor to that of the traditional dictatorship, Linz presents a model of a political system with "limited, not responsible, political pluralism; without elaborate and guiding ideology (but with distinctive mentalities); without intensive or extensive political mobilization (except at some points in their development); and in which a leader (or occasionally a small group) exercises power within formally ill-defined limits but actually quite predictable ones" (page 297). Particularly relevant for this discussion of the transitional process is Linz' comment that "Authoritarian regimes are a likely outcome of the breakdown of such [Weberian] traditional forms of legitimacy. This results from a partial social and political mobilization and a questioning of the traditional principles of legitimacy (largely due to their secularization) by significant segments of the society. Authoritarian regimes—even those we might call reactionary—are modernizing in the sense that they represent a discontinuity with tradition, introducing criteria of efficiency and rationality, personal achievement and populist appeals. . . . In our times authoritarian rule almost inevitably leads

47. See Irving Louis Horowitz, *Three Worlds of Development*.

to questioning traditional authority, if for no other reason than by making the people aware of the importance of the effective head of the government and its secular character. Authoritarian rule might be an intermediate stage in or after the breakdown of traditional authority."[48] A conceptual framework such as this, which attempts to relate types of dictatorships to levels of sociopolitical development and modernization (or decay), may enable us to provide better answers to the questions posed at the beginning of this section concerning the Trujillo regime and the implications of his rule.

Outline of Study

In this introductory chapter an attempt has been made to describe the physical setting in which the Trujillo regime came to power and to provide a theoretical framework in which his dictatorship may be considered in comparative perspective.

In the chapters that follow, the several important pillars of Trujillo's control are analyzed. Chapter 2 discusses Trujillo's rise to power and his position as "the dictator." Chapters 3, 4, and 5 deal with his control, respectively, over the armed forces, the government (including the use of the official party), and the national economy. Chapter 6 summarizes Trujillo's political ideology and its uses, and Chapter 7 considers the implementation of the ideology in terms of techniques of thought control and scrutinizes the regime's relations with the Church. In Chapter 8 the overthrow of Trujillo is analyzed.

The final chapter summarizes the findings of the study and, in returning to the theoretical discussion of the introduction, attempts to arrive at some conclusions concerning the nature of the Trujillo dictatorship, its place in the study of comparative political systems, and the implications of Trujillo's rule for the development and modernization of the Dominican Republic.

48. Linz, pp. 321-22. See also George S. Wise, *Caudillo,* for some interesting comparisons.

2. Trujillo: Man and Dictator

TOTALITARIAN RULE is necessarily personal rule. The totalitarian dictator, as C. W. Cassinelli points out, maximizes his authority by destroying or controlling all other centers of power; he shares power with no one, ruling alone and unchallenged.[1] It is necessary to make this point because it has often been stated that in the most prominent totalitarian systems the party (Stalin's Soviet Union) or the generals and big business (Hitler's Germany and Mussolini's Italy) really ruled and that the dictator was merely a figurehead. Enough evidence has been accumulated, however, to demonstrate that these dictators indeed exercised "dictatorial" power; though limited in certain areas, their authority was absolute to a degree unknown in the traditional dictatorships. Stalin, Hitler, and Mussolini were the actual rulers of their countries and their views were decisive. Through techniques of thought control, in addition, the totalitarian dictator becomes completely identified with his people in a mystical union, and this factor again serves to distinguish him from traditional kinds of dictators.[2] As Hitler himself wrote, "Extraordinary geniuses

1. "The Totalitarian Party."
2. Friedrich and Brzezinski, Chapter II; and Ebenstein, *Totalitarianism*, pp. 54-55.

permit of no consideration for normal mankind. From the smallest community cell to the highest leadership of the entire Reich, the state must have the personality principle anchored in its organization. . . . Surely every man will have advisers by his side, but *the decisions will be made by one man.*"[3]

What is required, however, is not simply an analysis of the function of the totalitarian dictator but also a consideration of his personality type. Though studies of the relations of politics and psychopathology are still somewhat limited, those who become totalitarian dictators do seem to be of a definite psychological type: the paranoiac, who has both systematized delusions of persecution and of his own greatness as well. The analysis of the personal element in totalitarian rule together with a fuller understanding of the totalitarian dictator as a personality type should be brought into the "syndrome" of totalitarianism.[4]

If consideration of the personal element is essential for a better understanding of most modern-day dictatorships, this is particularly true for the Trujillo regime. Trujillo's was a highly personal dictatorship in which power was not shared, even among a small clique, but concentrated in the hands of one man. The absolute power of the dictator was so great, indeed, that it tended to compensate for whatever other deficiencies might have existed in Trujillo's elaborate and refined system of dictatorial controls. Within the narrow confines of the Dominican Republic (and Trujillo frequently regretted the small arena in which he had to operate), his authority and power were nearly "total." Because of the importance, indeed, of charismatic authority in practically all dictatorial regimes—be they traditional or modern—and especially in the Dominican dictatorship, this study begins with a consideration of Trujillo himself.

Trujillo: A Political Biography

Rafael Leonidas Trujillo Molina was born in San Cristóbal,[5] the Dominican Republic, on October 24, 1891. He was the fourth of eleven children born to José Trujillo Váldez and Julia Molina

---

3. Excerpt from *Mein Kampf* in Betty B. Burch (ed.), *Dictatorship and Totalitarianism*, p. 59.
4. See the excellent discussion by Tucker, "The Dictator and Totalitarianism."
5. The city of San Cristóbal always received special treatment from Trujillo and was renamed Ciudad Benemérita, literally "Blessed City." It is noteworthy that this area later gave Juan Bosch, a long-time Trujillo foe, his largest

de Trujillo. His ancestry can accurately be traced back to José Trujillo Monagas, a Spaniard who came to the country from the Canary Islands during the 1861-65 Spanish protectorate of the Dominican Republic, and to Diyetta Chevalier, a Haitian who settled in San Cristóbal during the 1822-44 Haitian occupation of the country.

This relatively undistinguished genealogy did not prevent Trujillo's laudatory biographers from rewriting history and claiming that the dictator was of noble blood. His paternal heritage was thus officially considered to be in the line of the Spanish conquistadores, while on the maternal side, it was claimed, the lineage could be traced back to the French court under Napoleon, specifically to the Marquis of Philborou who accompanied General Leclerc, the husband of Pauline Bonaparte, to the island.[6] As we shall see, after being rejected by the traditional Dominican ruling elite, Trujillo attempted to demonstrate that he was of the purest nobility.

Trujillo's birthplace was a poverty-ridden, agricultural village on the southern coast, only fifteen kilometers east of the capital, and the Trujillo family, like the community, was poor. Rafael's father was a postal clerk and small-time businessman and as such was a member of the very small middle class. His salary was insufficient to feed his large family, and to supplement his meager income he is reported to have resorted occasionally to cattle-rustling.[7]

Little is known of Trujillo's early years. The official accounts say that he was taught to read and to write by his maternal grandmother Luisa Erciná Chevalier,[8] and there is a record of his having attended the Escuela Nacional grammar school in San Cristóbal. One of the dictator's fawning biographers wrote of young Trujillo, "A self-made man, making his way thanks to his strong will-power and industriousness, he learned the lessons of the hard school of life, and with faith in God and in himself, he struggled on, getting his bearings and proving himself a man of action, a veritable dynamo."[9] Though the above rhetoric tends to overglorify and complicate a simpler explanation, Trujillo was indeed a self-made man, a man of action, and one who seldom

majority (12-1) in the 1962 presidential elections. See the statistics compiled by the author in *Dominican Republic*.

6. See Pedro González Blanco, *Trujillo*, p. 17.
7. Germán Ornes, *Trujillo: Little Caesar*, p. 29.
8. The best of the official biographies is Abelardo R. Nanita, *Trujillo*.
9. González Blanco, *Trujillo*, p. 17.

tired. It is most likely that young Trujillo, like his friends and neighbors, received most of his early education and training in the streets of San Cristóbal and that Trujillo was better at getting ahead in this environment than were his fellows.

He worked as a telegraph operator and as the chief of a private police force on one of the large sugar plantations, in which capacity he is supposed to have received his earliest training in cruel and oppressive methods. Though the evidence is scanty, one author claims that young Trujillo was a hoodlum, cattle-rustler, procurer, forger, torturer, and murderer;[10] another states that he had been convicted for theft or forgery and that he had escaped punishment for other offenses by fleeing the country.[11] These accusations cannot be proved or disproved since a fire in the Supreme Court building in 1927 destroyed the criminal records. It is probable, however, that the fire was providential for Trujillo's laudatory biographers.

In 1916 the United States Marines occupied the Dominican Republic. One of the major effects of the occupation was the creation of the first modern, unified, and professional armed force in Dominican history. Trujillo was introduced to the officers of the occupying force by an uncle; after entering the Marine-created national constabulary, his biography can be more readily traced. Since the constabulary was regarded as a puppet of the Marines, the more patriotic Dominicans refused to join and it was extremely difficult to enlist capable men. Lacking able leadership, the constabulary's creators ignored Trujillo's questionable past and grasped at his proven ability to organize and command. In contrast to those Dominicans opposing the occupation forces, he served as a guide and informer and built up advantageous friendships with the Marine officers.[12] Trujillo is reported to have served under the infamous Captain Merckle, notorious for his persecution and oppression of Dominican nationals.[13]

In 1919 Trujillo received his commission as a second lieutenant in the national constabulary, and after receiving his first formal military training as well as his only higher education in the United States-created Haina Academy from August 15 to December 21, 1921, his commission was confirmed. Thereafter his rise to power

10. Albert C. Hicks, *Blood in the Streets,* pp. 27-30.
11. Ernest Gruening, "Dictatorship in Santo Domingo," p. 584.
12. Marvin Goldwert, *The Constabulary in the Dominican Republic.*
13. Luis F. Mejía, *De Lilís a Trujillo,* pp. 216-17; and Ornes, *Trujillo: Little Caesar,* p. 35.

was meteoric. In 1922 he was promoted to captain and assigned to the city of San Francisco de Macorís as a troubleshooter. His promotion to major in 1924, the year the United States Marines left the country, was facilitated by the assassination of his superior Major César Lora, Commander of the Department of the North.[14] As the new commander of the northern area of the Dominican Republic, Trujillo distinguished himself as an efficient administrator and attracted the favorable attention of President Horacio Vásquez. In 1926 he was advanced to lieutenant colonel and by 1928 had been chosen chief of staff of the newly renamed National Army.[15]

As conceived by the United States military planners, the Dominican constabulary was to be a non-political force whose sole function would be the preservation of internal order. But given the Republic's praetorian, caudillistic tradition, a non-political armed force was extremely unlikely. It is not surprising, then, that after becoming head of the army, Trujillo turned it into his personal instrument; through adroit maneuvering and handling of promotions and appointments, he secured the loyalty of the military and became the most powerful man in the country.[16]

As a brigadier general, chief of staff of the army, and thus a powerful figure, Trujillo sought admission to some of the country's exclusive social clubs. He was then in contact with the social and political leaders of the country and sought admission to the aristocratic elite to which he thought his rank entitled him. Membership implied acceptance and social standing on a level with the Dominican Republic's "first families." This was particularly important for the middle-class Trujillo who aspired above all else to achieve upper-class status. At first, however, he was rejected by the principal social club of El Seibo; and this snub helped build up his hatred of the aristocracy. In a society, where one's social and economic class standing is often the major determining factor in denoting one's place within the system, this blackball hurt Trujillo deeply. Later, after he had married for a

14. The events of this assassination are somewhat obscure, but at least two authors report that Trujillo divulged to the assassin the meeting place of his unfaithful wife and Major Lora. See Hicks, *Blood in the Streets*, pp. 31-32; and Ornes, *Trujillo: Little Caesar*, pp. 38-39.

15. Ernesto Vega y Pagan, *Military Biography of Generalissimo Rafael Leonidas Trujillo Molina*. Though written by Trujillo's official military biographer, this book contains a wealth of documents and provides some valuable factual information.

16. Luis Mejía, p. 147, and Ornes, *Trujillo: Little Caesar*, p. 39.

second time into a more socially acceptable family, he was admitted to the exclusive Union Club of Santo Domingo but under such humiliating circumstances that rejection was almost to be preferred to acceptance. His resentment grew. After becoming president in 1930 he forced the admission of his fellow middle-class military officers to the Union Club, eventually dissolved it in favor of a newly-created Club de la Juventud, and then helped organize the President Trujillo Club. The dictator continued to harass the oligarchy and to carry out recriminations against it at every opportunity.[17]

The change which took place in the Union Club reflected the transformation which occurred in the governing elite, both military and civilian. The upper strata of Dominican society, intensely nationalistic and patriotic, had refused to serve as officers in the United States-created constabulary with the result that the military leadership was soon dominated by new elements. The old elite had lost is monopoly on military training and leadership and thus forfeited what had historically been the major, and sometimes the only source of its political power. This shift from upper-class to middle-class leadership took place initially in the officer corps of the army; but after Trujillo came to power, the change was noticeable in the civilian governmental leadership as well. Trujillo personified these transformations.[18]

In 1930, it will be recalled, a revolution had been launched against the government of President Vásquez. Whether there was prior collusion between the rebels and Trujillo remains a matter of controversy among Dominican historians, but of the succeeding events there is no dispute. As the rebellious forces led by Rafael Estrella Ureña marched on the capital, Trujillo's army, with greater numbers and more and better weapons, remained in the barracks. After the government of President Vásquez subsequently toppled, Estrella Ureña became provisional president. But Trujillo had meanwhile collected the arms from the rebel forces and his position as arbiter of any political decision was assured. Elections were called and Trujillo secured the nomination of a coalition of small political parties. When it became apparent that the liberal appeal of Trujillo's opponents was gathering support and that the

17. Ornes, *Trujillo: Little Caesar*, pp. 41-42, and Crassweller, pp. 47, 57, 104.
18. Goldwert, pp. 14, 21. Some of these points have previously been mentioned in Howard J. Wiarda, "The Politics of Civil-Military Relations in the Dominican Republic."

opposition would win the election, Trujillo and *La 42,* a group of thugs named after the Forty-second Marine Company, unleashed a campaign of terror, dealing out beatings, breaking up opposition meetings, and jailing, exiling, or killing political foes. Unable to compete with these tactics the opposition withdrew. The elections were held and Trujillo was declared elected unopposed. On August 16, 1930, Trujillo was inaugurated President and for the next thirty-one years ruled the Dominican Republic with an iron hand.[19]

Eighteen days after Trujillo assumed the presidency a devastating hurricane almost leveled the capital city. To help meet the crisis the Congress suspended constitutional guarantees and invested the President with virtual dictatorial power. However, he used this legalized dictatorship not only to maintain order and rebuild Santo Domingo, but also to eliminate all remaining political opponents. While the budgets for other ministries were reduced to help service a pressing foreign debt, the army's appropriation went unaffected; and the military, at this time the sole pillar of Trujillo's control, was strengthened. The fledgling political parties which had emerged in the 1920's were snuffed out and in 1931 the Dominican Party, which would soon develop into a monolithic political apparatus completely at the service of the regime, was created in their place.

Trujillo's first term ended in 1934 and he sought re-election for a second four years. His opponents had by this time been silenced and the official Dominican Party was the only organized political group remaining in the country. Trujillo's slate of candidates then received a 100-per-cent endorsement, a pattern which was to become the norm. During this term a number of minor revolts continued to break out in the provinces against the government. They were quickly crushed, however, and this kind of uprising soon ceased to occur altogether. By the mid 1930's the domestic opposition had all but completely been snuffed out. Trujillo's megalomania also first became prominently noticed now: Pico Duarte, the highest mountain in the Antilles, was changed to Pico Trujillo and Santo Domingo, the capital city and the oldest permanent European settlement in the Western Hemisphere, was renamed Ciudad Trujillo. The dictator further consolidated his power by creating a new national police force, distinct from the

19. These events are followed in more detail in Ornes, *Trujillo: Little Caesar,* pp. 46-59.

army, to replace the old municipal police forces and by imposing ever tighter controls over the government.[20]

In 1937 the slaughter of some 15,000[21] Haitians—seasonal farm workers and their families who had settled within the largely undefined Dominican border—produced a revulsion abroad which posed a threat to Trujillo's rule. In an effort to vindicate himself, he spent untold millions on lobbyists, writers, and newspaper advertisements.[22] The sentiment against him continued with the consequence that Trujillo declined to be a candidate in the 1938 election. He had no intention of forfeiting any real control, however, as evidenced by his statement to the Dominican people declining a third term: "While my heart continues to beat my country will continue to have my vigilance and my services."[23] He then recommended Jacinto B. Peynado for the presidency and Manuel Troncoso de la Concha for the vice presidency, stating "These are my candidates."[24] Trujillo did not really intend to give up any actual power, but to assure the maintenance of his own legal authority he had the rubber-stamp Congress pass a law conferring on him the same rights and privileges as the president. Trujillo increased the strength of his official party and assured the loyalty of his puppet president. By the end of 1938, after he had stepped down, his power was as great as if he held office himself.[25]

Trujillo felt certain enough of his control to take an extended tour of the United States and Europe in 1939, but when the war broke out he hurried back to the Dominican Republic. Peynado died in 1940 and the presidency passed to Troncoso de la Concha. In 1941 the Trujillo Party was organized to serve as a complement to the Dominican Party, and the constitution was amended to extend the presidential term from four to five years. As the candidate of both the Trujillo Party and the Dominican Party in 1942,

20. A good term-by-term summary of Trujillo's rule may be found in Jesús de Galíndez, *La era de Trujillo*. An excellent, more recent history is Robert D. Crassweller, *Trujillo*.

21. The estimates of the number of those killed vary. Galíndez, *La era*, p. 380, states the "official sources" placed the number at 12,000 while other estimates ranged as high as 25,000. See also the dispatches of William D. Ryan and Quentin Reynolds, reporters who were in the area at the time.

22. Hicks, *Blood in the Streets*, p. 122.

23. Rafael Trujillo, *President Trujillo Molina Declines to be a Candidate for Reelection*, p. 14.

24. *Ibid.*, p. 6.

25. Vega y Pagan, *Military Biography*, p. 154.

Trujillo was unanimously elected to a third term as President.

When World War II began in Europe, the Dominican Republic at first declared its neutrality; but after the bombing of Pearl Harbor, Trujillo found it more advantageous to side with the Western Allies. The increasing wartime demand for Dominican products resulted in the first large-scale industrialization and growth of manufacturing in the country and swelled the income both of the Dominican government and of Trujillo personally. At the end of the war his business enterprises included hotels, banks, agricultural processing plants, textile mills, a number of factories, and air and shipping lines. He was acquiring monopolies or near-monopolies in sugar-refining (which produced the country's major export crop), salt, meat exportation, and cigarettes, and had become the country's largest merchant, industrialist, and landowner. Trujillo's control of the military and of the governmental machinery was now cemented by his control over the national economic life.

The wave of democratic sentiment which swept Latin America following World War II forced or prompted Trujillo to give his system more of the appearance of a democracy. Trade unions were permitted to organize, the subservient press was allowed to criticize the regime, and opposition parties, including the Communist Partido Socialista Popular, were initially encouraged to organize and campaign against him. But Trujillo received 92 per cent of the vote in the 1947 election, and shortly thereafter all opposition or potential opposition was again snuffed out. The late 1940's and early 1950's may be considered the plateau of Trujillo's power.

Trujillo's fourth term, 1947-52, produced controls which were still more strict. The workers were consolidated into a single official labor confederation and no strikes were permitted. The regime began to enter the field of totalitarian thought control with even tighter supervision and more clever manipulation of all communications media, education, and intellectual life. A military assistance pact was signed with the United States in 1951 and the armed forces were strengthened and given more and better equipment. Economic ownership by the Trujillo family was extended and its economic control over the populace thus strengthened. It was also during this term that two abortive invasion attempts were launched against the Dominican Republic by the growing number of exiles.

In the final year of his fourth term as president, Trujillo had his subservient Congress create the special position of commander in chief of the armed forces and the dictator was named to fill the post. His control of the military thus assured, Trujillo again stepped down from the presidency and in 1952 placed another puppet, his brother Héctor, in the office. After Héctor was inaugurated, however, Rafael was named special ambassador to the United Nations, secretary of state for foreign affairs, social welfare director, and secretary of religious affairs, and it became clear that the veteran dictator was making all important decisions.[26] As plenipotentiary to the Vatican he journeyed to Rome in 1954 and signed a mutually beneficial Concordat with the Holy See, the first such agreement in Dominican history.

By this time Trujillo had reached the height of his power. The economy had continued to boom in the post-World-War-II years and the Trujillo family became immensely wealthy. After some twenty-five years of rule, there was no internal opposition to Trujillo and his international position also seemed secure. Social change had accelerated during this period—a sizable middle class was emerging, peasants were increasingly being recruited into the industrial labor force, communication grids were being greatly expanded, and rural-to-city migration was rapidly increasing—but none of these changes seemed to pose an immediate threat to Trujillo's lengthy dictatorship. The mid-1950's may be considered the pinnacle of the Trujillo era.

In 1957 Héctor was reelected for a second term, though Rafael continued to be the real power in the country. Héctor was never particularly happy in the exercise of his office and in 1960 resigned in favor of Vice-President Joaquín Balaguer, a compliant intellectual. Balaguer remained in the presidency until Rafael was assassinated, and it was he who attempted initially to preside over the transition following the collapse of the entire Trujillo family dictatorship.

The chain of events leading up to the assassination of the Generalissimo are analyzed in Chapter 8 and need not be detailed here. It should be mentioned, however, that in addition to the external and the internal forces which gradually built up and

26. After 1930 Trujillo in fact maintained his absolute control whether he held an official position or not. Some Dominicans claim he filled such posts as commander in chief only because they provided an excuse for him to wear the many dress uniforms he loved.

eventually coalesced to overthrow the regime, there are persistent reports that in his last years Trujillo (who was sixty-nine when he was killed) was quite sick, physically or mentally and likely both, and had begun to lose control. These reports cannot be fully verified since there have thus far been few published disclosures by Trujillo intimates, either family members or close collaborators,[27] but it seems clear that the old Generalissimo was indeed losing his hold. He behaved more irrationally, lost his sense of restraint, and seemed on some occasions to be mentally unbalanced. On May 30, 1961, the thirty-one-year Trujillo era was violently ended just as it had begun—he was ambushed, machinegunned, and his body was savagely beaten.

Trujillo: The Leader

What kind of man was Rafael Trujillo?[28] It is already too late to answer this question with much assurance. As mentioned above, there exist few accounts by Trujillo intimates and few trained observers have written their impressions. But the problem is much more complex than simply a lack of on-the-spot analyses. Trujillo probably once had a believable personality, with all its contradictions, human traits, and paradoxes, but this has long vanished in mountains of one-sided prose. Trujillo was surely not the great historical figure, benefactor of his people, healer, teacher, statesman, and so on presented by his official biographers and propagandists both to his own people and to the outside world. Nor was he only the assassin, thief, and lecher described by his opponents during his rule and accepted almost universally, since his death, as the true picture. At this point it is nearly too late to fully recapture a full and accurate portrayal of Trujillo the man,[29] but if this is impossible, we can still attempt to offer a brief analysis of Trujillo the leader. Since the Trujillo dictatorship was so highly

27. Two published accounts by Trujillo intimates, a daughter and an intelligence officer, confirm that toward the end the dictator had indeed begun to lose his self-control. See Flor de Oro Trujillo, "My Life As Trujillo's Daughter," p. 62, and Arturo Espaillat, *Trujillo*. See also Crassweller, Chapter 27.

28. The question is posed but not fully answered by Rodman, pp. 150-51. The most sophisticated explanation is Crassweller, *passim*.

29. For some comments on the works of both Trujillo's official propagandists and his bitter enemies, see the bibliographic note. Trujillo has also become the prototype of "the dictator" for several novelists who, without much real inside information, have succeeded in describing many of the human complexities. See, for example, Albert J. Guerard, *The Exiles*, and Bruce Palmer, *Hecatomb*. See also the review of the Palmer book, by Howard J. Wiarda.

personalistic, it becomes necessary to describe the personal aspects of his rule.

Personally, Trujillo presented an imposing sight. He was not particularly tall, though at five feet nine inches he was a bit taller than most of his fellow Dominicans. His air was sometimes haughty and aloof which gave him the manner of a leader. Until his last years, he was exceptionally healthy and vigorous (and spent long hours and much money on aphrodisiacs and "miracle" foods). His eyes could be soft or hard, depending on his mood. Most women considered him handsome. His clothes were expensive and his wardrobe extensive. Particularly in one of his dress uniforms, Trujillo looked the imposing dictator that he was.[30] He had a magnetic personality and was in many ways a charismatic leader.

Perhaps the major key to Trujillo's personalistic grip on the Dominican Republic was that he worked harder and longer than any of his opponents, competitors, or subordinates. When asked once to explain how he had maintained his lengthy tenure, he is reported to have answered, "Because I work at my job."[31] His working day began early and cabinet ministers and advisers were frequently roused by pre-dawn telephone calls from his office. His black limousine usually arrived at the Palace before 7:00 A.M. and the chain of consultations, business, papers, and audiences continued through the lunch hour. Following a half-hour walk and two-hour siesta, Trujillo returned to the Palace for several more hours of state and private business, though at times he remained at home during the afternoon and with the aid of a team of secretaries did his work there. It was not unusual for Trujillo to spend ten hours at his desk and it was reported that he had not missed a Sunday morning at his office in twelve years.[32] In his book Yo fuí secretario de Trujillo (I Was Trujillo's Secretary) José Almoína rightly states that "working with Trujillo leaves time for neither rest nor relaxation; he is physically and intellectually made of steel and his speed at work allows neither pause nor delay." There is no doubt that Trujillo had more strength, energy, and endurance than his rivals or potential rivals.

There can also be little doubt that in addition to being an

---

30. Germán E. Ornes and John McCarten, "Trujillo."
31. Ornes, Trujillo: Little Caesar, p. 74.
32. Ibid., pp. 74-75. It is particularly significant that even bitter critics like Ornes are impressed by Trujillo's capacity for work.

indefatigable worker, Trujillo was an excellent organizer and administrator. The best evidence for this assertion is his long rule and the way the regime was run, and once again even his most violent critics, such as Ornes and Mejía, who wrote that he had "martial energy and undeniable qualities of command," were forced to admit this.[33] Perhaps the most objective evidence comes from the reports by his Marine superiors when Trujillo was a young officer. These reports describe him as being "calm, even tempered, forceful, active, bold, and painstaking" as well as possessing "initiative, intelligence, and good judgment." Other Marine reports described his work as excellent and himself as efficient, and he was regarded as one of the best officers in the military.[34] It has already been pointed out that his ability as an organizer and administrator enabled him to rise meteorically in the armed forces hierarchy, and these traits stayed with him and were more sharply practiced and refined once he took power.

Trujillo had other assets which enabled him to rule for thirty-one years. He probably knew his country and its people better than anyone before or after him in Dominican history. He was aware of the strong and weak points both of those who worked with him and of his enemies and was particularly astute at manipulating these strengths and weaknesses. He apparently had an incredible memory which permanently fixed in his mind the details of the one-page reports that crossed his desk. His personality was forceful, powerful, and dominating and his will imposing; those who dealt with him came away from interviews with the impression that he could literally see right through them. Trujillo usually remained unruffled by major events and did not often lose his temper; in his stuffy office and in full uniform he never perspired, which gave him a large psychological advantage over those who stood before him sweltering, nervous, shaken, and perspiring in the tropical climate.[35]

Though he had very little formal education, Trujillo was far from unintelligent. He was not the genius that his propaganda often presented but his official biographer Nanita was essentially correct in seeing in Trujillo "a very clear intellect; an intelligence which is keen, sagacious, penetrating, and profound, quick to

33. See Ornes, *Trujillo: Little Caesar*, p. 37, and Luis Mejía, p. 216.
34. See the documents reprinted in Vega y Pagan, *Military Biography*, pp. 53-56.
35. Espaillat, pp. 32-35.

understand and swiftly decisive in moments of crisis."[36] He was a wily, cunning, master politician of the pure Machiavellian sort who, in the words of his crack intelligence chief, "elevated the law of the jungle into a science."[37] Almost instinctively, it seemed, he understood and operated upon the principles of political combat as they existed in the Caribbean area. Perhaps astute is the best word that may be used to describe him.

Trujillo had many of the qualities required for a Latin American political leader. He was *muy macho* (very much a man), and tales of his sexual exploits and conquests were about the only jokes about him which were allowed. There was a good deal of flamboyance to Trujillo's character and also an element of charlatanism and fakery. He thought of himself, and was thought of by most of his subjects, as a *patrón*, a great teacher and father who must educate and lead his people. In this role he served as godfather and hence as overseer of thousands of Dominican families. He thought in terms of absolutes, demanding absolute loyalty, absolute obedience, and absolute power. It is therefore not contradictory that he could be kind, considerate, and generous to friends and relatives and ruthlessly cruel to enemies or those who crossed him.

Trujillo had a role to play, and he played it to perfection. Like many Latin American politicians, he had a seemingly natural flair for the dramatic. The Dominican Republic was his stage and he a natural but also carefully cultivated actor. He was the lead in a Latin American drama in which life must be not just lived, in which the players must not only exist, but in which one must fully act out his part; the drama required the characters and the events to be larger than life and to heighten reality. The all-powerful male, who must cultivate an air of mystery, flirt with death, but finally conquer, and conquer with grace and drama—the flamenco dancer, the bullfighter—Trujillo was this kind of leader. In many ways Trujillo was a product of Dominican and Hispanic culture and history, and much of his behavior had its origins in these traditions.

Trujillo's affinity for the dramatic and skill at theatrics was ultimately a factor in his overthrow. Toward the end of his rule he began to reach too far and, as we shall see, his overreaching started the chain of causes which led to his downfall. He felt

36. Nanita, *Trujillo, passim.*
37. Espaillat, p. 38.

inferior to and persecuted by the older Dominican aristocracy, and at the same time had delusions of his own grandeur. He was a megalomaniac who demanded and received constant adulation, and here again he went too far. For Trujillo changed from a man who constantly placed his image before the public in a highly skillful political way to a man obsessed. It is in this sense that some observers have written that he began to lose his self-control toward the end.

Trujillo had one other disadvantage as a political leader and dictator: he was not a good public speaker. Unlike many other modern dictators, his power and success were not based on the emotional appeal of his words; he could not move vast masses of men by force of speech. His voice was high pitched and seemed ludicrous for a great leader. Trujillo realized this weakness, however, and did not allow it to hamper his rule; he came to rely on equally effective techniques of mass mobilization and control.[38]

The question of motivation remains to be discussed: Why did Trujillo do it? Why did he rule as a bloody tyrant and dictator? Why did he exercise power in the particular way he did? What drove him to power and what prompted him to stay there once power was attained? No complete answers can as yet be given to these questions, since Trujillo's ultimate motivations remain obscure. The desire for power itself is, however, a good starting point. As Selden Rodman has written, "Power for its own sake, personal aggrandizement over men and possessions—concentrated, hoarded, and flaunted in a vulgar display—were the beginning and the end of Trujillo's drive."[39] There is, in fact, little doubt that Trujillo was driven by the urge to dominate. He used money, wealth, people, even sex to that end. He was cunning and shrewd in the manipulation of power and almost instinctively seemed to sense and play upon others' ambitions and desires. His unquenchable ego, his craving for money and property, his absolute dictatorship may all be explained if one takes into account that the driving force was Trujillo's constant desire for total power.

The power instinct goes a long way toward explaining Trujillo's motivation, but it does not tell us why that instinct was so intense and does not explain why he was driven to seek power and to hang on to it for so long. At least part of the explanation for

38. Flor de Oro Trujillo, p. 50; and Ornes, *Trujillo: Little Caesar*, p. 73.
39. Page 143. The theme of the power instinct also dominates the Crassweller and Ornes books.

Trujillo's inordinate drive lies in the makeup of the Dominican social structure and belief system which, from the time of Columbus, has been based on rigid class-caste stratification and on absolutism. Traditionally a very few, who constitute the nobility, the elite, or the oligarchy, have ruled the Dominican Republic politically, socially, and economically. Beneath this ruling group has historically come a small middle class and a large lower-class peasantry, and the lines between these classes are so fixed that there is very little upward mobility in the society. Trujillo was born in the middle sector and, like so many in the Latin American countries born to that station, desired first and foremost to live in the fashion of the elite and be accepted by it. But Trujillo had not been able to gain acceptance into the aristocracy, and his sense of social rejection was particularly acute. He was an intensely ambitious man—and in some ways a very talented and able man—living in a hierarchically organized society where access to the top ranks was closed. Trujillo's fervent desire to reach the top may be seen prior to his entrance into the military when, as his first daughter recalls, he was proud and arrogant, despising his home town as "vulgar" and its people as "common."[40] His intense ambition for power plus his feeling of social rejection help explain Trujillo's rise to power in the military, a rejection of his first family and his remarriage into the social elite, his seizure of power and rejection of the old order, his constant harassment and humilitation of the traditional elite once in power, his megalomania, his claim to nobility, his extraordinary desire for wealth and prestige, and his maintenance of absolute personal power for thirty-one years. In a society where class and social standing are all-important the middle-class Trujillo felt constrained by his environment, wanted above all else to rise to the top, and to stay there once in power. He wanted to pull down the elite and the high-born, in the words of Robert D. Crassweller, to dominate every facet of a hostile society by money and the fist, to force all men and women to be dependent on and subject to him, and to set himself above all others.[41]

In Trujillo's Dominican Republic all decisions were made by one man. He ruled alone and unchallenged, sharing his authority neither with other individuals nor with a group. Trujillo's was thus an extremely personalistic kind of rule. In order to maximize his

40. Flor de Oro Trujillo, pp. 50, 52.
41. Pages 82-83; and Bosch, *Trujillo, passim.*

personal power, it was required that he completely destroy or control all other centers of power. In the next several chapters we shall examine those pillars of his power: the armed forces, the governmental machinery, the national economy, thought control, education and intellectual life, and the Church.

3. The Armed Forces

THE FIRST and most important instrument of Trujillo's control over the Dominican Republic was the armed forces.[1] It was through the national constabulary that he rose to power and by military strength that he first assumed the presidency. After he became President, the armed forces were transformed into an efficient apparatus of the regime and were used to suppress any opposition and to maintain Trujillo in power. Though most authorities differ in their methods of categorizing the Turjillo dictatorship,[2] all are agreed that the military, at least initially, was the backbone of the regime. And despite the totalitarian-like controls which were later established over the rest of the society, the armed forces remained the ultimate source of Trujillo's authority. This chapter examines the size, strength, and composition of the armed forces; demonstrates Trujillo's control

1. Some of the materials in this chapter were previously summarized in Wiarda, "The Politics of Civil-Military Relations in the Dominican Republic," *Journal of Inter-American Studies,* VII (October, 1965), 465-84.
2. Miguel Jorrín, *Governments of Latin America,* p. 201, simply called Trujillo's regime a "military dictatorship"; Gómez, p. 98, categorized it as a "personalistic caudillo" dictatorship; and Edwin Lieuwen, *Arms and Politics in Latin America,* p. 151, referred to it as an "exceptionally predatory military regime."

over this immense military apparatus; and analyzes its service to the regime.

Size, Strength, and Composition of the Armed Forces

Prior to the United States Marine occupation, 1916-24, there had been no centrally organized, professional armed forces in the Dominican Republic. Rag-tag armies had been put together at times to repel foreign invaders and personalized bands had been formed to promote the domestic political purposes of rival generals or politicians; but these forces were untrained, disorganized, mutinous, and devoid of discipline, professionalism, administrative technique, and effective weapons.[3]

The United States occupation forces created the first standing Dominican armed force organized along professional lines. Prior to 1916 the administration and control of the military forces were weak and divided; now they became strong and unified. Before the Marines the Dominican armed bands were fragmented and inept; after the United States took control they became centralized and efficient. The recruits were now paid regularly, given free board and room, medical assistance, and clothing, as well as standardized training and weapons. The previously semi-independent provincial governors, municipal authorities, and local caudillos were divested of their military power. Indeed, the organization of a modern constabulary and the centralization of military administration were probably the major historical effects of the United States occupation.[4]

After becoming chief of staff of the National Army and later president of the republic, Trujillo carried the work of the Marines forward. Employing his considerable organizational and administrative skill, he further tightened central control, purchased the most modern equipment, strengthened discipline and efficiency, and increased the size of the military until it became one of the largest and strongest forces in the Central American and Caribbean area.

The exact size of the Dominican armed forces was always a well-kept secret. Official figures showed a standing army of 12,000 men,[5] though few doubted that it was many times this number.

3. Otto Schoenrich, *Santo Domingo*, pp. 317-18, 332-33.
4. See Goldwert, pp. 5-13; and Vega y Pagan, *Sintesis Histórica de la Guardia Dominicana*.
5. See S. H. Steinberg (ed.), *The Stateman's Year Book, 1961-1962*, p. 957.

All male Dominicans who were between the ages of sixteen and fifty-five were subject to the draft, and at the age of eighteen a year of military service was mandatory.[6] Selective service rolls listed the names of 467,704 men between eighteen and thirty-five who had "freely volunteered to register," though this inordinantly high figure was no more accurate concerning actual army strength than the official figures of the standing force. It is known, however, that in addition to the regular army, some 60,000 had received a seventeen-week course in basic military training and that Trujillo had frequently boasted that he could field a force of 100,000 men.[7] Including irregulars, 75 to 80 thousand would probably be a fairly accurate estimate.

Early in Trujillo's rule the army was equipped with the most modern weapons. By 1935, five years after he had taken power, the arms included Springfield, K. C., Monitor, and Remington rifles, .30 caliber automatic rifles, Colt anti-aircraft guns, German automatic rifles, Thompson machine guns (the type used by the F.B.I.'s famed Elliot Ness), .35, .75, and .77 caliber cannons, and .26 and .34 caliber small mortars.[8] This fire power had never previously existed in Dominican history or, for that matter, in the histories of most Latin American armies, and it foredoomed any armed uprising against the regime (the traditional method of transferring power in the Dominican Republic) to failure. Trujillo continued throughout his rule to provide the military with the best and most up-to-date weapons.

The size of the Dominican navy was estimated in 1957 at four thousand men and thirty-nine combat and auxiliary vessels. The ships included two destroyers, eight frigates, six patrol boats, two landing craft, and seven coast guard vessels.[9] The strength of this comparatively huge sea force was greater than that of Mexico and could have overpowered any other navy in the Caribbean or Central American area with the possible exception of the Venezuelan.[10] Though himself an army man, Trujillo displayed a marked preference for the navy and seemed to derive special pleasure from acting as "admiral of the fleet."

During the 1950's the Dominican air force grew into the most

6. Vega y Pagan, *Historia de las Fuerzas Armadas*, II, 150.
7. Ornes, *Trujillo: Little Caesar*, p. 132. See also Horacio Ortiz Alvarez, *La obra del Generalisimo Doctor Trujillo Molina en el Ejército Nacional*.
8. Vega y Pagan, *Sintesis Histórica*, pp. 236-47.
9. *Jane's Fighting Ships*, pp. 170-74.
10. The United States and its Atlantic Fleet is, of course, also excepted.

powerful of the services. It was composed of an elite corps of some 3,000 men and in 1952 had 16 airports and 132 combat and training planes.[11] The signing in 1953 of a mutual assistance pact with the United States resulted in an even greater preponderance of strength for the air force, since this was where United States aid and training were concentrated.[12] The air force, in addition, was strong on the ground for, by a strange quirk, and reputedly due to the influence of a German ex-military officer, it controlled the infantry tanks. The air force continued to be the dominant service, though by 1960, after the countries of the Americas, including the United States, had refused to sell additional arms to Trujillo, he was forced to buy from European producers, chiefly Great Britain and Sweden.[13]

A centralized police force was also formed during the Trujillo era. Prior to the 1930's the country had only municipal police forces, which meant that they were largely at the service of local caudillos or provincial governors, and Dominican presidents exercised only nominal jurisdiction over them through the executive ministries. Trujillo created the National Police in 1936 with a centralized command and thereby, as with the three regular services, unified still another armed force under the control of the regime. The National Police, to be distinguished from the several secret police agencies which also came into existence and which will be discussed shortly, numbered between three and four thousand.[14]

A number of irregular and paramilitary forces, finally, were also created during the Trujillo period. These were formed at times of national crisis, particularly when the threat of foreign or exile invasion loomed. Thus in the late 1950's three of these auxiliary forces—the Cocuyos de la Cordillera led by Trujillo's brother, General José Arismendi Trujillo, the Legión Extranjera, and the Jinetes del Este—were organized to protect the wobbly dictatorship. A reported five thousand men were mobilized in these three groups alone.[15]

Not only were Trujillo's armed forces comparatively huge in size and strong in equipment, but the Dominican Republic be-

11. Vega y Pagan, *Historia*, pp. 497-98.
12. Ornes, *Trujillo: Little Caesar*, p. 135.
13. This last aspect, which contributed to the overthrow of the regime, is treated in a different context in Chapter 8.
14. Rafael Martínez Hiciano, "La creación de las fuerzas armadas y la policía nacional" (dissertation).
15. *Hispanic American Report*, XIV (October, 1961), 699.

came nearly self-sufficient militarily. Considering that the country had almost no industry prior to 1930, this factor was particularly significant. In the 1940's machinery was purchased in Switzerland, Belgium, and Germany, and by the early 1950's factories were producing nitric and sulphuric acids, gunpowder, and dynamite. An electric oven for the production of steel alloys was built, and by 1955 small arms up to 105 mm. artillery were being manufactured.[16] The 1957 report of United States Senator George D. Aiken, head of a study mission to the Caribbean, bore out the fact of the country's near self-sufficiency in the military realm when it stated that the Dominican Republic "appears to be quite independent of outside supplies so far as arms necessary to maintain internal order is concerned" (page 12).

The size and scope of the armed forces are also reflected in the increased share of the budget allotted to the military during the Trujillo era. In 1931, a year after he came to power, $1,141,000, or 11.5 per cent, of the national budget, went to the military. In 1936 the figure had risen to $1,690,000, or 16.1 per cent of the budget. By the 1956-57 fiscal year $28,685,110, or 25 per cent of the government's expenditures, went to the armed forces.[17] This was by far the largest single item in the budget, but even the last figure cited did not include the $1,000,000 in United States military aid for that year, the special secret funds set aside for the purchase of planes, ships, tanks, and other heavy equipment, or the money budgeted to other ministries but channeled to the armed forces. (For example, the funds for the National Police were budgeted to the Ministry of Interior.) Trujillo's military biographer estimated that the scope of military expenditures and activities tripled during the era of the dictatorship,[18] but this may be a conservative estimate.

The immense armed forces were well disciplined, organized, trained, and equipped, and remained completely loyal to Trujillo. Their strength bore little correspondence to the threat of foreign invasion; rather, the major function of the Dominican military machine was the internal maintenance of the regime.

16. Vega y Pagan, Historia, pp. 407-9.
17. Ornes, Trujillo: Little Caesar, p. 138, and Hicks, Blood in the Streets, p. 80.
18. Vega y Pagan, Historia, p. 291.

Trujillo's Control of the Armed Forces

Realizing that the final source of his power and also the greatest potential threat to his continued rule were the armed forces, Trujillo attempted to maintain an absolute personal control over them. While in some totalitarian systems the military establishment has been able to maintain some degree of independence from the regime,[19] in the Dominican Republic the armed forces were not an "island of separativeness." There had been no long-standing military establishment prior to Trujillo; the armed forces were in large measure his creation and he kept them under his absolute authority. There could be no divided loyalties or divisions of command; power and decision-making were vested solely with Trujillo.

As commander in chief Trujillo had full constitutional and legal authority over everything that affected the armed forces. This position meant that he was in charge of military organization, distribution, administration, quartering, clothing, equipment, transportation, communications, conduct, efficiency, discipline, inspection, mobilization, retirements, promotions, rations, fortifications, revenues, resolutions, supplies, and declarations of war. He alone could propose legislation which affected the armed forces; all questions, particularly those relating to their force, distribution, and morale, were subject to his consideration; and reports of every activity undertaken by them had to be submitted to him.[20]

Even when not in the presidency, Trujillo retained full legal control of the armed forces. When he stepped down in 1938 and placed the puppet Peynado in the presidency, the Congress, it will be recalled, passed a resolution conferring on Trujillo the same rights and privileges as the president;[21] and when Vice-President Troncoso took over upon Peynado's death, Trujillo was named Secretary of War and Navy.[22] In 1952 brother Héctor's first official act as president was to designate him commander in chief of the armed forces.[23]

Trujillo's control over the armed forces, however, was by no means limited to his constitutional and legal powers. He em-

19. Friedrich and Brzezinski, pp. 239, 273-81.
20. Vega y Pagan, *Historia*, pp. 219-20, and Joaquín Balaguer (ed.), *El pensamiento vivo de Trujillo*, pp. 77-78.
21. Vega y Pagan, *Military Biography*, p. 154.
22. *Ibid.*, p. 147.
23. Vega y Pagan, *Historia*, p. 396.

ployed a wide variety of politically astute techniques as well to further cement his authority.

Among the major methods by which Trujillo maintained his control over the military was the constant shuffling of its personnel. No officer was allowed to become entrenched in a position long enough to build up his own personal following; the entire organization was shuffled periodically to prevent a potential rival from gaining an independent power base. These shake-ups in the structure of command were not limited to the highest positions but occurred all the way up and down the military hierarchy; not only were the secretaries of the several services frequently shuffled and reshuffled in and out of their positions but any officer who commanded a regiment, battalion, or special service, particularly those in the outlying areas, could expect to be replaced every few months. After one of these shuffles, for example, a former head of the navy might find himself serving as chief of the National Police, or a former lieutenant general as a colonel. As Germán Ornes remarks, the entire process resembled a game of musical chairs, and it proved to be a particularly effective means of keeping the armed forces atomized.[24]

Trujillo buttressed this control by constant surveillance of the armed forces. He held periodic inspections, arriving unexpectedly at the various posts to review personally the men and the proceedings.[25] In 1942 he created a special corps of inspectors with the rank of major whose function was to tour all the military installations, sometimes under cover, and report back personally to Trujillo.[26]

The armed forces were kept content in large measure by largess, though their condition was not so prosperous as the official spokesmen for the regime suggest. Elaborate pension, health, and retirement programs were worked out, though many of these benefits existed only on paper.[27] Nevertheless the military, both officers and enlisted men, were extremely prosperous when compared with the rest of the population of this poverty-stricken nation. The soldiers received three square meals a day, comfortable quarters, health and entertainment facilities, clothing, and regular pay, all

24. *Trujillo: Little Caesar*, p. 139. See also Charles Porter and Robert J. Alexander, *The Struggle for Democracy in Latin America*, pp. 147-48, and *New York Times* (April 5, 1960), p. 18.
25. Vega y Pagan, *Historia*, p. 520.
26. *Ibid.*, p. 306.
27. Nanita, *Trujillo*, p. 191, and Vega y Pagan, *Historia*, p. 310.

of which was far more than the overwhelming majority of the non-military population received. Trujillo pampered the soldiers by granting frequent bonuses and used the proceeds from the national lottery to provide enlisted men with low-cost housing (though low-cost, they were far better than the shacks from which the soldiers had come.)[28]

The armed forces also served as an avenue of social mobility; in a society where one's socioeconomic class standing was so important, the military enabled men from poor (and darker) families to rise in the social scale. Those who rose in this fashion were not allowed to forget that Trujillo was their "benefactor" and that he could as easily break them as make them. And for their continued loyalty and subservience to the Generalissimo, those who climbed the ladder of the military hierarchy received even greater benefits; an officership meant admission to one of the exclusive military clubs, implied equality with the country's elite, and became one of the most profitable occupations in the country.[29]

Though obviously underpaid by United States standards, other economic advantages accrued to members of the armed forces. Their incomes were supplemented by activities which the government either condoned or chose to ignore. Gratuities were given out by illegal gambling establishments and houses of ill repute in return for "protection," and fees were paid by employers to ensure "labor peace" and to guarantee against the enforcement of inconvenient government regulations. Though servicemen on active duty were forbidden by law from engaging in business activities, many found opportunities for "investment" in real estate, farming, small businesses, or other profitable activities. The government reportedly overlooked these activities since (1) it might otherwise be forced to pay higher salaries, (2) they served as substitutes for possible maneuvering against the regime, and (3) Trujillo kept the offenders under threat of revelation and punishment and thereby tied to him.[30] The Dominican armed forces remained loyal out of fear, habit, and self-interest.

An *esprit de corps*, carefully nurtured by Trujillo, helped maintain the unity of the armed forces and their loyalty to the regime. The military was isolated and pampered and was con-

28. Galíndez, *La era*, p. 307, and *Hispanic American Report*, V (June, 1952), 18.
29. Galíndez, *La era*, p. 307, and *Miami Herald* (May 12, 1962), pp. 1-A, 9-A.
30. Ornes, *Trujillo: Little Caesar*, pp. 142-43.

ditioned to think of itself as an elite element in the society. Whereas before Trujillo there had not been a distinct military caste, now there were military songs, military libraries, military holidays, military hospitals, military schools, and, though members of the armed forces were almost immune from prosecution, special military courts.[31] Exceptional service was rewarded by rapid promotion, the granting of special military medals, and appointment to one of the orders of military merit established by Trujillo. The armed forces were granted all sorts of special rights, privileges, and immunities, and these "fueros," as Professor L. N. McAlister writes, offered the soldiers "a measure of relief from their depressed status and an opportunity to evade the law." The military came to occupy a position of prominence in the social system and, again quoting McAlister, "the possession of special privileges enhanced its sense of uniqueness and superiority."[32]

Trujillo packed the armed forces with his relatives and cronies, who were chosen more for their absolute loyalty to him than for their military talents. Many of those at the top of the armed forces hierarchy were not even able to read or write, but were advanced to high-ranking positions by faithfully serving the dictatorship. Brother Héctor served as chief of staff of the army, and as secretary of war and navy; brother Romeo was a high-ranking army officer; and brother Aníbal also served as chief of staff of the army. Brother Virgilio served as minister of interior and police until it was discovered that he was cultivating a following of his own and was promptly sent abroad on an extended diplomatic mission, and brother Arismendi was a lieutenant general until it became apparent that he too cherished political power. Son Rhadamés was made an honorary major while still a child and son Rafael ("Ramfis") who had been named a brigadier general at the age of nine, served as chief of staff of the air force. Brothers-in-law José García and José Román Fernández were generals in the army and the former served as chief of staff. Nephew José García Trujillo was secretary of the armed forces and nephew Virgilio García Trujillo also headed the army. At one time over a hundred Trujillo family members held armed forces posts.[33]

31. Vega y Pagan, *Historia*, pp. 193-200.
32. *The "Fuero Militar" in New Spain*, p. 30. Though obviously written for a different time and place, many of McAlister's comments concerning the "fuero militar" are applicable to today's Latin America.
33. Galíndez, *La era*, pp. 358-66, and Ornes, *Trujillo: Little Caesar*, pp. 222-26.

Perhaps learning from the United States Marine occupation forces that a disarmed population could not easily fight back, Trujillo carried the principle to its logical conclusion. Not only were civilians and government officials not allowed to own a gun without special authorization, but the armed forces were not allowed free use of them either. Large caches of arms and ammunition were stored in secret hideaways, but only enough for target practice was allotted and only the best and most loyal troops were taught to use firearms. The armed forces had to often enforce Trujillo's will only with clubs or machetes. Basic training was limited to drilling and indoctrination since it was felt that, should the need arise, the use of guns could be taught in a short time; and Trujillo feared that the weapons might otherwise be turned against his government.[34]

The society came to resemble a garrison-like state. Armed forces life was glorified and inculcated in the youth. Military training was introduced into the school curriculum and children of nine and ten could be seen daily marching and drilling in the streets. But though military life was glorified and though the armed forces were pampered and occupied a position of prominence, Trujillo never permitted the military to forget that he was the Generalissimo, and the training program stressed the invincibility and infallibility of the "first soldier."[35] Indeed, no aspect of armed forces activity was immune from Trujillo's authority. With the armed forces thus securely under his control, Trujillo employed this military strength to completely dominate the country.

The Uses of the Armed Forces: The Terror

The mere presence of the powerful Dominican military machine, loyal to and under the firm control of Trujillo, was sufficient to discourage all opposition, but it was further used to impose an all-pervasive terror on the population.

When the Trujillo regime first came to power in 1930, the technology of totalitarian terror had not yet been fully developed, and the kind of oppression employed by Trujillo's armed forces was not much different from that used by other traditional dictatorships. During Trujillo's first two terms of office all opposition

---

34. Ornes, *Trujillo: Little Caesar*, p. 132, and Hicks, *Blood in the Streets*, p. 179.
35. C. A. Thomson, "Dictatorship in the Dominican Republic," p. 37.

was overcome through the comparatively unrefined techniques of beatings, murders, or forced exile.[36]

It was not until after World War II, at precisely the same time that the methods developed in Stalin's Russia and Hitler's Germany were becoming more widely known to the world, that the more refined and systematic procedures of totalitarian all-pervasive terror were developed. Not only did beatings, murders, or exile continue, though now on a reduced scale because these traditional techniques were no longer as necessary, but a vigilant and unremitting surveillance was maintained over every aspect of Dominican existence. By such means as those previously developed by more advanced totalitarian systems, secret police and espionage agencies rendered any deviant thinking or expression dangerous. And usually those who did deviate were efficiently brain-washed: "persuaded" of their "mistakes" and brought back into compliance with the official dogma.[37]

The kind of development outlined above, from the relatively simple oppression and elimination of the opposition to all-pervasive terror and brainwashing, is not unusual in totalitarian systems. A dictatorship must first eliminate its enemies, but it does not become totalitarian until repressive measures are extended to include everyone in the society. Trujillo first destroyed his opponents, but he later came to use preventive terror to ensure that no further opposition developed. As Hannah Arendt remarks, "Only after the elimination of real enemies has been completed and the hunt for 'potential enemies' begun does terror become the actual content of totalitarian regimes."[38]

Espionage agencies and secret services functioned under various names and jurisdictions throughout the Trujillo era. *La 42,* the original strong-arm squad which had terrorized the opposition into withdrawal in Trujillo's first election compaign, was soon replaced by a number of new services. The Army Intelligence Service came to concentrate on the discovery of "Communist" plots, while the "inspectors" scrutinized activities of government employees. Others included the Naval Intelligence Service; Trujillo's

36. Ornes, *Trujillo: Little Caesar,* pp. 46-59.
37. Juan Isidro Jiménes-Grullón, *Una Gestapo en América, passim.* See also Peter Wiles, "Comments on Tucker's 'Movement Regimes,'" p. 291, in which probably more emphasis than is wholly accurate is placed on Trujillo's technologically refined terror.
38. Arendt, *Origins of Totalitarianism,* see especially pp. 387 ff., concerning the role of the secret police. See also Friedrich and Brzezinski, Chapter 13.

bodyguards, whose activities went far beyond the simple guarding of their chief; and the prefect's corps at the University of Santo Domingo which checked student friendships, habits, and political views and which was headed by a former official of the disbanded La 42. The exact nature and extent of the activities of each of these several branches was never known by the others, and frequently two or more intelligence agencies were assigned the same task. Their secret activities and overlapping jurisdictions enabled Trujillo to use them to scrutinize each other as well as the rest of the population.[39]

The several espionage services were unified in 1957 into the all-encompassing State Security Secretariat. Major General Arturo Espaillat, the Dominican Republic's first West Point graduate and one of Trujillo's toughest and cleverest henchmen, was named to head the new ministry, though later his duties were largely taken over by Johnny Abbes García (nicknamed "Gillette" for obvious and appropriate reasons). The security department included the National Police; the "Spanish police," a hard corps of about one hundred former Spanish secret servicemen; the "Veterans"; the immigration service; the Military Intelligence Service (SIM), which under Abbes became the most ruthless, efficient, and feared of all the services; and various other foreign and domestic espionage agencies.[40]

The State Security Secretariat came to number some five thousand men, which made it larger than the regular National Police force as well as two of the regular armed forces. It was in charge of the issuance of passports, the enforcement of immigration regulations, the registry of foreign agents and companies, the issuance of arms permits, the vigilance of foreign visitors, the surveillance of gambling operations, the enforcement of security, the exercise of censorship, and the control of all organizations, meetings, and public movements. The personnel of the security department was recruited particularly from the criminal element. One writer plausibly claims that Trujillo preferred this type since he had found that men who could be imprisoned for past crimes proved more manageable and willing to employ terroristic methods.[41]

The large size of the armed forces and intelligence services

39. Ornes, Trujillo: Little Caesar, pp. 111-13, and New York Times (April 5, 1960), p. 1.
40. For a fascinating, though at times incredible, account of the politics of espionage and intelligence in the Caribbean setting, see Espaillat, passim.
41. Ornes, Trujillo: Little Caesar, pp. 111-12.

meant that throughout the country no one was ever far from a soldier or secret policeman. Armed traffic officers were stationed on nearly every street corner in some areas of the capital city, though the traffic was light. Each principal town (of roughly 15,000 or more population) had a large fort with guards who stood with fixed bayonets; and the police headquarters or army post was, along with the offices of Trujillo's official party, the most impressive building in every city. Army or police check points with huge bumps in the road ("sleeping soldiers") to prevent an automobile from speeding through were established every twenty miles throughout the countryside, where travelers were required to show their *cédula* (identification card) and give their name, residence, and destination.[42]

The secret services and intelligence sources were not limited to those in uniform, however. Wherever people congregated, plain-clothesmen kept close tabs on what was said and done. In addition, the kind of system developing in the Dominican Republic meant that nearly everyone was forced, to some degree, to be a collaborator. Informers could and did include almost everyone— taxi drivers, fellow workers, friends, and relatives. Employees of hotels, bars, casinos, and restaurants doubled as government spies.[43] These civilians were forced to collaborate with the regime since they lived under constant threat of loss of family or of job security.

Secret police or informers were suspected of being present at every gathering, whether in the flesh or represented by a hidden microphone. The mail was censored, and wiretapping in the modern telephone system installed by Trujillo was common. It became a regular cloak-and-dagger regime complete with spies, secret listening and recording devices, informers, the eavesdroppers at the bar, the mysterious missing persons, and the accidents that strained credibility.[44]

The effectiveness of Trujillo's armed forces and secret police and espionage services rendered any divergence from the official line extremely dangerous. Anyone who desired to alter the established order or who criticized the regime represented to Tru-

42. Ornes, *Trujillo: Little Caesar*, p. 107, and "How One-Man Rule Works on Doorstep of U.S.," *U.S. News and World Report*, p. 76.
43. Tad Szulc, "Uneasy Year 29 of the Trujillo Era," p. 9.
44. The best accounts of these efficient, technologically developed surveillance techniques are the dispatches of E. C. Burks, *New York Times* (April 5, 1960), p. 18, and (April 6, 1960) p. 1.

jillo the worst of "Communist" revolutionaries.[45] The result was that freedom did not exist—neither political, intellectual, religious, economic, nor educational freedom—except in Trujillo's unorthodox definition of that term.[46] Liberty of thought and of action was replaced by dogma, terror, and regimentation, and arbitrariness became institutionalized.

Not only was there no freedom of opposition in the country, but those who were merely neutral or apathetic toward the regime were also persecuted. In addition to all real opposition, being purged, every individual and every group which might form a potential opposition was obligated or forced to become an active supporter and collaborator. The comments of some competent observers are relevant to this point. Max Frankel wrote, "Fear stalks the Dominican capital. Missing are all dignity and choice; there is not only no freedom to speak, but no freedom to remain silent."[47] Germán Ornes stressed the same point when he wrote that one was assumed to be either a collaborator with the regime or a subversive; those who were merely indifferent were sub- versives by definition.[48] Charles Porter and Robert Alexander stated: "This is the world's worst dictatorship. Not in any of the Iron or Bamboo Curtain countries is the terror exercised by the government over the populace as great as it is in the Dominican Republic."

The terror was institutionalized legally as well as politically and psychologically. A 1933 law declared that all persons who in their writing, letters, speeches, or in any other way spread informa- tion of subversive character, injurious to the authorities or de- famatory of the government, would be tried as criminals.[49] Capital punishment had been unconstitutional in the Dominican Republic since 1924; yet soldiers, policemen, and the numerous special forces were authorized to deal arbitrarily with the population without fear of legal punishment. In this fashion, any expression of resentment against or disloyalty to Trujillo was nipped before it could grow into a threat. By the late 1940's preventive terror was a characteristic of the regime and one of the primary reasons for its longevity.[50]

One result of the terror was a stifling silence in an otherwise

45. Balaguer, *El pensamiento,* p. 280.
46. See the discussion of Trujillo's political philosophy in Chapter 6.
47. *New York Times,* Sec. 4 (June 4, 1961), p. 4.
48. *Trujillo: Little Caesar,* p. 114.   49. Hicks, *Blood in the Streets,* p. 78.
50. Porter and Alexander, p. 149, and Ornes, *Trujillo: Little Caesar,* p. 122.

volatile, talkative, and friendly country. Dominicans learned not to speak to outsiders, particularly those who spoke their language. The person talked to might subsequently have made an unflattering remark about the regime or have written something derogatory about Trujillo, and the teller would then have been considered equally guilty. Or, the person talked to might have been an *agent provocateur*, and any expression of disloyalty would then have been reported to the secret police.[51]

Political prisoners were usually arrested on some fabricated charge. They were frequently placed in solitary confinement in exceedingly small cells, with dirt floors and no windows, and furnished only with a bucket. Discipline was harsh and cruel and the jails were full of rats, vermin, and disease. Often several prisoners were placed in the same five by five cell, which made it impossible for one to stretch to his full length. One of the regime's favorite methods was to refuse the prisoner any liquid other than his own urine. The inmates were repeatedly threatened with death, and false stories about relatives or associates were planted.[52] As Friedrich and Brzezinski state: "A slow disintegration affecting all human relations sets people against each other and causes mutual distrust so that ordinary people are alienated from one another, all the bonds of confidence in social relationships are corroded by the terror and propaganda, the spying, and the denouncing and betraying, until the social fabric threatens to fall apart" (page 166). Usually these conditions and techniques ensured the prisoner's future collaboration with the regime.

When indoctrination and brainwashing failed, the dictatorship resorted to relentless physical torture. Those who survived were so ruined, physically and mentally, that Trujillo had little to fear from their release. Some were disposed of by being "shot while attempting to escape," while another was reported to have "hung himself in his cell." Unfavorable reactions abroad to these lame excuses forced Trujillo to further refine his methods. Prisoners were then reported to have confessed their guilt and then committed suicide in remorse. Frequently the executioners also disappeared after the commission of their charge.[53]

51. *New York Times* (September 14, 1955), p. 18; Porter and Alexander, p. 144; Ornes, *Trujillo: Little Caesar*, p. 120 all have the same account.
52. Hicks, *Blood in the Streets*, p. 40, and Ornes, *Trujillo: Little Caesar*, p. 121.
53. Hicks, *Blood in the Streets*, pp. 40, 48n, and Ornes, *Trujillo: Little Caesar*, p. 124.

Those who opposed the regime but whose death or disappearance would have proved embarrassing to the regime were frequently sent to distant diplomatic posts. General Ramón Vásquez Rivera, for example, who was thought to be the leader of a planned military coup in the 1930's was arrested, jailed briefly, and then exiled to Bordeaux, France, as consul general.[54]

In the post-Trujillo years Dominican Attorney General Antonio García Vásquez conducted an investigation of the atrocity stories previously silenced by the terror of the dead Trujillo's army, secret police, and strong-arm squads. The investigation validated many of these tales. According to García Vásquez, the Military Intelligence Service ran the torture chambers, *La Cuarenta*, on 40th Street in Ciudad Trujillo, and "Kilometer Nine," on a highway nine kilometers east of the capital. Some of the devices found included an electric chair employed for mild shocks or electrocutions; the *pulpo* ("octopus"), another electrical apparatus with long tentacles which were attached to all parts of the body and a cap which was attached to the skull by means of screws; a rubber collar which went around the victim's neck and could be tightened enough to sever his head; and an electric cattle prod used for shocking particularly sensitive areas.[55]

Political prisoners often had their nails extracted; some were castrated, others burned alive. One of the most notable cases investigated by the Dominican Attorney General was that of General René Román Fernández who was implicated in the plot to kill Trujillo. Román Fernández reportedly had his eyelids stitched to his eyebrows and left in that state for days, was beaten with baseball bats, exposed to swarms of insects, drenched in acid, shocked repeatedly in the electric chair, and finally machine-gunned.[56] The list of examples and illustrations could be greatly extended.

The terror was not confined to the Dominican Republic nor was the list of those disposed of limited exclusively to Dominican citizens. The long tentacles of the Trujillo regime covered most of Central America, the Caribbean, and the United States and reached out to include Dominican exiles, other Latin American

54. Hicks, *Blood in the Streets*, pp. 53-54.
55. "Dominican Republic: Chamber of Horror," *Time*. These reports were periodically published in Dominican newspapers during the post-Trujillo period. See especially the atrocity stories in *El 1J4* and *Unión Cívica* during 1961 and 1962.
56. "Dominican Republic: Chamber of Horror."

opponents, and United States citizens. Mauricio Báez, a prominent Dominican labor leader who was forced into exile, "disappeared" in Havana in 1950. Andrés Requena, novelist and editor of an anti-Trujillo newspaper, was shot in New York in 1952. Eduardo Colón y Piris, a Puerto Rican youth who had spoken disrespectfully of Trujillo while touring the Dominican Republic, vanished and was never heard from again. Charles R. Barnes, an Episcopalian clergyman, was found dead in the Dominican Republic after smuggling accounts of the 1937 Haitian massacre out of the country. Probably the most prominent Trujillo victim was Jesús de Galíndez, an exiled Basque scholar, former instructor at the University of Santo Domingo, and author of the Columbia University doctoral dissertation *La era de Trujillo* which was a vigorous indictment of the regime; he disappeared from New York in 1956.[57] The Galíndez disappearance was later linked with the suicide of Gerald Murphy, a United States pilot who worked for Trujillo.[58]

The total number of those killed through Trujillo's systematic terror cannot be estimated accurately. Mention has been made here of only a few of the most prominent. Albert C. Hicks concluded his 1946 book (pages 227-30) with a list of 134 names of those whom he claimed were murdered by Trujillo. But this list did not include the estimated 15,000 Haitians massacred in 1937. Even more significantly, Hicks' list was compiled before the transition from oppression of oppositionists to complete terrorization of the entire population had fully taken place. There are no figures or even accurate guesses as to the number who were killed in the late 1940's or early 1950's, though the immense changes which were occurring during this period in the social, economic, and political realms meant that the number was undoubtedly very high. It was probably higher than the 5,700 which Attorney General García Vásquez estimates as the number of those

57. The Galíndez affair focused attention on Trujillo and helped precipitate his overthrow. See Chapter 8.
58. Galíndez, *La era*, pp. 265-68; Ornes, *Trujillo: Little Caesar*, pp. 121-20 and Chapter 19; Porter and Alexander, p. 146; Hicks, *Blood in the Streets*, *passim;* and Noel Henríquez, *La verdad*, Chapters 5, 7, 8, 10 and 11, describe these and other examples of those killed by Trujillo's terroristic methods. Much of the evidence is circumstantial but the basic patterns and formulas have been repeated so often and the excuses of accident, suicide, or disappearance employed so many times that it is difficult to doubt the authenticity of many of the charges. In addition, there comes a point at which circumstantial evidence becomes overwhelming.

murdered or missing and presumed murdered in the last five years of Trujillo's rule.[59]

Trujillo's terror, administered by the powerful armed forces, secret police, strong-arm squads, and civilian informers (all under his personal control), was all-pervasive and affected the entire nation. The terror was a result of planning and organization and proved to be a technologically advanced and efficient instrument for the maintenance of the regime.[60]

After a time, however, the terror became somewhat less bloody. One reason for this is that after some twenty-five years of absolute dictatorship, there was simply less resistance. Few Dominicans any longer had the will to resist; physical oppression and terror was used less often as passive resignation set in. Another reason for the reduction of the blood-letting aspects of the terror is that by this time Trujillo had devised other equally effective controls over the populace. As Galíndez wrote in his 1955 book: "The Trujillo dictatorship is not so bloody as the exiles assert. The Trujillo style is characterized more by a bloodless type of domination; hunger, the knowledge that it is impossible to earn a living without proving an active adherence to the regime, is much more effective. Trujillo prefers to force the collaboration of a former enemy rather than eliminating him completely" (page 244). It is to these other techniques of control and domination that we now turn.

59. "Dominican Republic: Chamber of Horror."
60. For an interesting attempt at comparison between Trujillo's terror and the techniques employed by earlier totalitarian systems, see Jiménes-Grullón, *Gestapo, passim*. See also Wiles, p. 291.

4. The Government

TRUJILLO had risen to a position of preeminence through the national constabulary and in 1930 had used the army to gain the presidency. Once in office, and with the support of the armed forces, he established control over the entire governmental apparatus. The constitutional system was only a parody which masked Trujillo's absolutism; the formal governmental machinery functioned only as the dictator willed; the bureaucracy was subservient and loyal to the regime; and a single official political party carried out special activities for Trujillo. All the branches of the government were dominated by him, every action received its ultimate authority from his office, and all governmental officials were dependent on him for their positions. The governmental structure was highly monolithic, and all power and decision making were concentrated in Trujillo's personage.

The Constitutional Parody

The Constitution of 1955, echoing the words of the twenty-odd Dominican constitutions going back to 1844, established as an immutable principle that the country had a civil, republican, democratic, and representative government. On the United States model, the traditional three branches of government—executive, legislative, and judicial—were coequal and independent in their respective governmental functions. An impressive list of human rights was included.[1] In this and in the earlier constitutions in effect during the Trujillo era, the country appeared to be governed by the entire formal structure of a Western democracy.

The appearance, however (that of a constitutional democracy), bore little resemblance to Dominican political reality. Elections were held periodically but the returns were manipulated and the results falsified. The legislature was frequently called into session but only to approve without discussion measures demanded by the National Palace. The Supreme Court was likewise subservient, and the constitution was changed when it was convenient for Trujillo. Dominican constitutionalism was thus a reflection of Trujillo's personal desires but also of his wish to rule absolutely within a constitutional framework. The letter of the constitution was always upheld with great and perhaps excessive vigor, but the spirit of constitutionalism was wholly ignored. The constitution was a façade, a part of the attempt to hide the excesses of the dictatorship; it was honored in the breach but it did not limit the power of the dictator. The system, as Jesús de Galíndez remarked, was a "constitutional parody."[2]

Latin American dictators have often attempted to give the semblance of constitutional democracy to their regimes, but Trujillo's techniques were somewhat more subtle. Instead of merely paying lip service to constitutionalism, as many recent hemispheric strong men have done, he made a mockery of it. Instead of maintaining only the external trappings of democratic rule, he scrupulously observed its precepts. To overcome some constitutional provision which restricted his authority, he would not ride roughshod over it but carefully and constitutionally amend its contents or see that it was reinterpreted. For this reason the constitution was purposely ambiguous; and when the ambiguities could not possibly be reinterpreted in a required new light, the constitution was simply rewritten or amended, as occurred in 1934, 1942, 1947, and 1955. There was thus a vast gulf between the constitutional structure and the actual political realities of the regime, a fact which was carefully disguised, particularly for foreigners.

1. *Dominican Constitution of 1955.*
2. *La era,* p. 189.

A careful reading of the constitution reveals, further, that despite the elaborate system of checks and balances among the three branches of the government, the Dominican president was granted virtually absolute power. Contained in the constitution were provisions that in effect gave him *carte blanche* authority to rule as a constitutional dictator. There were no restrictions on the number of terms a president could serve. He had the authority to appoint and remove all public officials without congressional consent or confirmation; to issue special regulations and rule by decree; to declare a state of siege and suspend human rights; to regulate at all times matters concerning the armed forces, to command them personally or through someone designated by him, to fix the number of these forces, and to deploy them personally for purposes of "public service"; to expel anyone whose activities were "harmful to the national interest"; to initiate legislation and to veto congressional proposals; to extend the regular sessions of Congress, call special sessions, or dissolve it altogether.[3] It goes without saying that only Trujillo could decide what was meant by such vague terms as "public service" and "national interest."

The Formal Governmental Machinery

Trujillo's principal method of controlling the governmental machinery was the constant shuffling and reshuffling of political officeholders. He had the constitutional authority, first of all, to appoint and remove almost all government personnel and he used this power extensively. In addition, he kept a file of signed but undated resignations for all government employees, and officials frequently arrived at work only to learn that Trujillo had filled in the date and that they had "resigned."[4]

The technique of shuffling government personnel was employed for the same reason as Trujillo's frequent changing of the armed forces and police commands. One could never be certain of the permanence of his position and the government was thus kept in a state of flux. Anyone who gained a powerful position could expect to be replaced before he could consolidate his hold and build a political following independent of the dictatorship. No potential opposition power centers were allowed to develop. Trujillo's technique was to fragment the power of the many and, correspondingly, to concentrate all authority in his own hands. As

3. See especially Articles 49 and 54.
4. Ornes, *Trujillo: Little Caesar*, p. 264.

Germán Ornes stated, "No place in the pyramid of command is for keeps and no authority except Trujillo's is more than provisional."[5]

The game of musical chairs, as the constant shuffling of government employees implied, was played among all the deliberative or decision-making branches formally established by the constitution. Thus cabinets during the Trujillo era were not policy-making bodies or even effective administrative agencies, but a group of very temporary assistants. During Trujillo's third term, for example, which is chosen not because it is exceptional but because the figures are readily available, the personnel of the cabinet were frequently shuffled. From August to December, 1942, there were six changes in its makeup, five in 1943, sixteen in 1944, twelve during 1945, thirteen in 1946, and fifteen in 1947.[6]

The fortunes of the ousted officeholders provided a ready gauge as to whether one was rising or falling in Trujillo's favor. It also served to indicate the degree of the fallen official's "sin" and whether he might one day be back in Trujillo's good graces and restored to a higher position. Thus, if the sin were not too bad, the former cabinet member would be demoted to the Congress. After a trial period he might again be allowed to occupy a higher position. On the other hand, if the sin were great, he was ordinarily not allowed even a congressional post and was completely dropped from government service.[7]

But no legislator could be certain that he would be allowed to fulfill his mandate. During Trujillo's first term as president, 1930-34, the two houses of the legislature remained relatively stable: among 12 senatorial seats only two vacancies occurred, one by assassination and one by voluntary exile; and among 33 deputy positions there were 19 "resignations." During his second term, among 13 senatorial positions there were 12 resignations and among 35 deputy positions there were 46 resignations. From this time on there were always considerably more resignations among the membership in both chambers of the Congress during a given term than there were seats. From 1938-42 only three from a membership of 16 in the senate completed their terms while among the other 13 positions there were 30 resignations. In the

5. *Ibid.*, p. 260.
6. Galíndez, *La era*, p. 235.
7. Jesús de Galíndez, "Un reportaje sobre Santo Domingo." See also Ornes, *Trujillo: Little Caesar,* p. 264, and, especially, Crassweller, *passim.*

lower house during this period among 50 deputy positions there were 83 resignations. Trujillo's third term in the presidency, 1942-47, saw the same method continued when among a membership of 19 in the upper house there were 32 resignations and among a membership of 42 in the *Cámara* there were 139 resignations. From 1947 to 1952, among 21 senatorial positions there were 41 resignations and among 49 deputy positions there were 122 resignations.[8] Though the figures are unavailable, the same technique of constant removals and appointments in the Congress continued through the years of Héctor Trujillo's presidency.

The shuffling of magistrates and judges in the court system followed a parallel pattern. Criminal judges, Supreme Court justices, and the personnel of civil courts all had to submit signed but undated resignations on the day they took office. Trujillo family members and friends of the regime received special treatment in the courts unless the dictator willed otherwise. Though the Supreme Court was constitutionally given the power of judicial review, it could not act independently and did not pass on the constitutionality of Trujillo legislation.[9]

Other high state officials were also appointed and removed at Trujillo's will. The rector of the University of Santo Domingo, the president of the administrative council of the Federal District, as well as all provincial and municipal officials were rotated periodically. Trujillo had such wide appointive powers (literally from janitors to presidents) that his system of pre-signed resignations proved especially effective. The frequent removals served to demonstrate his power, but they also revealed how congenital his fear and distrust were.[10]

The method of filling vacancies that occurred further demonstrated Trujillo's absolute control over appointments. Congressional approval, first of all, was unnecessary for most appointments so that the dictator could appoint almost anyone he wished. Congressional confirmation was constitutionally required for vacancies in the legislature, however. When a vacancy occurred, the president of the party to which the ousted representative belonged submitted a list of three names to the Congress and the Congress picked a successor from that list. But since there was only a single official party with Trujillo at its head, the system meant that

8. Galíndez, *La era*, pp. 210-18.
9. *Ibid.*, p. 240.
10. Theodore Draper, "Trujillo's Dynasty."

professional "yes men" were selected from a list submitted by the Dominican Party. Trujillo usually approved the list beforehand and placed his choice at the top. Congressional confirmation of the appointment, then, was just a part of the legal and constitutional façade, but served the function of helping preserve the appearance of constitutionality.[11]

Elections.—Voting in the Dominican Republic was obligatory for those eligible, and failure to vote was interpreted as an expression of indifference toward the regime. Opposition parties, except when fomented by Trujillo, did not function legally after 1930 and opposition candidates did not run. In keeping with the constitutional façade, elections were regularly held, campaigns conducted, and ballots formally cast and counted. The elections were usually unanimous, however, and no dispute of them was allowed. Eventually the electoral board no longer bothered to distinguish between the number of votes cast and the number received by the official Dominican Party. The regime's candidates, unless Trujillo willed otherwise, received 100-per-cent endorsements.

The election of 1930, Trujillo's first, demonstrated what the likely pattern would be in future elections. In the weeks preceding the balloting, Trujillo's soldiers terrorized the opposition. The constitution required that the army remain in its barracks on election day; but despite the withdrawal of all opposition candidates, soldiers patrolled every polling place.[12] Of a total of 225,614 votes cast, Trujillo received 223,714 or 99 per cent.[13]

The number of votes cast for Trujillo in the 1930 election exceeded the number of eligible voters with the result that the still-existent opposition parties claimed fraud and brought the dispute to court. The district court of El Seibo upheld the claim and the Dominican Supreme Court supported the district court's decision. Trujillo's strong-arm squad, *La 42*, thereupon invaded the Supreme Court chambers and forced the judges to resign.[14] In subsequent elections Trujillo so dominated the governmental machinery that appeals to the courts were not even attempted.

The presidential elections after 1930, with one exception, were unanimous. In 1934 Trujillo was elected president for a second

11. See Porter and Alexander, p. 147, and Szulc, "Uneasy Year," p. 44.
12. Gruening, p. 584.
13. *Gaceta Oficial*, No. 4257 (June 13, 1930). These and other returns are accurately cited in Galíndez, *La era*, pp. 202-4.
14. Carleton Beals, "Caesar of the Caribbean," p. 33, and A. H. Sinks, "Trujillo," p. 167.

term with all the 256,423 votes cast.[15] Similarly in 1938, Jacinto B. Peynado, Trujillo's choice for the presidency and the candidate of the official Dominican Party, received all 319,680 votes.[16]

In 1941, as the new ally of the United States against the Axis Powers, Trujillo felt obliged to extend the democratic façade by creating an opposition party, and so the Trujillo Party was formed. But Trujillo was the presidential candidate of both the new creation and his old official party. Under the Trujillo Party banner he received 190,229 votes and as the candidate of the Dominican Party he polled 391,708; the total of both parties, 581,937, meant that Trujillo had again received 100 per cent of the votes.[17]

In deference to the wave of democratic sentiment which swept the world immediately following World War II, Trujillo again fomented an opposition. The Communists organized in the Partido Socialista Popular were allowed, and even encouraged, to carry out extensive activities, though they were soon suppressed. The newly formed National Democratic Party and Labor Party were even permitted to conduct an election campaign and to run candidates. The election returns, however, showed Trujillo and the Dominican Party with 781,389 votes, the National Democratic Party with 29,765, and the Labor Party with 29,186.[18] The artificiality of the opposition was demonstrated by the fact that in the pre-election campaign the presidential candidate of the Labor Party had signed a petition favoring Trujillo's re-election. These two "opposition" parties disappeared immediately following the election.[19]

In the 1952 and 1957 elections Trujillo did not bother with the creation of an opposition and his brother, Héctor, won both unanimously. As another election date approached, Trujillo, under heavy pressure from the United States to democratize his regime, again created two opposition parties and even allowed them to win some minor posts in off-year "elections"; but the dictator was assassinated before the next scheduled presidential elections could be held.

The president was not the only official elected unanimously. The Dominican Party's candidates for constitutional conventions, for the legislature, and for local offices always received 100 per

15. *Gaceta Oficial*, No. 4684 (May 29, 1934).
16. *Gaceta Oficial*, No. 5180 (June 6, 1938).
17. *Gaceta Oficial*, No. 5749 (May 17, 1942). For an account of this campaign see Galíndez, "Un reportaje."
18. *Gaceta Oficial*, No. 6632 (May 27, 1947).
19. Albert C. Hicks, "Election Day in Santo Domingo."

cent of the vote unless Trujillo wished differently. In a 1949 election in the province of Independencia, for example, Abelardo R. Nanita, Trujillo's official biographer, received all the 8,374 votes cast for senator, and Juan Bautista Lamarche and Manuel María Santamaría each received all 8,374 votes cast for the two positions as deputies. In the village of Pepillo Salcedo in Monte Cristi province, the three candidates of the Dominican Party for the three positions as regidores ("councilmen"), their three suplentes ("alternates"), and the three candidates for the three positions as síndicos ("mayors") each received all the 2,149 votes cast.[20]

Lawmaking.—The principal function of the Dominican Congress was to give legislative sanction to the policies and programs previously decided by Trujillo. When he declared a measure urgent, the law was passed instantaneously, and at his request the Congress approved measures which concentrated power in his own hands. No bill was initiated without the previous consent of Trujillo's office unless it was an expression of homage to the chief of state. The legislators did not discuss or debate proposals; their only responsibility was to vote affirmatively. The Congress was thus only one of many mechanisms by which Trujillo maintained the appearance of constitutionality.[21]

Many of the laws were designed to strengthen Trujillo's personal economic and political power. The constitutional reforms of 1934, 1942, 1947, and 1955, for instance, were enacted to justify procedures already practiced by the regime.[22] Trujillo had special laws enacted conferring extraordinary powers on his office or giving him a special legal and constitutional position when out of the presidency. Other laws made it a crime to resign a government position while Trujillo was abroad, and various tax exemptions and financial provisions were specifically designed to favor the Trujillo commercial, agricultural, or industrial enterprises.[23]

Some of the most flagrantly obvious special laws involved Trujillo's family or marital relations. In 1935 Trujillo sought a divorce from his second wife, Bienvenida Ricardo, whom he had married six years earlier and by whom he was childless, in order to marry his mistress, María Martínez Alba, who had already borne him a

20. *El Caribe* (November 6, 1949), p. 5.
21. Thomson, p. 33.
22. Galíndez, *La era*, pp. 193-95, and Ornes, *Trujillo: Little Caesar*, pp. 26-27.
23. Ornes, *Trujillo: Little Caesar*, pp. 26-27.

child. He therefore had Congress pass a law declaring that a couple could be divorced after five years of childless marriage if one of the partners so desired. Trujillo was divorced from Bienvenida and married to María within a matter of days.[24] When Trujillo's daughter Flor de Oro's marital and extramarital exploits had damaged Trujillo's prestige and image at a time when these were being carefully cultivated, Congress passed a bill enabling a father to disavow wayward children.[25] Two of Trujillo's favorite children, Rafael, Jr., and a child by Lina Lovatón, a mistress, had been born out of wedlock. Hence in 1939 a law was passed which gave equal legal rights to illegitimate children.[26] These measures all demonstrate how farcical, yet how carefully hidden from the outside, was Trujillo's constitutional parody.

Local government.—According to the constitution, Dominican provinces and municipalities were supposed to be autonomous and self-governing. Indeed, in the era prior to Trujillo the officials of the provinces and municipalities, usually in alliance with the first families of the area, maintained their own armed forces and ruled as nearly absolute sovereigns within their respective districts. Decision-making was highly diffused, and several areas of the country were almost independent sovereignties.

Trujillo maintained the appearance of local autonomy while at the same time he centralized decision-making. One of the principal agents of the centralization process was the official Dominican Party which maintained a large office in each city and which channeled many local matters to the National Palace. Even minor administrative questions were handled at the top by Trujillo or one of his henchmen. The party thus not only kept the regime in touch with local problems and needs but also helped destroy municipal and provincial autonomy and further concentrated power in the dictator's hands.

Trujillo's control of local affairs was further enhanced by his wide appointive power. Constitutionally, he had the power to appoint local officials in case of vacancies. As with other governmental positions, Trujillo controlled provincial and municipal authorities by first creating the vacancy and then filling it with a more compliant or loyal official. In the early years of his rule

24. Galíndez, *La era,* p. 369.
25. For her own tragic but amusing story see Flor de Oro Trujillo, "My Life as Trujillo's Daughter."
26. Galíndez, *La era,* p. 369.

while Trujillo was seeking to rapidly centralize authority, he sent out special commissioners with the power of the president's office behind them to bring the provincial governors and regional military commanders into line. Local officials were thus divested of their power, and the influence of Trujillo was extended to the remotest areas of the interior.[27]

The regime's control over local affairs was cemented by the creation of a municipal association. All cities were required to join and the association was administered through the Ministry of Interior (police). Though the association performed certain beneficial services for provincial towns and cities, its chief purpose was again to centralize decision-making. According to its statutes the association provided administrative, engineering, and legal serv ices for the municipalities; loaned them money for development projects; distributed national subsidies; and bought, sold, or loaned equipment, such as road-building machinery. In fact, however, few of these services were performed and the municipal association's major function was to serve as a link between the local and national governments and thus help maintain centralized control over local affairs.[28]

The Bureaucracy

The Dominican civil service before the Trujillo era was very small. Prior to 1930 the country was still essentially more traditional than modern; the dominant modes of bureaucratic behavior were personalism, nepotism, lack of specialization, diffusion of decision-making, particularism, and inefficiency. There were few services for the government to perform, in addition, which meant that there was no need for a larger administration.

Under Trujillo the area of government operations and activities immensely expanded. The many controls which the regime exercised over the society required an enlarged governmental apparatus. The bureaucracy grew particularly because of Trujillo's growing industrial, commercial, and agricultural holdings, which required managers, technicians, laborers, and so forth. As we shall see, it was often difficult to tell where Trujillo's holdings left off and the government's began. Suffice it to say for the moment that the entire governmental machinery was put at the service of

27. *Ibid.*, p. 241; and Crassweller, pp. 93-94.
28. John B. Blandford, *Public Administration in Latin America*, pp. 34-35, and Abraham F. Lowenthal, *Hydraulic Resource Development*, pp. 2-4.

Trujillo's personal economic enterprises and that this development required an increasingly large number of specialized and efficient personnel.[29]

The Dominican dictatorship always remained a highly personalistic, one-man operation, and Trujillo had few close advisers. He did, however, maintain a shifting body of henchmen, cronies, and hangers-on who assisted in carrying out his programs but who did not themselves make important decisions. This group resembled a "kitchen cabinet" and its members were at times called upon for advice. They were chosen primarily for their personal loyalty to Trujillo but were not delegated much independent authority and were not allowed to remain in their positions of favor long enough to secure private power.

These subordinates were not as close to Trujillo as might be expected. They seldom learned the complete inner workings of the regime or the plans of its leader. Each member of the inner circle was usually given only a small part in any assignment and was informed only about the particular aspect of a program which he was to carry out. Only Trujillo knew all the aspects and ramifications of every program and he kept this to himself. One author writes that Trujillo atomized and isolated his subordinates in this fashion because he did not want to give any one of them or the whole group sufficient power to pose a threat to the regime and also because Trujillo realized it had often been the case that a president had supplied the power to the one or ones that overthrew him.[30] Trujillo's official biographer has written accurately that Trujillo did not delegate leadership, formulated his policies alone, reserved his thoughts for himself, and carefully watched those close to him.[31]

Few of those who had originally helped Trujillo gain power in 1930 remained in the administration during its entire thirty-one years. Rafael Estrella Ureña, Rafael Vidal, and Roberto Despradel, all early collaborators, were among the first to be purged. It has been suggested that these prominent politicians sought to dominate Trujillo, thinking the young president could be easily manipulated, or perhaps Trujillo felt they constituted a real or potential threat to his rule. The exact motivation is unclear, but

29. Herman Bernholz, "Survey of the Dominican Administration" (unpublished).
30. Draper, p. 23. See also Crassweller, *passim.*
31. Nanita, *Trujillo,* p. 128.

all of the regime's earliest political allies were soon removed. Some of those purged later worked their way back into favor and were allowed to occupy government posts, but they did this under Trujillo's auspices and never regained their former power.[32]

Completely free of political allies and possible rivals, Trujillo now placed his own personal friends in the highest advisory positions. Many were fellow military officers. These remained active in the government longer than the old-time politicians; but by the end of World War II this second line of henchmen was also removed. Trujillo continued to confide occasionally in his cronies and sometimes allowed such men as Virgilio Alvárez Pina, Ricardo Paíno Pichardo, Félix Bernardino, General Federico Fiallo, Ramón Marrero Aristy, General Arturo Espaillat, Anselmo Paulino, and Johnny Abbes García fairly extensive power, but even these close aides were not trusted for long or granted too much independent authority. Periodically even the closest of Trujillo's cronies were stripped of power.[33]

As the Dominican economy, society, and polity became more complex following the war, Trujillo came to rely increasingly on a large, non-political bureaucracy. The expanding civil service was well trained, fairly professional, and impersonal; unlike the traditional system, it provided little opportunity for nepotism (the Trujillo family was of course excepted), for personal favoritism, or for the building up of competing political power centers. These bureaucrats, as Ornes states, were "hard-working messenger boys" and "perfect boy scouts."[34]

Discipline was deeply ingrained in the civil service. The machinery of government functioned with military precision and efficiency. Trujillo was, of course, an army man, and the bureaucracy was a reflection of his barracks training. Like Trujillo himself, the bureaucracy was highly disciplined, well organized, and capable of large amounts of work. Clerks and employees were not allowed to arrive late to work, to loaf during office hours, or to spend government time in private pursuits. To make certain the machinery was functioning smoothly and efficiently, Trujillo frequently made unannounced visits to various agencies and departments and immediately fired anyone he found not working hard enough.[35]

32. Ornes, *Trujillo: Little Caesar,* p. 260.
33. See Espaillat, *passim;* and Crassweller, *passim.*
34. Ornes, *Trujillo: Little Caesar,* pp. 259-60.
35. *Ibid.,* p. 262.

The Dominican bureaucracy under Trujillo was well trained and oiled and proficient in turning out its heavy load of routine, day-to-day assignments. Though this bureaucracy was technically competent, complacence and satisfaction with the status quo were deeply ingrained. All traces of independent action and initiative were eliminated. In some respects, such as the strict separation of functions and the hierarchy of decision-making, the civil service approached a perverted form of Max Weber's "ideal type"; nothing was ever decided, including the most minor administrative matters, without first being approved in the National Palace.[36]

While in many respects technically capable of carrying on the everyday business of government, the public servants, particularly those at the level of department or agency heads, were not always chosen primarily for their competence. Rather, the primary consideration was personal loyalty to Trujillo. For this reason, the bureaucracy was composed of men of widely differing levels of ability, intelligence, and performance but with the common element of allegiance to *el jefe*. This requirement ensured the subservience of the civil service to Trujillo, and because it sometimes produced mediocrity at decision-making levels, helped keep authority in his hands.

Dominican government employees were required to submit to extensive loyalty checks. The Comisión Depuradora de Empleados Públicos (Commission for the Purification of Public Employees) was established to weed out security risks. A 1945 form prepared by the Commission had to be filled out by almost all applicants for even minor posts. The form was a sworn affidavit of loyalty to Trujillo and required detailed information concerning the political views of the applicant plus those of his friends and relatives. The questionnaire asked which political rallies had been attended, the nature of any political articles written or speeches made, attendance at patriotic *Te Deums*, membership in the official party, political work, and details of cooperation with the government.[37]

These elaborate initial security checks were supplemented by additional, subsequent investigations. A letter was once circulated among all civil servants requiring information about anyone thought to be opposed to or indifferent toward the government. And at frequent intervals the Coordinator of Public Employees

---

36. Draper, p. 23; Porter and Alexander, p. 148; Ornes, *Trujillo: Little Caesar*, p. 263.
37. Ornes, *Trujillo: Little Caesar*, pp. 105-6.

conducted investigations of the morals, efficiency, and political views of the civil servants.[38]

Trujillo did not allow the formation of any kind of clique or grouping within the government which could become a possible danger to his rule. Even personal ties and individual friendships among his subordinates were regarded with suspicion and distrust. Though not openly declared reprehensible, such friendships were discouraged. Trujillo himself often personally destroyed private and family associations. An individual would be summoned to the Palace and told an unpleasant truth, usually gathered by the secret police, about his personal life or public conduct. The source of the story would be ascribed to a friend or relative with the implication that he had been betrayed by someone very close to him. Many friendships and families were broken up in this fashion.[39]

The technique of denunciation was later further refined. Letters would appear in the newspapers accusing out-of-favor bureaucrats and public servants of immoral behavior, crimes against the state, or disloyalty to Trujillo. Though the letters were unsigned, there was little doubt that their origin was the National Palace. Such a letter was expected to elicit a reply from the accused official denying the charges and expressing his eternal loyalty to Trujillo. The possibility of having one's name mentioned in the letters-to-the-editor column was a constant cause for dread and fear among public officials.[40]

Trujillo's dealings with all government employees were characterized by constant mistrust and innate suspicion. Even the dictator's official biographer wrote that he never fully trusted either friends or enemies.[41] He bullied all his subordinates, yet demanded and received absolute fealty.

The Generalissimo's distrust of subordinates included even his puppet presidents. His special position as commander in chief of the armed forces, even though others occupied the presidency, has been mentioned previously. In addition to this post he became, when not formally chief executive, a kind of super-president. In 1938, when Trujillo first stepped down, the Congress created the special ministry of Secretary of State for the Presidency which

38. *Ibid.*
39. *Ibid.*, p. 261.
40. Porter and Alexander, p. 148.
41. Nanita, *Trujillo*, p. 128.

enabled him to maintain direct control over the government. He was always recognized by the populace, government officials, foreign governments, and international organizations as the actual head of state, even though others were at times in the presidency.[42] Trujillo's position as super-president produced a number of comical situations. As the constitutional president, brother Héctor's signature was required on all official documents and aides were forced to scurry back and forth between the wing of the Palace where decisions were actually made and the wing where the papers were signed. The press carried a list of Rafael Trujillo's daily appointments and not those of the president. At state dinners and diplomatic receptions, complex protocol problems were raised by the presence of both the nominal and real heads of state. Only Trujillo took credit for everything accomplished by the government after 1930 when, technically, he was not president for thirteen of those thirty-one years.[43]

Another technique by which Trujillo maintained his control of the government service was to pack it with his relatives. As in the armed forces, Trujillo family members held most of the important positions. Indeed, there were even more Trujillos in the bureaucracy than in the military. A 1953 survey revealed that a total of 153 relatives was employed by the government or by businesses closely intertwined with the government. At this time Trujillo himself was minister of foreign relations, minister of social security, ambassador at large, and special ambassador to the United Nations. Family members held the presidency, two senatorial posts, six major diplomatic assignments, and the positions of commander in chief of the armed forces, undersecretary of defense, chief of staff of the air force, inspector general of the army, inspector of embassies, plus a great number of less important posts.[44]

The Dominican Party

The Partido Dominicano (PD) was founded the year after Trujillo first took office and served for thirty years as the personal political machine of the dictator to assist him in controlling politics and the governmental machinery. This party was created to replace the fledgling parties which had emerged prior to Trujillo's

42. Hicks, *Blood in the Streets*, pp. 136, 155, and Ornes, *Trujillo: Little Caesar*, p. 26.
43. See Galíndez, *La era*, p. 368.
44. *New York Times* (March 28, 1953), p. 7.

assumption of power and which were crushed in the first years of his presidency.

The first to be destroyed was the Alianza Nacional Progresista whose candidates, up until their withdrawal, had been the front-runners in the 1930 presidential campaign. After this organization had been broken up and its principal leaders sent into exile, Trujillo turned on the parties which had supported his candidacy. The two strongest were the Partido Liberal and the Partido Republicano, both of which disappeared when their major chieftains were assassinated or exiled. The minor parties—the Coalición Patriótica de Ciudadanos, the Partido Obrero Independiente, the Partido Nacionalista, and the Partido de Unión Nacional—soon dissolved.[45]

To replace the suppressed opposition Trujillo created his own official party. The Dominican Republic became a one-party state and the Dominican Party became an integral part of the government, yet it never ran the government and its subservience to its founder was maintained. The Party did not have a genuine popular following and never became an independent political organization; rather, it was used by Trujillo as a personal tool to implement his programs, rubber-stamp his decisions, and carry out certain specialized functions for the regime.[46] As William Ebenstein has written, "the totalitarian political party is not an organization of private citizens seeking to have its candidates elected to political office in open competition. It is, in effect, an agency of the government, no more independent than the army or the police."[47]

Members were required to swear allegiance to the Dominican Party, its statutes, and its motto of "Rectitude, Liberty, Work, Morality." (The initials of the party's motto "Rectitud, Libertad, Trabajo, Moralidad" were also the initials of its founder Rafael Leonidas Trujillo Molina.) Government employees were required to join and to pay 10 per cent of their salaries to it. Within a year after its founding, the PD claimed a membership of 80 per cent of the electorate.[48] Recalcitrants were jailed until they agreed to join and at times the police boarded the buses and *públicos* in Ciudad Trujillo requiring the passengers to show their Party membership cards. The lack of a Party card was regarded

45. Galíndez, *La era*, pp. 147-48.
46. Max Uribe, *Función del Partido Dominicano en la era de Trujillo*.
47. *Totalitarianism*, p. 52.
48. Thomson, p. 33.

as prima facie evidence that one was an oppositionist, and to have one's membership revoked for some offense was usually a prelude to more serious difficulties with the government.[49]

The Party had a branch for everyone. The children were organized into the Sección Juventud while high school and university students had their own organizations. The creation of the Sección Feminina led to a great outpouring of emotional rhetoric describing Trujillo as the greatest feminist in the country's history. Women were also organized into Clubs de Madres.[50] An attempt was thus made to mobilize and enlist all within the Party's ranks.

The structure of the PD's organization was hierarchical and monolithic, patterned on Lenin's concept of "democratic centralism." There were neighborhood assemblies, sectional assemblies, municipal juntas, provincial juntas, and a central governing junta. Though the members of each assembly or junta supposedly elected representatives to the next highest body (thus again maintaining the appearance of democracy), in fact all party officials were nominated by Trujillo. Further, the various juntas had no power. Policy was made only in the top echelon by an executive committee whose permanent chairman was Trujillo. The committee passed on all measures necessary for the development of the party and the realization of its ideals and programs, maintained absolute supervision over all branches and subdivisions, and nominated all candidates for public office.[51] The entire structure in itself was conducive to total dominance by Trujillo.

The Party's statutes, in addition, demonstrated that Trujillo alone made all important decisions. Article 27 stated that the Party's executive committee "cannot dispose of any matter which conflicts with the decision of the Supreme Chief." Article 42 recognized Trujillo as its chief and director. According to Article 43, Trujillo had the exclusive right to appoint the Party chairman and all its salaried employees, to resolve all disputes, to veto all resolutions, to authorize all expenditures, to eliminate all traitors, and to name all prospective candidates. His authority was "undiminishable and untransferable."[52]

Trujillo's decisions were final in all matters concerning the party; he not only determined policies but had to be consulted on

49. Robert J. Alexander, "Dictatorship in the Caribbean."
50. Galíndez, La era, p. 147-48.
51. Articles 7-12 and 20-34 of the Dominican Party's statutes in José F. Penson, El Partido Dominicano, pp. 67-74.
52. For complete text of the statutes see ibid.

minor administrative details as well. His control of the PD's finances was particularly important, for only he kept tab on the Party balance sheets and the records were never made public.[53] Despite the elaborate by-laws and large bureaucracy, little independent action was permitted PD officials and nothing of importance was undertaken without Trujillo's approval. As C. W. Cassinelli has pointed out in his article on the totalitarian party, totalitarian rule is necessarily the personal rule of a dominant individual.

The Party was founded to render assistance to the regime in all its activities. According to its statutes and Declaration of Principles, it assisted in the administration of justice, instilled in the youth respect for Trujillo, implemented his labor legislation, defended constitutional guarantees, and urged the observance of legislation in favor of marriage, motherhood, the rights of illegitimate children, and the obligations of fathers. The PD was charged with raising the standard of living of the rural peasants; the construction of parks, clinics, hospitals, churches, streets, hotels, libraries, and schools; the printing of books and newspapers; and the showing of movies.[54]

The more important uses of the Party to Trujillo, however, were not stated in its statutes and official declarations. The chief of these was the dissemination of propaganda. Trujillo had to be constantly eulogized and the PD was employed as an instrument of adulation. Party publications sang the "glories" of his rule and were constantly read over radio and television and printed in the newspapers. The propaganda was aimed at convincing the people that Trujillo and his government could do no wrong.

One night per week in each of the Party's fifty-four headquarters thrughout the country was devoted to a compulsory course on Trujillo's patriotic deeds.[55] The PD gathered signatures on a petition asking that the name of the capital city be changed from Santo Domingo to Ciudad Trujillo and often rounded up gigantic crowds called "civic reviews" to yell "Viva!" when the Generalissimo appeared in public.[56]

53. Ornes, *Trujillo: Little Caesar*, p. 150.
54. See points 3-10, 34, and 41 of the Party's "Declaration of Principles" in Partido Dominicano, *Declaración de Principios y Estatutos del Partido Dominicano*. Also valuable is Partido Dominicano, *Acción y obra del Partido Dominicano*.
55. Ornes, *Trujillo: Little Caesar*, p. 156.
56. George Kent, "God and Trujillo," p. 15.

The Party's functions included the dispensing of charity, always in Trujillo's name and usually accompanied by a kind letter over "El Benefactor's" signature. The feminine section of the Party administered milk stations and a scholarship program; its sub-division, the Clubs de Madres, helped in literacy campaigns and advised expectant mothers on health matters.[57] While some of these programs existed only on paper, others were actually operative: milk was at times given to starving infants, sewing machines to poor widows, and once a wooden leg to an indigent soldier.[58]

When Trujillo visited an outlying village, the people were frequently invited to present their requests to him personally and, if within reason, these requests were often granted immediately. Sums of cash were many times given away in this fashion.[59] However humanitarian some of these services and grants were, their chief purpose was the favorable publicity received. The Party sent lengthy press releases praising Trujillo's "proverbial generosity," along with pictures of the grateful beneficiaries, to the newspapers where they received front-page coverage.[60] The *patrón* system, characteristic of traditional Latin American dictatorships, was being refined along more propagandistic, Madison-Avenue lines.

Another major function of the Party was to unite into an organic whole all the diverse and divisive factions, cliques, and personalities which had traditionally existed in the Dominican Republic. In the words of one of the apologists for the regime, the PD was a link between the family, the school, the society, and the state.[61] It was, in its founder's own view, an organization which would help create "mass subordination to the principle of authority."[62]

The Party thus performed a "transmission belt" function. It enabled Trujillo to maintain closer contact with those he governed since the PD served as a channel of communications from the people up to the regime and back down again. Its numerous offices throughout the nation served as the eyes and ears of the dictatorship; the Party kept in touch with local needs and problems, sampled public opinion, sifted this information, and passed

57. Galíndez, *La era*, pp. 187-88.
58. Ornes, *Trujillo: Little Caesar*, p. 155.
59. Espaillat, pp. 25-26.
60. Kent, p. 15.
61. Fabio A. Mota, *Un estadista de América*, pp. 70-187. See also Rafael Peña Roulet, *Raiz y escencia del Partido Dominicano*, p. 9.
62. Rafael Trujillo, *The Evolution of Democracy in Santo Domingo*, p. 22.

it on to Trujillo. Because of the vast networks established, Trujillo came to know his country and its people—their wants, their strengths, and their weaknesses—more intimately and in greater detail than any Dominican before or since.

The PD also gathered information and kept elaborate files on the background, habits, personal character, and political views of each politically conscious Dominican[63] and all foreign residents. No one was permitted to oppose the regime or to deviate from the official dogma. The Party's informers were called "inspectors" and it became known that "good services" to the regime were well rewarded. One of the major sources of information was the servants of prominent politicians and leading families, and it is reported that a disguised school of domestic science and home economics trained maids to be informers until PD officials discovered that graduates of the "school" were being boycotted.[64]

The Dominican Party had an income of several million dollars per year. In addition to the 10 per cent deducted from every government employee's salary, it exacted large contributions from businessmen and also engaged in highly profitable business ventures of its own. In 1957, for example, its investments were valued at more than $6 million. When it dispensed shoes or milk to the poor or built low-cost housing, the Party made a handsome profit on its reimbursement from the government. At one time it owned *La Nación* and until 1954 was the second largest stockholder in *El Caribe*, the two daily newspapers of the capital city. It had vast holdings in real estate and provided the capital for many agricultural, commercial, and industrial enterprises. The PD became one of the few profit-making political organizations in the world. Trujillo was also enriched by its charitable activities since he owned the factories from which it bought shoes, cement, and building blocks, and the dairy monopolies from which it purchased milk. He used it as a clearing house for many of his own business activities and periodically transferred funds from the Party treasury to his own pocket.[65]

Only incidentally did the Partido Dominicano perform the functions of what is normally thought of as a political party. Almost as

63. The qualifier "politically conscious" was used to exclude much of the rural peasantry who were unintegrated into the nation's social, economic, and political life and who thus posed no potential threat to the regime.
64. Ornes, *Trujillo: Little Caesar*, p. 155.
65. Ornes and McCarten, p. 71, and Bosch, *Trujillo: Causas*, p. 161.

a sideline did it provide candidates for public office, devise party platforms, and run election campaigns. Even then, as we have seen, there was no genuine opposition and the elections were all fixed, though for the unaware and the unsuspecting the Party did lend another element to the constitutional façade. The Party was also useful to Trujillo as a patronage agency.

The Dominican Party was one of the principal instruments by which Trujillo maintained his control over the Dominican Republic. It was not a disciplined elite with a fanatical faith in a creed, nor was it a large popular or mass movement. Almost all Dominicans were forced to become members not so much out of devotion but as part of a routine. It was, in short, a personal apparatus of the dictator, with little pretension to ideology, and with a large body of followers professing allegiance to Trujillo. The Party's chief purpose was to provide Trujillo with another means of control over a large number of people who were not themselves directly employed by the dictatorship.[66]

66. In many respects, Linz' model of the "authoritarian party" is thus not appropriate or relevant in the case of Trujillo's Dominican Party. For some interesting comparisons, however, see, pp. 311-15.

5. The National Economy and Socioeconomic Groups

THE THIRD MAJOR PILLAR of Trujillo's control over the Dominican Republic was the near-monopoly which he established over the national economy and over all socioeconomic groups. He had risen to power through the constabulary and used military force to take over the government. Now, with the armed forces and the political and governmental machinery safely under his control, Trujillo also sought to bring the economic life of the country under his power.

Most traditional Latin American caudillo dictatorships, we have emphasized, have been almost exclusively military and political; the control which these traditional dictators exercised was usually limited to the armed forces and the government. Trujillo, however, went a step further: the armed forces and the government served as instruments at the service of his desire for wealth, and the country was converted into his personal fief. The state functioned as the legal servant of Trujillo's agricultural, industrial, and commercial enterprises, the armed forces as its security guards, the national territory as its field of operation and exploration, and the populace as its labor force, producer, and consumer. In transforming the Dominican Republic into a kind of vast private es-

81

tate, Trujillo was, as Juan Isidro Jiménes-Grullón remarked, perhaps "more Croesus than Caesar."[1] His control over the national economic life cemented his control over the country and its people.[2]

The Control of the Economy

Trujillo so dominated the economy of the Dominican Republic that he was its foremost businessman, its largest landowner, its greatest storekeeper, and its only important industrialist. Though privately owned monopolies were explicitly forbidden by the constitution, almost every profit-making organization in the country was either owned by Trujillo or paid tribute to him. The title of the pseudonymous Gregorio R. de Bustamante's book *Un Satrapía en el Caribe* (*A Satrap in the Caribbean*) was appropriate. The country, as Juan Bosch has written, was transformed into a capitalistic enterprise with Trujillo as the major entrepreneur; the Dominican Republic was converted into an economic cartel with the appearance of a sovereign state.[3]

The observations of some other popular commentators concerning Trujillo's manipulation of the national economy are not wholly inaccurate. Thus A. H. Sinks wrote (page 169) that the Dominican government could be summarized by the single word "grab" and that the grabbers were Trujillo and the many members of his family. Sinks commented further (page 171) that "the republic remains the most corporative of states with the Trujillo family controlling 100% of the stock in the corporation." Writing in *Inter-American,* George Kent stated (page 14), "This republic, so called, is run like a private business in which the boss is absolute." *Time* once commented: "While dictators in many countries have fumbled their way to economic disaster, Trujillo has turned into a brutally efficient businessman. Name of the business: The Dominican Republic."[4]

It remains impossible still, several years after the overthrow of the Trujillo regime, to determine the exact nature and extent of his vast possessions. His holdings in land, business, and industry were so vast and so complex that a United States accounting firm, hired by the post-Trujillo Council of State government in January, 1962,

1. "Trujillo," p. 485.
2. On the importance of Trujillo's economic control as an instrument of the dictatorship, see especially Bosch, *Trujillo: Causas, passim,* and Jean Ziegler, "Santo Domingo."
3. Bosch, *Trujillo: Causas,* p. 139. See also Galíndez, *La era,* p. 348.
4. Quoted in Ornes, *Trujillo: Little Caesar,* p. 239.

to survey his properties, had not yet untangled the web six months later.[5] Indeed, it is doubtful if the complexities of the Trujillo properties and accounts can ever be completely cleared up.

Trujillo's vast holdings in land, for example, were never accurately surveyed. The pattern, however, was that the Trujillo family would simply take possession in their entirety of the plushest and richest valleys and tablelands in the country. The dictator also owned few corporations outright and had few investments formally registered in his name. Rather, he preferred to legally register ownership in the names of family members and close friends and to work through dummy private and government corporations. Since the ownership of these properties changed frequently, just like the personnel who served the regime, it was difficult to tell where Trujillo's holdings ended and the government's began. Perhaps the best method of distinguishing the ownership of property was contained in the popular Dominican expression that if it loses money, it is government-owned, and if it makes money, it is Trujillo's.[6]

Though exact figures will probably never be available, an estimate of Trujillo's holdings can be made. It is estimated, for example, that between 50 and 60 per cent of the arable land belonged to him or his family.[7] This included roughly 700,000 acres of the best farming and grazing lands in the country.[8]

One tabulation concluded that the Trujillo family owned, in addition, 119 enterprises accounting for some 80 per cent of the volume of business in Ciudad Trujillo. At the time of Trujillo's assassination, it was discovered that he had an interest ranging from only a small percentage to total ownership in at least fifty-five corporations. The total assets of the fifty largest corporations were found to be $78 million, of which Trujillo's share was about $25 million. Trujillo, his family, and their associates controlled an estimated three-quarters of the country's means of production and probably an even greater share of the national income.[9]

Any list of Trujillo's holdings is perforce incomplete. A full index would likely fill an entire volume, yet even a partial and

5. See the report by David Kraslow in *Miami Herald* (June 8, 1962), p. 1-B.
6. Ornes, *Trujillo: Little Caesar*, pp. 237-38.
7. Kraslow, p. 1-B, placed the figure at 50 per cent while Jiménes-Grullón, "Trujillo," put it at 60 per cent.
8. Bosch, *Trujillo: Causas*, p. 148.
9. Ornes, *Trujillo: Little Caesar*, pp. 241, 258. See also Kraslow, 1-B.

necessarily incomplete listing must be attempted to demonstrate their vast extent.[10] The salt monopoly, obtained through a state concession, was the initial base of the Trujillo family fortune. Trujillo soon gave himself the state tobacco concession and was the country's largest cattle rancher. He had a monopoly on the natural riches of the country and received deferential, preferred treatment in exporting the products of his lands—sugar, coffee, rice, beef, sisal, cacao, coconuts, and wood.

The demand for Dominican products fostered by World War II brought large-scale industrialization to the country for the first time. Whereas Trujillo's properties prior to this time had been largely limited to land and its products, mineral wealth, and small businesses, they were now expanded into industry and larger commercial and manufacturing establishments.

Industrialization was initially limited to the processing of Dominican agricultural and food products. As the country's largest rancher and cattle raiser, Trujillo opened the only pasteurizing plant, controlled the distribution of milk, dominated the national slaughterhouse business, and held a monopoly on meat exportation and animal fats. With the state tobacco concession he became the major manufacturer of cigarettes and placed restrictions on foreign brands, while the manufacturer of matches paid him a license fee. His factories were soon producing cans, beer, arms, explosives, phonograph records, flour, peanut oil, leather, textiles, fruit juices, sacks, chocolates, rope, shoes, alcohol, furniture, hardware, paints, and clothes.

The sugar industry best exemplified these changes. Sugar, by value, accounts for about 60 per cent of the country's exports. With his vast holdings in cane-producing lands, Trujillo soon expanded into the processing and refining of sugar and the production of its major by-product, rum. After his entry on a large

10. This index of Trujillo's holdings is taken from a report by Herbert L. Matthews in *New York Times* (March 28, 1953), p. 7; Galíndez, *La era*, pp. 348-58; Ornes, *Trujillo: Little Caesar*, Chapter 15; Bosch, *Trujillo: Causas*, pp. 147-65; Kraslow, p. 1-B; Thomas P. Whitney, "The U.S. and the Dominicans"; and *El Caribe* (December 5, 1961), p. 1, and (December 8, 1961), p. 1. Chronologically, Matthews' analysis appeared first and it was later validated by the more complete accounts of Galíndez, Ornes, and Bosch. The Kraslow, Whitney, and *El Caribe* accounts were all based on post-Trujillo events and official investigations. Though differing in a variety of details, the similarities between all these independent analyses is remarkable and hence probably fairly accurate.

scale into the sugar business, that product took up an even greater share of the economy in a time of falling prices. He owned twelve of the country's sixteen sugar mills and built the huge Haina complex which, at the time, was one of the world's largest. Trujillo's holdings in sugar alone were valued at an estimated $120 million.

Following World War II, as economic development continued, Trujillo's ownership of business and industry was expanded into other previously nonexistent areas. The Ozama Construction Company, for example, was a complete industrial and commercial complex including cement, asphalt, steel, gravel, lumber, and concrete blocks. In addition to controlling exports and imports through the manipulation of the governmental machinery, Trujillo owned the shipyards, drydocks, and the only two shipping lines. Control of the Dominican Aviation Company and Caribbean Atlantic Airlines enabled him to monopolize the aviation industry and air transport. He owned Santo Domingo Motors, Dominican Motors, and Caribbean Motors and thus monopolized the sale of automobiles, trucks, and their accessories.

The ownership of other business establishments further consolidated his hold over the economy and the nation. He owned or controlled the country's two major daily newspapers and had a monopoly on radio and television. Trujillo's concerns thus received preferential advertising. The Bank of Agricultural and Industrial Credit was established to serve as a clearing house for his private transactions. He charged enormously high rents on his many properties and controlled the distribution of all medical supplies. It is easy to see how the near-monopoly which Trujillo had over the economy could be used as a further instrument of political control.

The vast web of the entrepreneurial dictatorship seemingly covered every facet of the economy. Organized vice and gambling were Trujillo family monopolies. His entrance into the insurance business was accompanied by the passage of a worker's compensation law and a bill requiring all employers to carry insurance on their employees. The national lottery was also a Trujillo family concession. The agricultural, commercial, and industrial enterprises under Trujillo's ownership made the Dominican Republic truly a personal economic empire.

In the midst of an extremely poor country, Trujillo became immensely wealthy. Though the per capita income of the Dominican population was around $200 per year, he accumulated a fortune estimated at some $800 million.[11] The Trujillo family fortune, in the relatively short span of thirty years, came to be ranked with the greatest fortunes in the world. He achieved this huge fortune by squeezing the population, cutting off almost all public consumption, and literally starving his people to death for the sake of building up his own private income.

Some of the profits from Trujillo-owned enterprises were reinvested into the economic development of the Dominican Republic, but the greater percentage was transferred into hidden investments, silent holdings, and numbered bank accounts in Europe and did not at all profit the country or its people. While many indices of economic development—gross national product, industrial output, manufacturing, exports, agricultural production, and so forth—rose rapidly, little of the new wealth trickled down to the general population. The Trujillo era was one of rapid national economic expansion, but the bulk of the Dominican people received none of the benefits of the new prosperity. As in most dictatorships, the streets were kept clean and great public works and buildings were constructed; but it is difficult not to conlude that few, if any, projects were instigated which did not materially benefit the regime or its reigning family.[12]

Some of the public works (highways, water systems, and so forth) did contribute to a slightly better standard of living for the great mass of the population; some of Trujillo's fiscal practices were beneficial to the economy, and there was undoubtedly a degree of material progress during the Trujillo era. It is most likely, however, that economic development in the Dominican Republic during this thirty-one-year period, reflecting a world-wide pattern, would have occurred anyway, with or without Trujillo.

What was most tragic for the Dominican Republic is that during this period much of the country's wealth was being drained off

---

11. The estimates of the amount of the fortune vary. Kraslow, p. 1-B, put it at $500 million; both Ornes, *Trujillo: Little Caesar*, p. 234, and Jiménes-Grullón, "Trujillo," p. 485, stated that it was "more than $500 million"; Ziegler, p. 101, placed it in the neighborhood of $800 million; and *Hispanic American Report*, XIV (July, 1961), 412, estimated it at $1 billion. The figure of $800 million was chosen because (1) it is roughly the average of the several estimates, and (2) this is the figure at which the highly respected "National Zeitung" of Basel, Switzerland (Trujillo's principal bankers) arrived. See Geoffrey Bocca, "A Dictator's Legacy," p. 5.

12. Galíndez, *La era*, p. 357.

and not being poured back into the economy or used for national development. Despite the occasional beneficial projects, a large share of the profits almost always accrued to Trujillo. Much of the profits then found their way to Switzerland. Some funds trickled into Geneva via various front companies, at least seven of which were based in Liechtenstein; other funds were deposited directly in the secret and silent numbered accounts. To expedite transactions after the dictator was assassinated, Trujillo's son and heir Ramfis bought up the banks (70 per cent of the Banque Genevoise de Commerce et Crédit of Geneva and a large share of the Société Holding Bancaire et Financière Européene S.A. of Luxembourg).[13]

Trujillo's control over the national economic life was most important because it enabled him to impose still further controls over the Dominican people. His most efficient method of terror was to deprive an individual or a family of its security and well-being, a particularly effective technique since nearly everyone was dependent on Trujillo for his everyday livelihood. At least 75 per cent of the gainfully employed population, according to one estimate, worked for the regime directly or indirectly—directly in one of Trujillo's agricultural, commercial, or industrial enterprises, indirectly as members of the vast government service.[14] Juan Bosch broke the number down further when he estimated that 45 per cent of the labor force worked for Trujillo directly and 35 per cent indirectly as part of the bureaucracy.[15] Trujillo could hire and fire whom he pleased when he pleased. Since the great majority of the population was thus absolutely dependent on him for day-to-day existence, his control over it was assured.

In the traditional Latin American caudillo dictatorships, the tyranny was usually confined to control of the armed forces and, with the backing of the military, the governmental machinery. In these dictatorships a degree of independent individual or group action was usually possible since the dictator did not dominate the national economic life. Economic independence usually resulted in at least a degree of political independence, even in the severest dictatorships. But in the Dominican Republic there was so little economic independence that even a bare minimum of political independence was impossible. The Dominican people,

13. Bocca, p. 5.
14. Jiménes-Grullón, "Trujillo," pp. 485-86.
15. Trujillo: Causas, pp. 147-48.

forced to produce and consume Trujillo's products, were the ultimate guarantee of his economic control and hence of his continued rule.[16]

Trujillo's manipulation of the nation's economy for his own profit was not unique, for many Latin American dictators have transferred untold hundreds of millions of dollars out of their countries while holding power. Juan Perón of Argentina, Marcos Pérez Jiménez of Venezuela, and Fulgencio Batista of Cuba are only a few recent examples of dictators who became enormously wealthy. While enriching themselves in private and public dealings, however, these dictators did not exercise anywhere near total control over their nations' economies. What was unusual in Trujillo's Dominican Republic was his near-monopoly of the entire national economic life as an instrument of control; he used his wealth to further increase his power.

Another unique feature was the spirit of fraud which impregnated all government and business dealings. Germán Ornes wrote: "What makes the Dominican situation particularly abhorrent is the sheer corruption and hypocrisy that pervades the actions of Trujillo or the small group of men who carry out his ill-fated policies. . . . With 'Operation Big Swindle' in full swing . . . government has been turned into a permanent exercise in thievery, embezzlement, bribery, blackmail, and all the known unlawful devices evolved by contemporary lords of the underworld."[17] Dominican business and government came to resemble what Ornes colorfully called "the virtues of a bawdy house."[18] Trujillo exacted tribute and fealty and, by whatever methods, legal or violent, declared or undeclared, used his power to impose his personal monolithic control.

The entire Dominican government became the legal servant of Trujillo's business dealings; he used the dictatorship to further facilitate his control of the economic life. Legislation was designed to benefit his business empire, while the tax structure, customs and tariffs, and economic controls and restrictions were intended to benefit Trujillo, his family, and his friends. Direct taxes, for example, accounted in 1954 for only 12 per cent of the national tax revenues. The incidence of most taxes fell indirectly on the great mass of the population; and property owners, of which

16. *Ibid.*, p. 141.
17. *Trujillo: Little Caesar*, p. 252.
18. *Ibid.*, p. 253.

Trujillo was the largest, bore little of the tax burden. The incomes of the dictator and his immediate family were by law also exempt from taxation.[19]

The national banking system was designed especially to help finance his enterprises, and one bank served specifically as a clearing house for these transactions. Ambassadors were sent abroad not so much to perform the normal diplomatic functions, but to act as lobbyists for Trujillo's products, particularly to secure increases in the sugar quota given the country by the United States.[20] Government agencies such as the Sugar Commission worked only for Trujillo. Indeed, the sugar industry most clearly exemplified the interlocking system of Trujillo's power and control. Trujillo's sugar companies were awarded a general tax exemption, government-owned construction equipment was used to clear land and build refineries, the cane was planted on lands watered by a government irrigation project, access roads were built with government funds, soldiers and convicts formed the labor force, the armed forces stood guard along the barbed wire enclosures, and army trucks transported the sugar to Trujillo's shipyards.[21]

The cruder forms of economic exploitation flourished. The government became one of the most lucrative of entrepreneurs making highly profitable deals with contractors and businessmen and finding new occasions for enrichment wherever a highway or public building was constructed or whenever private business required a franchise or favor.[22] There was no such thing as conflict of interest; private capital was made of the public domain.

Trujillo was, of course, the major beneficiary of this peculation. He often bought businesses or property from the government at low prices and sold them to private investors at enormous profit. When one of his investments failed, it was unloaded on the government. Many properties went back and forth between the government and Trujillo several times. One farm, "Altagracia Julia," is reported to have changed hands so many times that no one was ever certain of its owner.[23]

Trujillo received a 10 per cent cut of everything the govern-

19. Jiménes-Grullón, "Trujillo," p. 485, and New York Times (March 28, 1953), p. 7.
20. Bosch, Trujillo: Causas, p. 149; and Henry C. Wallich and Robert Triffin, Monetary and Banking Legislation of the Dominican Republic.
21. Ornes, Trujillo: Little Caesar, pp. 239-40.
22. Draper, p. 24.
23. Ornes, Trujillo: Little Caesar, p. 255.

ment bought or sold, even from his own construction firms. These procedures came most prominently to light during a 1957 United States Senate Finance Committee investigation of income tax evasion. It was learned that the Internal Revenue Service, operating under pressure from the Department of State, had allowed the Lockjoint Pipe Company, a New Jersey construction firm, to deduct as a business expense a $1.8 million bribe split between Trujillo and an intermediary for a contract in the Dominican Republic. Under questioning, Tax Commissioner Russell C. Harrington is reported to have testified that such bribes were "an ordinary and necessary business expense."[24] If such graft were indeed "ordinary and necessary," it probably helps explain the extent of Trujillo's public works projects.

Payoffs and corruption were widespread in almost all areas of enterprise. Under the jurisdiction of brother Romeo Trujillo, protection was granted to illegal gambling establishments, numbers rackets, and houses of ill repute. Brother Virgilio Trujillo was reported to have earned the title of "Señor Supreme Court" because of his placing, for a fee, of the family name behind one side or another in lawsuits. Mysterious fires broke out in the peanut oil factory when the plant became obsolete and in the sisal warehouse when the price was dropping, and in both cases the insurance was paid without investigation. Another fire destroyed the only paint factory in competition with Trujillo's.[25]

When questioned and arrested on another tax evasion charge, Jack B. Cooper of Miami Beach admitted helping Rafael Trujillo, Jr., embezzle public funds and stated, "I was not alarmed by the graft arrangement. . . . To me this was the accepted practice of doing business in the Dominican Republic." Cooper's testimony revealed further that Trujillo, Jr., while head of the air force, had signed sham contracts for the purchase of forty-two fighter planes, listing the prices higher than they actually were and pocketing the difference.[26]

It becomes clear that in addition to using the Dominican economy as a means of enriching himself and of exercising control over the 75-80 per cent of the labor force who worked for him, Trujillo frequently employed his economic power to destroy his political opponents. Banks could and did, on a political basis,

24. This incident is reported *ibid.*, pp. 253-54.
25. *Ibid.*, pp. 255-56.
26. *Miami Herald* (April 6, 1962), p. 1-A.

refuse loans and foreclose mortgages; government agencies refused export or import permits to out-of-favor businessmen; property was destroyed by "unknown" gangs; electricity or phone service was interrupted; and streets and sidewalks in front of selected business establishments were torn up. A good example of these techniques is provided by the case of Germán Ornes, who at one time was owner-editor of Cuidad Trujillo's major newspaper *El Caribe*. After falling out of favor with the dictator, Ornes went to the United States where he wrote a letter to Trujillo stating that he did not intend to return to the Dominican Republic and offering to sell the newspaper. But without prior notice the finance company foreclosed and *El Caribe* became the property of the regime.[27]

Trujillo thus utilized his near-monopoly of the national economy to further secure his control over the country. The title "President," as Theodore Draper remarked, was merely a concession to a foreign fad; everyone worked hard but it was primarily for the national entrepreneur.[28] Daniel James accurately stated that "It is impossible to eat, drink, smoke or dress without in some way benefitting *el benefactor* or his family. The Dominican pays him tribute from birth to death."[29]

The Control of Socioeconomic Groups

In addition to his near-monopoly of the national economic life, Trujillo made a determined effort to keep all socioeconomic groups in the country under his control. No group was allowed to become a nucleus for power to rival or compete with the dictator's personal authority. For "old" or "traditional" and "new" or "modern" sectors[30] of the population alike, success and satisfaction of demands depended on the extent to which these groups were subservient to Trujillo.

Independent interest associations were thus not permitted to exist other than as fronts or servants for the regime. As Ornes states, almost every day was "loyalty day" for some sector of

27. Julian Díaz Valdeperes, "La Cuestión de '*El Caribe*,'" and Ornes, *Trujillo: Little Caesar*, pp. 196-200.
28. Draper, p. 22.
29. Quoted in Bosch, *Trujillo: Causas*, p. 164.
30. Terms like "traditional" and "modern" are used advisedly to denote ideal types. See especially the Introduction by Gabriel A. Almond, "A Functional Approach to Comparative Politics" in Almond and James S. Coleman (eds.), *The Politics of the Developing Areas*, pp. 3-64.

Dominican society. One day the labor leaders or armed forces chiefs gathered arm in arm with Trujillo before the cameras; the next day it would be the turn of the dentists, the rice-growers, or the university student leaders.[31] No organized group or socio-economic sector could function independently as an intermediary between the government and the governed; Trujillo's rule was direct and hence more absolute.[32]

The rural peasantry.—Prior to 1930 the rural peasantry (*campesinos*) existed largely outside the nation's social, economic, and political life, and, for the most part, they remained unintegrated, unmobilized, and uninvolved throughout the thirty-one-year Trujillo era. Accurate figures are not available for the first part of Trujillo's rule, but even by 1960, despite some industrialization and increasing urbanization, the Dominican Republic remained 65 per cent rural.[33] Only about 20 per cent of this rural population could obtain seasonal employment, mostly on the large plantations, while four-fifths continued to exist by subsistence farming.[34] With an illiteracy rate in the countryside of 80-90 per cent, outside the market money economy, and unaffected by decisions made in the capital, the *campesinos* held an unimportant political role. They produced little, consumed little, bought almost nothing, and continued to live in the manner to which they had traditionally been accustomed.[35]

The peasantry remained, during the Trujillo period, the most atomized of all Dominican social sectors. In the case of the peasantry, however, this lack of solidarity or organization and of group self-consciousness was, by and large, not accomplished through a forced campaign of purposeful atomization on the part of the regime. The *campesinos* had historically been isolated and without much contact or awareness of national politics. The Dominican peasantry was not a revolutionary force and posed no threat to the dictatorship. Trujillo, therefore, seldom bothered with it.

Because of the isolation and nonrevolutionary character of the

31. Ornes, *Trujillo: Little Caesar*, p. 7.
32. On the role of interest organizations as intermediaries which tend to serve as checks on absolute government, see especially Kornhauser, pp. 74-76.
33. The criterion of an urban person is anyone who lived in a town of 1,000 population or more. See Dyer, *passim*.
34. *Informe sobre la Republica Dominicana* (Anon., typed carbon copy), p. 11.
35. Alberto Arredondo and Carlos M. Campos, "Las condiciones de vida del campesino dominicano."

peasants, Trujillo made little attempt to enlist them in a mass movement of the totalitarian type. Indeed, as Friedrich and Brzezinski (Chapter 21) point out, the agricultural sector presents difficulties for any would-be totalitarian state. The nature of agricultural production and pre-industrial rural life is such that it is especially unsuited for large-scale organization and mass control. No totalitarian system has been completely successful in mobilizing, regimenting, and bringing under total control the rural peasantry.

Realizing that the *campesinos* were not a major source of potential danger to his rule, Trujillo's efforts to bring them under the control of his system were feeble and halfhearted. If their children went to school, they received the same *trujillista* indoctrination as other schoolchildren; but few attended school. The official Dominican Party had a peasant branch, but this organization existed almost exclusively on paper.[36] Some *campesinos* were appointed to minor government posts in the rural areas, but the number of these was insignificant. Under the Trujillo agrarian reform much of the less fertile land in the country was distributed to dispossessed and landless peasants and the entire program was accompanied by widespread propaganda, but this effort never reached the dimensions of a full-scale mass movement.[37]

The closest the regime came to organizing mass support in the countryside was its stress on nationalism and its propagation of Trujillo as the personification of the nation. Through immigration and forced resettlement of the population, Trujillo sought to make the Dominicans clearly distinguishable from their traditionally hated Haitian neighbors. The regime's propaganda incessantly stressed nationalistic themes—the Dominicanization of ownership, the settling of the previously undefined Haitian border, the payment of the foreign debt which had often made the country prey to foreign powers, increased power and prestige—and pictured Trujillo as the country's greatest hero, ruler, and savior. He became the godfather and *patrón* of numerous *campesino* children. In the popular mind, even in isolated areas of the countryside, Trujillo was the nation and the nation was Trujillo.[38]

Despite some totalitarian ventures in the countryside and the incorporation of more and more peasants into the national eco-

36. The first national congress of peasants in Dominican history was actually called by son Ramfis *after* Trujillo had been assassinated. See *El Caribe* (September 29, 1961), p. 1, and (November 1, 1961), p. 1.
37. Manuel Valldeperes, *Acción y pensamiento de Trujillo*, p. 160.
38. Mota, pp. 160-62.

nomic life, however, Trujillo did not fully succeed in integrating the entire rural population into his regime. Most peasants remained subsistence farmers and did not achieve political significance. The government did little to improve farm-to-market roads or to expand communications facilities to isolated areas, both of which would probably have brought the *campesinos* to a greater awareness of the system of which they were a part. Trujillo could afford to ignore many of these needs and wants because he realized that such an unorganized and diffuse group posed no threat. The rural peasantry thus remained largely isolated and unintegrated into the national existence; and Trujillo, for the most part, preferred that they remain in that atomized state. In Trujillo's Dominican Republic the peasants were subjects of the system, but not fully participant members of it.[39]

The rural-urban workers.[40]—Prior to the Trujillo era, an organized labor movement was almost nonexistent in the Dominican Republic. The lack of workers' organizations was a reflection of the almost total absence of industry and of the traditional, unmechanized, agrarian economy, conditions which persisted into the 1920's. It was not until 1929, only one year before Trujillo came to power, that the first national labor organization, the Dominican Confederation of Workers (CDT), was formed as a consequence of the worldwide boom of the 1920's. Labor remained a weak force, however, throughout the early years of Trujillo's rule and it was not until the 1940's, again with the stimulus of the war and the continued expansion of the economy, that the workers became sufficiently strong and well enough organized to constitute a potential threat to the regime.

The CDT from the time of its founding was the largest labor federation. But though relatively large in comparison with the other fledgling workers' organizations, it remained politically unimportant until the ranks of its membership were swelled by Trujillo's efforts to industrialize and stimulate overall economic development. The CDT's success was indicated by the fact that from 1940 to 1943 it was the only labor organization to enjoy official recognition. Its success, however, sealed its doom. Following World War II the CDT became even more dependent on the

39. See *Informe*, p. 10.
40. The materials in this section were previously summarized in Howard J. Wiarda, "The Development of the Labor Movement in the Dominican Republic," *Inter-American Affairs*, XX (Summer, 1966), 41-63.

government and was used by Trujillo as an instrument to control the labor movement and to effect political action. The CDT was "coordinated" with the regime—labor completely lost its freedom and independence, and the workers' organizations became non-autonomous bureaucratic agencies of the government.[41]

Only one major strike occurred during the thirty-one years of the Trujillo era. Previous small-scale demonstrations in 1942 and 1945 had been ruthlessly crushed by Trujillo's army; but in January, 1946, the sugar workers struck for higher wages. The regime took no action against the workers during the two-week shutdown and even acceded to many of their demands. Repressive measures were only taken later against the leaders of the strikes; Manuel Frías Meyreles was arrested for inciting a riot and Mauricio Báez was forced to take asylum in the Mexican Embassy. Báez, now considered the father of the Dominican labor movement, later "disappeared" from the streets of Havana, and was presumed killed by the regime.[42] Three months after the settlement of the strike Trujillo delivered a public address in which he declared that "in no case can the workers decide to stop work or declare a strike."[43]

Subsequent to the 1946 work stoppage, various measures were enacted by the rubber-stamp Congress which brought the labor movement under the even more strict control of the government. Labor legislation was authored providing for minimum wages, social security, sick leave, and paid vacations.[44] The legislation was a cruel hoax on the workers since they received few benefits, and the government's concessions to and patronage of labor destroyed its independence and brought even tighter controls. These measures culminated in 1951 with the promulgation of the celebrated Trujillo Labor Code by which all labor organizations were amalgamated into the official CDT. From that time on, though Trujillo continued to profess his belief in free trade unions and in labor's rights, absolutely no independent labor activity of significance was permitted and the workers were systematically exploited for the benefit of the ruling family.[45]

During the 1950's, as the country continued to industrialize, the

41. Galíndez, *La era,* p. 299.
42. *Ibid.,* pp. 301-4.
43. Rafael Trujillo, *Discurso pronunciado por el Excmo.,* p. 15.
44. Narciso Elio Bautista y de Oleo, "La protección de la clase obrera en la era de Trujillo" (dissertation).
45. "El régimen de Trujillo y los sindicatos," *Combate.*

labor force inevitably grew. Though the official figures are probably exaggerated, they do serve to indicate the increasing numerical strength of the rural-urban workers. At the height of its power the CDT claimed to have within its organized ranks 156 unions with a total membership of 250,000 persons.[46] In addition, there were a few independent associations of craftsmen organized locally in the smaller towns, but these were closely scrutinized and not permitted to organize nationally. Significantly, in Trujillo's private enterprises, particularly the all-important sugar industry, even the government-controlled labor organization was not allowed to function.[47]

The development of a strong, independent labor movement, a vital element in a free and democratic society, was, despite the numerical increases, interrupted, frustrated, and perverted during the Trujillo period. An informal survey carried out in mid-November, 1961 (the time when the last Trujillos left the country), revealed that an overwhelming majority of the workers had no conception of the ends, means, or nature of labor unions. Indifference to their existence or ignorance of their functions was the most common response of those interviewed. Some 90 per cent had no idea of what a trade union was supposed to be; most respondents considered it as something "official" or like a social club.[48]

This ignorance of the nature of trade unionism and of the labor movement may be better understood if one goes behind the legalistic façade and examines realistically the condition of labor and of the workingman during the Trujillo era. When Daniel Benedict of the AFL-CIO and Raúl Valdivia of the Cuban Sugar Workers Federation visited the Dominican Republic in the late 1950's as a delegation representing the International Confederation of Free Trade Unions, they reported that there was no freedom of association in the country, that the trade unions were not independent and were strictly controlled by the government, that there was no collective bargaining, that working men received almost no social welfare benefits, and that forced labor was practiced in many Trujillo-owned enterprises.[49] These conditions pre-

---

46. Lázaro Euclides Pimental Castro, "Evolución de los sindicatos en la República" (dissertation), p. 22. See also Franklin J. Franco, *República Dominicana*.
47. See Jorrín, p. 286, and Galíndez, *La era*, p. 294.
48. "Sobre el Sindicato," *Unión Cívica*.
49. *Inter-American Labor Bulletin*, IX (May, 1958), 1.

vailed throughout the Trujillo era but especially during its last fifteen years.

The middle sectors.—Not only do industrialization and economic development draw peasants out of rural areas and give rise to a labor force, but they also tend to promote the growth of a variety of middle sectors[50] such as technicians, businessmen, professionals, and bureaucrats. Prior to 1930 the middle sectors were an exceedingly small fraction of Dominican society; the vast majority of the population was at the bottom of the socioeconomic scale, there was a small but powerful group at the top, and very few in between these two extremes. During the Trujillo era, however, the importance of these middle sectors grew and so, correspondingly, did their numbers. Though still a relatively small percentage of the population, the middle groups represented a growing force. As their size and importance increased, Trujillo found it necessary to subject them and their organizations to the same kind of controls which he held over other sectors of the population.

Trujillo was able to gain the initial support of much of the business community because he provided peace and stability, but many aspects of the dictatorship soon proved unfavorable to the interests of the merchants, traders, and commercial elements. They were obliged to join the official Dominican Party and were dependent on the government for the issuance of passports, business licenses, and import and export permits. These and other political controls made the businessmen dependent on the regime for their everyday negotiations.

Trujillo's greatest control over the business community came from his dominance of the national economy. He frequently forced prospering enterprises to cede a share of their profits to Trujillo family members and their friends. Other businesses were forced to purchase "protection." At one time Trujillo established a 10-per-cent ad valorem import duty which was paid in cash to his henchmen and for which no receipt was given. Trujillo reached into all private economic transactions to impose penalties against any person or firm which was unsympathetic to the regime. It was impossible to employ anyone in any enterprise who did not give at least lip service to the government. Even foreign firms had to have special permission from the executive power to employ

50. For a discussion of some of the political implications of the emergence of middle sectors in Latin America, see John J. Johnson, *Political Change in Latin America.*

Dominican nationals. And, of course, few businesses were allowed to compete with those of the ruling family.

Despite the various controls, many businessmen maintained a degree of individual independence from the regime. While they were not allowed to oppose Trujillo openly, most were not forced to become vocal and active collaborators either. Those who were reluctant were not generally coerced into accepting government positions or working directly for the regime. This was particularly true of the smaller commercial shopkeepers, craftsmen and artisans, and petty businessmen, especially those who lived outside the capital.[51]

Many of the more prominent professionals were also extremely cautious in their dealings with the regime. Manuel Arturo Peña Batlle, Rafael Bonnelly, and Manuel Troncoso de la Concha were among those eminent lawyers who worked closely with the government and rose to occupy high positions in it, but many of the lawyers limited their activities to joining the party and occupying lesser government posts so as not to be accused of being enemies of the regime. Their dependence on the regime for much of their business made them subject to many of the same controls as the business elements, but most lawyers, like the businessmen, were not forced into active collaboration.[52]

Other middle-sector professionals collaborated with the regime and came under its control in varying degrees. The doctors, because of the nature of their profession, were more independent and usually cooperated with the regime only to the extent of serving for a time in the Ministry of Health or teaching in the national university. Engineers and architects were, of necessity, more closely involved in the regime's activities since the public works and construction programs of the government offered them about the only available employment; but these too hesitated to accept government positions. Few professionals or businessmen became legislators, ministers, or governors.[53]

Though Trujillo could not force the active collaboration of many businessmen and professionals, he did control their organizations. Formerly respected civic groups like the Rotarians, Odd Fellows, or Masons were turned into Trujillo fronts; and when he needed the backing of internationally known groups for foreign consump-

51. Bosch, *Trujillo: Causas*, p. 148, and Galíndez, *La era*, pp. 334-38.
52. Galíndez, *La era*, p. 338.
53. *Ibid.*, p. 339.

tion, he called upon these organizations.[54] Trujillo presented himself as the "first doctor" and "first lawyer" and was made honorary president of most business and professional associations.[55] Before enacting any measures, business conferences customarily elected him or brother Héctor honorary chairman.[56] Trujillo's control over the nation was so absolute that any group or association faced dissolution if it failed to carry out his wishes.

All the organizations of the middle sectors, both social and professional, were thus either not allowed to organize or were tightly controlled by the regime. While many businessmen and professionals were not forced into active collaboration and therefore maintained a degree of individual independence, they were not allowed to organize freely or to carry out functions and activities independently of the regime. Without any independent organizations the emerging middle elements were kept atomized, isolated, and powerless.

The elite.—The Dominican Republic was traditionally a two-class society composed of many poor and a few well-to-do members. Unlike many of the Latin American countries, however, there is almost no "landed oligarchy" on the island which traces its ancestry back to colonial times. Rather, the present-day Dominican elite emerged only after the 1822-44 Haitian occupation and grew increasingly prosperous, more socially prominent, and politically strong in the latter half of the nineteenth and early twentieth centuries. The elite constituted a very small percentage of the population; its size has been estimated at no more than a hundred families.[57] The names of Cáceres, Cabral, Troncoso, Espaillat, Vásquez, Jiménez, and others became most prominent during this period and, prior to Trujillo's seizure of power in 1930, these families had begun to emerge as the ruling class.

Trujillo, who came from middle-class origins and was thus never fully accepted by the aristocracy, displayed a continued bitterness toward the elite and attempted to destroy its social and political power. He had destroyed the Union Club by forcing the admission

54. Ornes, *Trujillo: Little Caesar*, p. 14.
55. See, for example, Pascasio A. Toribio Piantini, "El progreso médico en la era de Trujillo," p. 71, and Hipólito Herrera Billini, "La era de Trujillo y la Jurisprudencia Dominicana," p. 66.
56. Ornes, *Trujillo: Little Caesar*, p. 17.
57. Marcio Antonio Mejía Ricart, *Las clases sociales en Santo Domingo*, pp. 23-24, and Juan Isidro Jiménes-Grullón, "Estructura de Nuestra Oligarquía." See also Juan Bosch, *Crisis de la Democracia de América en la República Dominicana*, p. 62.

of his military and political cronies, then compelling the loftiest Dominican heads of family to serve on its board of directors, and finally dissolving it altogether. Ornes feels that because Trujillo was considered a parvenu and was rejected by the elite, the eventual destruction of the Union Club and of the aristocracy was assured.[58] While this may be an exaggeration, it remains true that retaliations against the upper strata continued to be carried out.

Trujillo's humiliation of the aristocracy was at first confined to the social and political realms. In addition to controlling the elite's social organizations, he forced its members to serve in his government. Trujillo's constant shuffling of political officeholders and his dependence on no one but himself seemed to be designed not only pragmatically to ensure his own absolute power but also emotionally to humiliate those aristocratic elements who had rejected him. He apparently enjoyed seeing the country's traditional rulers being subservient to and serving him.

In the 1940's and 1950's Trujillo's domination over the old elite became economic as well as social and political. His dominance of the entire national economy meant that he was able to secure control over both that part of the elite which had acquired land and latifundia and that part which had begun to go into business, industry, commerce, and the professions. Trujillo thus forced some of the elite to give up their lands and demanded a share of the business of others. Indeed, the economic power which he held over the oligarchy was probably more important than any other controls.[59]

The elite was kept atomized in much the same fashion as other sectors of the population. Two of the major centers of aristocratic recreation which existed in Ciudad Trujillo in the 1950's, the Country Club and the *Club de la Juventud*, gave occasional parties which Trujillo at times condescended to attend; but there was no comparison between their simple functions and the lavish reception in the National Palace.[60] And when Trujillo later claimed to be the descendent of nobility, he further humiliated the elite by becoming the greatest aristocrat of them all. As with other groups, the elite was kept atomized and without an independent power base.

58. Ornes, *Trujillo: Little Caesar*, p. 42.
59. *Ibid.*, p. 241.
60. Galíndez, *La era*, p. 337n.

A newly rich class of high government officials, military men, Trujillo family members, and friends of the regime largely replaced the older elite. They built ostentatious houses, sent their children to the best boarding schools in the United States and Europe, staffed their homes with an overabundance of servants, and spent lavish amounts on automobiles, art, and clothes. The new aristocracy entered a period of conspicuous consumption and their social grace and taste were sometimes questionable, but they provided Trujillo with an official elite to lend window dressing to his regime.[61] Because this element was personally loyal to Trujillo and because it owed its enhanced status to him, the new elite was also dependent on Trujillo and his control over it was assured.

61. Ornes, *Trujillo: Little Caesar,* p. 5.

6. Trujillo's Political Ideology

AMONG THE UNIQUE features of modern totalitarianism, as distinguished from traditional dictatorships, is the employment of a single, all-encompassing official belief system or ideology. The totalitarian ideology (1) embraces all human thought and values, being a "total" belief system, (2) allows no competitive or rival beliefs, (3) demands fanatical adherence on the part of members of the society, (4) reduces human existence to a prescribed set of monolithic principles, and (5) seeks to achieve dominance over all man's life and thought.[1] As defined by Friedrich and Brzezinski (page 74) the totalitarian ideology is "a reasonably coherent body of ideas concerning practical means of how totally to change and reconstruct a society by force, or violence, based upon an all-inclusive or total criticism of what is wrong with an existing or antecedent society." The ideology forms "an official body of doctrine covering all vital aspects of man's existence to which everyone living in that society is supposed to adhere."[2]

In this perspective the possibilities for the effective use of totalitarian ideology have only come into existence in the twentieth century. While traditional-style dictatorships may have attempted to impose an official set of beliefs on their citizens, their success

1. Ebenstein, *Totalitarianism*, p. 50.   2. *Ibid.*, p. 9.

102

was limited by the lack of means, particularly modern communications, by which to carry out mass indoctrination. Totalitarian ideology, like several of the other aspects of totalitarianism, is thus intimately linked to modernization and to development; it becomes possible, as Harry Eckstein and David E. Apter state, "only when certain ideas become cojoined with certain technical capabilities and social conditions, and that conjunction of ideas and forces became possible only in the twentieth century" (page 435).

Whether Trujillo had such a totalitarian ideology is a question which must be considered. The titles of some of the more widely known books on the man (Germán Ornes' *Trujillo: Little Caesar of the Caribbean* and Arturo Espaillat's *Trujillo: The Last Caesar*) imply that the Trujillo regime was more in the traditional "Caesarist" style of dictatorship. Indeed, two of the more comprehensive studies of the Trujillo era, that by Ornes and that by Galíndez, conclude that the dictator had no political philosophy and that his sole motivating principle was power for its own sake.[3] Even Crassweller, who has written perhaps the best and most comprehensive biography of Trujillo, gives insufficient consideration to this aspect of his regime and concludes that Trujillo most closely resembled the oriental despots of ancient times.[4] As we shall see, these authors have all largely ignored the large body of materials containing Trujillo's political philosophy and they did not adequately comprehend the functions which his ideology served.

There is little doubt that Trujillo had something which can be roughly identified as an ideology. Some of it emerged in the form of *post-hoc* rationalizations for policies already practiced by the regime. It is also true that Trujillo was not the author of some of the pretentious writings and speeches which appeared under his name—even though he undoubtedly subscribed to the ideas expressed in these volumes. Further, Trujillo's regime never became totally immersed in the ideology, nor was ideology its great driving force, as was the case in the European totalitarian systems of Stalin and Hitler. Nevertheless, the Trujillo dictatorship was clearly going in that direction; the simple kind of caudillo rule in the historic pattern was a thing of the past. The Trujillo ideology

---

3. See especially the subchapter entitled "La defensa doctrinal del régimen" ("The doctrinal defense of the regime") in Galíndez, *La era;* and Ornes, *Trujillo: Little Caesar,* p. vii.

4. Crassweller, *Trujillo,* p. 4.

came to be an important ingredient in his honeycomb of power and control.[5]

The period during which Trujillo first began to formulate a self-conscious ideology is also significant. When he came to power in 1930 and during the early years of his rule, Trujillo did not attempt and, indeed, saw no need for a justification of his rule. Since many of the analyses of the regime were based on studies of the early period, this may help explain why most writers on Trujillo ignored or were unaware of his attempt at a doctrinal defense of the regime. For it was not until the post-World-War-II years—at precisely the same time that the regime was becoming increasingly totalitarian in other aspects—that the dictator, in several important speeches, began to formulate and put forward a number of thoughts concerning his rule. By the 1950's these random ideas had been pulled together into a statement of his political philosophy.

Trujillo's Political Philosophy

Trujillo's political philosophy may best be ascertained from his numerous discourses, speeches, and proclamations and from two attempts at a more systematic presentation of his ideas, *The Evolution of Democracy in Santo Domingo* and, more importantly, *The Basic Policies of a Regime.* Though there is no adequate secondary account, additional notes and comments on Trujillo's political philosophy do exist: Fabio A. Mota's *Un estadista de América: obra socio-política de Trujillo—filosofía, historia, estadística* (*A Statesman of America: The Socio-Political Work of Trujillo —Philosophy, History, Statistics*), Teodoro Vegueriza's *Acción y doctrina de un régimen político* (*Action and Doctrine of a Political Regime*), Manuel Valldeperes' *Acción y pensamiento de Trujillo* (*Action and Thought of Trujillo*), Joaquín Balaguer's *El pensamiento vivo de Trujillo* (*The Living Thought of Trujillo*), and Tulio Cestero Burgos' *Filosofía de un régimen* (*Philosophy of a Regime*). These works have either been ignored by those who have written on the regime or the implications of their contents have not been fully understood. Trujillo's political philosophy, while not a full-fledged totalitarian ideology, did serve certain important functions and was an effective and useful device for further cementing the regime's control.

General principles.—The major principles of Trujillo's political

5. *Ibid.,* p. 118.

philosophy appear to be logically cohesive and unified, if not wholly intelligible. In keeping with the definition of a totalitarian ideology proposed by Friedrich and Brzezinski, Trujillo begins with a critique and a rejection of the antecedent system: "In 1930 our situation was still at its starting point. After eighty-six years of bloody warfare, social unrest, poverty and want we had failed to solve any of our problems: there were still no schools, no hospitals, no employment, no boundary, no roads, no currency, no banks, no agriculture, no industry (except the sugar latifundium), no public buildings, no irrigation system, no bridges, no money, no appreciable production."[6] Trujillo's major purpose and the cornerstone of his ideology was to reverse and correct the mistakes and abuses of the preceding eighty years, to build a true nation-state, and to lift the Dominican Republic from an anarchic and chaotic past to an orderly, peaceful, stable, and constructive present. His fundamental goal, he stated, was to convert his country into a "noble, dignified, and free Fatherland."[7]

Trujillo's political philosophy thus had to provide a rationale for the goals he sought and for the methods he used to achieve these goals. Trujillo first attempted to prove that he alone had possession of Dominican reality—past, present, and future—and that he was the personification of the nation. He alone realized the needs and aspirations of the Dominican people. As Trujillo stated, his political philosophy was founded on his knowledge of and faith in his country; and his knowledge and faith were based upon a mystique, which he alone possessed, identified with the nation, its history, and its life. It was, Trujillo claimed, not an ideology based on vague and meaningless principles but a practical philosophy inspired by his intimate knowledge and understanding of Dominican reality.[8]

Trujillo sought to place himself in the tradition of the country's great national heroes who had stressed the necessity for peace, order, stability, and work. For in order to achieve the desired material progress, these principles had to be firmly established. Though in actual practice he fully succeeded in establishing peace, order, stability, and work, the philosophical underpinnings of these principles did not appear very clear. According to Trujillo, peace was God, since it was impossible to think of a generous God full

6. Trujillo, *Evolution of Democracy*, p. 12.
7. Trujillo, *Basic Policies*, p. 198.
8. Valldeperes, *Acción y pensamiento*, p. 16.

of rancor and suffering. Order was equated with country, since anarchy and libertinism were considered the greatest threat to true patriotism. And work was freedom because, according to Trujillo, man was only free when he earned his bread by the sweat of his labor.[9] Whatever was meant by these definitions, it was clear—and more important—that the principles of peace, order, stability, and work were securely implanted and enforced, and a tightly knit, organic, and corporate state established.

Trujillo's ideals were also defined in a rather unorthodox fashion. He claimed to adhere to the "eternal principles of Moral Right, Liberty, and Democracy,"[10] and stated that "the vital mainsprings of my work have been faith, tenacity, and a constructive spirit."[11] His policies, based on the unification of the economic and political systems about a principle of psychological authority, were called "neodemocratic." What Trujillo meant by such time-honored and lofty principles as freedom and democracy, however, was not at all in keeping with the more common and traditional meaning of these terms. Rather, they were redefined to serve the purposes of the regime.

These, then, were the general principles on which Trujillo based his political philosophy. It has become clear already that although often unclear and ambiguous, these principles do have a certain coherence. With this overall view of Trujillo's guiding ideals, the major topics briefly mentioned above may be considered in somewhat more detail. An attempt is made in the following pages to present Trujillo's ideology as he himself expressed it with a minimum of commentary. Commentary and interpretation will be reserved until the end of the chapter.

Trujillo and reality.—Trujillo wrote in his most sophisticated attempt at a full-fledged political ideology, published only a year before his assassination, that the histories of the various Latin American countries demonstrate the incongruity of attempting to adapt foreign political philosophies to the hard realities of their national experiences. The tumultuous political lives of the Latin American countries stem from a single primary cause: at the time of the separation from Spain and during their later development, these nations attempted to adjust themselves to predetermined theories rather than to their own realities. French and English

9. Balaguer, *El pensamiento,* p. 64.
10. Rafael Trujillo, *Position of the Dominican Government,* p. 60.
11. Rafael Trujillo, *Address to the Congress,* p. 14.

constitutional frameworks and governmental practices were studied and copied, and in many countries the United States Constitution was simply translated into Spanish and adopted. These documents and their abstract principles created conditions not in accord with those which characterized Latin American colonial history and were not relevant or applicable to these new nations.[12]

Trujillo claimed that no foreign theoretical approach could be of absolute value in the organization and administration of a specific society or nation, for any approach must be adaptable to the country's unique reality.[13] "Dignity, liberty, justice, and democracy," he wrote, "must be in accord with the psychology, the education, and the traditions of each nation."[14]

The history of the Dominican Republic, particularly, "drifts like a ship without a course." The nation was originally founded on foreign principles which did not reflect true Dominican existence and which were inappropriately given the Dominican historical experience. As a result, the country was subjected to the arbitrary rule of successive caudillos and petty war lords. It was diverted from its rightful destiny and its problems were compounded until they became tragedies. Solutions were sought not in cold and hard reality but in compromises, truisms, and past formulas, and their ineffectiveness and inappropriateness culminated in national humiliation.[15]

Trujillo, upon coming to power, sought to correct these mistakes. He claimed to seek his inspiration in reality and not in "immaterial abstractions." He was never swayed by "hazy and impractical theories," "verbal mirages," or "conventional and ephemeral definitions."[16] His beliefs and convictions were adjusted to the human, historic, social, and economic realities of the Dominican Republic.[17] Trujillo stated: "I have used my tenure of office without prejudice and avoiding policies which would have been contrary to the whole Dominican reality."[18]

According to Trujillo, Dominican reality required governing principles which were stark and palpable, elastic and flexible. Trujillo took various elements into account in formulating his

12. Trujillo, *Basic Policies*, pp. 5-6.
13. *Ibid.*, p. 21.
14. Trujillo, *Position of the Dominican Government*, p. 51.
15. Trujillo, *Basic Policies*, p. 6.
16. *Ibid.*, p. 10.
17. *Ibid.*, p. 161.
18. Trujillo, *Address to the Congress*, p. 12.

picture of Dominican reality: the country's geography, the land and its productivity, the social composition, the historical experience, and the human being, with respect to his social and cooperative nature, his tendency to regulate his actions by a moral law guaranteeing material security, his instinct for association, and his Christian faith. All of these elements must be in harmony, for any theory of the state based on the supremacy of any one of these constitutive elements would be unbalanced and hence weak and precarious.[19]

Not only did Trujillo claim to have a true grasp of Dominican reality, but he also claimed to be personally highly realistic and practical. He wrote, "Throughtout my life, both public and private, I have always obeyed a strong practical sense which has caused me to face up to problems objectively." For Trujillo, impractical theories, beautiful utopias, and "pure" ideology were without substance and could not be realized. "My sense of the practical," he wrote, "has always prevailed over the fantastic." Essentially material problems, by which he meant economic development, could not be solved with feverish political illusions, abstract definitions, or theoretical syllogisms. "Always I have kept my feet planted on the ground of realism," Trujillo claimed. "My policy has been to act decisively and in a manner adequate to the circumstances."[20]

Trujillo as the personification of the nation.—From Trujillo's analysis and total rejection of the antecedent Dominican society and his claim to have fully understood the true essence of Dominican reality, it was but a short step to the claim that *he alone* understood that reality and was therefore the personification of the nation.

Trujillo claimed to have grasped the true psychology of the Dominican people. Each country has its own consciousness, he wrote, and he had sought out this consciousness, identified its nature, and acted upon that knowledge.[21] He felt himself to be identified with the republic's destiny which, he said, was at the very core of his soul.[22]

Trujillo alone understood the essence, or spirit, of the Dominican nation and he sought to change and mould it and bring the country into the modern era. A general atmosphere of anarchy, timidity, aggression, pessimism, combativeness, and lack of discipline had

19. Trujillo, *Basic Policies*, pp. 8-9.   20. *Ibid.*, p. 7.
21. Rafael Trujillo, *Message Declining to be a Candidate for President*, p. 17.
22. Trujillo, *Address to the Congress*, p. 15.

prevailed in the past, he wrote; and these national characteristics had had a cumulative effect on the formation of the national mentality. It was necessary to reform the Dominican state of mind, as well as its political, social, and economic structure, and channel it into fervent feelings and actions, ardor, optimism, and dynamic cooperation. But these character traits of the people could not be transformed suddenly, since any change would meet resistance; they would have to be changed gradually over a long period of time and under the direction of a single man. The national consciousness would have to be adjusted to twentieth-century conditions; and since only Trujillo was completely aware of the "hard realities of the psychological structure," he alone could carry out these accomplishments.[23]

For Trujillo, the government represented the nation and the presidency personified the government. Since Trujillo was the president, he was also the government and the nation.[24] As Vegueriza, one of his apologists, states, the Trujillo regime was intimately united with the existence of the Dominican nation.[25] Another apologist, Valldeperes, reflected official thinking when he wrote that *trujillismo* was a national force, a national political credo, and that "the true Dominican is Trujillo" (pages 52-53).

Nationalism.—Once it was accepted that Trujillo alone fully understood the true nature of Dominican reality, that he was the government, and that he personified the nation, any number of implications could follow. Trujillo's political philosophy turned, first of all, to play upon and manipulate the rising sense of Dominican nationalism.

Trujillo sought to foster, develop, and channel for his purposes a new social and political myth, that of *Dominicanismo*.[26] In a society which had long been divided into various cliques and factions and in which loyalty and allegiance frequently went more often to rival families and competing caudillos, Trujillo used intense nationalism to cut down and eventually eliminate real and potential rivals. Loyalty and allegiance went now to the nation rather than to local or provincial military or political chieftains. But since Trujillo himself personified the nation, allegiance to the nation meant loyalty to Trujillo personally.

23. Trujillo, *Basic Policies*, pp. 29-30.
24. *Ibid.*, p. 17.
25. *Acción y doctrina*, p. 31.
26. Manuel Antonio Patín Maceo, *Dominicanismo*.

Dominicanism meant many things, but each of these was manipulated in such a way that it helped identify nationalism with Trujillo. The term Dominicanism was, in fact, applied to almost everything the regime accomplished. By the same token, to oppose or be indifferent to the policies of the regime or of Trujillo meant that one was not a Dominican patriot.[27]

Trujillo thus came to identify his own rule and programs with the hopes, fears, and aspirations of the nation. Dominicanism meant increased military might to ward off foreign and domestic foes and to increase national prestige; it meant the whitening of the population to make it increasingly distinguishable from neighboring Haiti; it meant the paying of the foreign debt which had made the country prey to foreign powers for half a century; and it meant the bestowing on Trujillo of the title "Restorer of the Financial Independence of the Country." The fact that the all-important sugar industry, dominated by foreign interests in the past, was now controlled by Dominicans (Trujillo himself) was undoubtedly a major source of national pride. Dominicanism was also identified with public works projects and overall economic development; whenever a new bridge or new highway was opened or a new law enacted, this was accompanied by a great patriotic outpouring.[28] It mattered little that these developments were chiefly for the benefit of the Trujillos. What was important was the regime's manipulation of nationalistic sentiments for its own purposes.

Dominicanism was, in the words of Trujillo and his apologists, a new mode of thought combining creative feeling and action. It was the harmonization of past, present, and future Dominican history; it was a call to work, to produce, and to give. Indeed, in all facets of Dominican life, wrote Mota, the social spirit of Dominicanism was present.[29] Trujillo thus effectively identified himself and his rule with Dominican nationalism. He became the country's foremost nationalist, and those who disagreed with his regime were *ipso facto* unpatriotic.

The organic state.—Since Trujillo claimed to have grasped the essence of Dominican reality, since he personified the society and the nation, and since his regime, as Vegueriza put it, was "united with the existence of the Dominican nation," it followed that there

27. Mota, *Un estadista de America*, p. 178.
28. *Ibid.*, pp. 160-62.
29. *Ibid.*, pp. 160-80, and Vegueriza, *Acción y doctrina*, p. 31.

could be no division of authority within the country. Each societal group or economic interest had its special duties and functions but all remained under Trujillo's absolute authority. The Dominican Republic thus came to resemble the corporate ideal with each group or interest knowing its place and harmonizing into an organic whole.

Trujillo sought to achieve a consonance of interests in the nation. He wrote that a government leader only becomes a true statesman when he can coordinate each citizen and group into a movement which contributes to the common good. His purpose was to "harmonize the common efforts and multiply the results methodically obtained."[30] This coordination became possible when the various forces had been defined, arranged, weighed, analytically measured, and systematically evaluated.[31] Because only Trujillo knew Dominican reality, this "analytic and systematic evaluation" presented no difficulties.

The Dominican Republic was therefore organized into corporate sectors—justice, instruction, sanitation, police, communications, army, immigration, administration, and the like. All of these sectors, societal and governmental, were united into an organic state which would work, not for the exclusive benefit of any one group or individual, but for the good of the entire nation.[32] The government's rule was thus blended with the social reality, and the success of the regime became the agent of and identical with the public well-being.[33] Mota accurately called the government a force for "institutional cohesion,"[34] and Trujillo himself wrote, "It was essential that we should work as a team, in a spirit of friendship, and accustoming ourselves to the idea that a nation can only achieve political maturity through a proper social conscience, entirely different from each individual's particular position."[35]

The implications of this organic coordination, in Trujillo's thinking, were several. The integration of the state, the nation, the society, and the regime extended to the three traditional branches of government. The executive, legislative, and judicial branches, according to his conception, could not function as three separate authorities, checking and balancing each other, but as three or-

30. Trujillo, *Basic Policies*, p. 33.
31. *Ibid.*, pp. 27-28.
32. Vegueriza, *Acción y doctrina*, p. 39.
33. Mota, pp. 25, 57.
34. *Ibid.*, p. 69.
35. Trujillo, *Address to the Congress*, p. 6.

gans of one government acting in unison on the basis of one philosophy, with one plan of action, and striving for cooperative success in a single sphere.[36]

Nor could there be any territorial divisions of authority. The Dominican Republic had never been a federal state but because of inadequate communications, transportation, and other facilities, the central government had traditionally been limited in the amount of control which it exercised over provincial and local authorities. In the monolithic, highly centralized regime of Trujillo there could be no regional or provincial authority and no local self-government. Sectionalism or decentralization, Trujillo wrote, was not possible since these smaller units could only develop in coordination with the rest of the nation "as parts of an indivisible unit."[37]

The complete integration of the entire society, finally, implied that there could be no social or economic class distinctions in the country. Dominican society was to be unified to the extent that the previous lines of cleavage would disappear and the separate classes would become one. There could be no class conflict or antagonisms in Trujillo's harmonious and coordinated society.[38] The dictator wrote, "In sum, the function of a statesman blessed with a real sense of country must always further the coordination of the efforts of those associated for the common welfare. . . . By this I mean that the Dominican society which I would establish had for its purpose the harmonization of man and social environment into a well-defined balance of rights and duties. To achieve this I proposed to lessen the differences dividing each group, encouraging a universal spirit of cooperation, allay simultaneously the pride of the powerful and the agitation of the weak—in short, stimulate harmony and consideration in the unfolding of the common effort. Achieving this, I would mobilize in behalf of the nation all the now-unified civic forces, each working in its own sphere, and from them would flow the strength needed for maximum accomplishments."[39]

Order, peace, and stability.—In order to carry out the goals of the regime, Trujillo required order, peace, and stability, and these, indeed, were obtained. For thirty-one years the Dominican

36. Trujillo, *Basic Policies*, pp. 47-48.
37. *Ibid.*, pp. 51-52.
38. *Ibid.*, pp. 84-85.
39. *Ibid.*, p. 82.

Republic experienced a period of forced and imposed stability which was in marked contrast to its previously chaotic independent history.

Trujillo rejected and sought to remedy the traditional pattern. He said, "The greatest need of the nation is order,"[40] and "What has not been tolerated is disorder."[41] The nation was to be transformed and a total revolution in Dominican psychology to be effected. "Above all," Trujillo wrote, "there would have to be security, peace and political stability."[42] He continued, "All my endeavors were placed at the service of peace, and later, to wage an incessant battle to preserve it and to make it permanent. In order to achieve this, it was necessary to re-establish the rule of law and respect for legally constituted authority, authority damaged by eighty years of separation from constitutional and legal norms. In order to preserve the peace, it was necessary to eliminate the causes of political unrest by fostering a balance between the social elements that produced the moral phenomenon called peace."[43]

Only the government, according to Trujillo, could secure the required peace, order, and stability. It was therefore necessary for the government to have the complete and undivided loyalty of the people and to secure the people's obedience to the government. Obedience to the government was seen as the best way to secure the nation's well-being, which insured the well-being of every individual.[44]

The creation of a principle of authority was thus an absolute imperative. Dominicans had to be forced to understand, Trujillo stated, that they had "the obligation of living in an orderly manner, respecting the law and honoring their undertakings."[45] The necessity of the principle of authority meant that the state itself must be strong, authoritative, and majestic, for it was the "driving force" in the nation and the "coordinator" of national values.[46]

The peace inaugurated by Trujillo, it would follow, also had to be an organic peace. The order and stability of the Trujillo period, wrote one of his apologists, was constructed with the human and

40. Nanita, *Trujillo*, p. 181.
41. Trujillo, *Address delivered at San Juan de la Maguana*, pp. 10-11.
42. Trujillo, *Basic Policies*, p. 30.
43. Trujillo, *Address at St. John the Baptist Fair*, pp. 7-8.
44. Balaguer, *El pensamiento*, pp. 275-76.
45. Trujillo, *Address to the Congress*, p. 6.
46. Trujillo, *Basic Policies*, p. 24.

lasting materials, liberty and social justice. The peace of Trujillo made tangible the new national spirit, transformed the ideal of the development of public and private wealth into a reality, guaranteed the functioning of the institutions of the state, and produced a permanent equilibrium of justice that facilitated the development of the collective life. It was a peace of all and for all, a peace without respite, a live, active, and permanent state of solidarity.[47]

Material progress.—The major task in the Dominican Republic, as Trujillo envisioned it, was twofold. The establishment of peace, order, and stability, first of all, was required to provide a spiritual, ethical, and psychological basis for the second task. That second task was economic development which would give rise to material progress.[48]

The development of the nation's wealth, Trujillo said, constituted the basis for the dignity of the Dominican people. By the same token, the republic's major plague and the cause which had prevented the fulfillment of her national destiny was poverty and underdevelopment.[49] Trujillo stated, "I have no doubts but that by guiding the common effort towards a goal of order and prosperity, we shall be able to develop fully our wealth and enjoy a standard of living as high as those of any of the prosperous nations on earth."[50]

Economic development, in Trujillo's ideology, thus became the basis of liberty. He wrote that a nation can only be free when its economy permits it to exist without compromising its sovereignty.[51] The many anomalies in Dominican agricultural and industrial life prior to 1930 had stemmed from a lack of order. Trujillo thus sought to establish stability which included guaranteed "suitable wages" and a planned and coordinated economy.[52]

The securing of order and subsequently the development of the economy, Trujillo called the "Dominican Revolution." His was a concept of "solidarity for the achievement of progress."[53] And further, "all progress, to be effective, must be harmonious."[54] He

47. Valldeperes, pp. 99-100. See also Ramón Emilio Jiménez, *Trujillo y la paz.*

48. Trujillo, *Position of the Dominican Government,* p. 45.

49. Trujillo, *Discurso pronunciado por Rafael Trujillo en el acto de inauguración del banco agrícola e hipotecario,* p. 19.

50. Trujillo, *Message Declining,* pp. 23-24.

51. *Ibid.,* pp. 6-7.

52. Trujillo, *Basic Policies,* p. 143.

53. *Ibid.,* p. 157.   54. *Ibid.,* p. 164.

concluded by linking Dominican nationalism with the economic development achieved by the regime: "A new nation has come into being. A new and dynamic society is on the march."[55]

The Dominican Republic did indeed make material progress during the Trujillo era, and the listing of these accomplishments formed a major part of his political philosophy. Nonproductive areas were made fertile, transportation and communications improved, farming techniques modernized, agricultural products diversified, and trade increased. Trujillo wrote of the old-age pensions, unemployment insurance, aid for orphans, health insurance, workers' retirement plans, and mobile medical clinics which he instigated. He built hotels, highways, docks, power plants, water supply systems, factories, canals, airports, and public buildings. The standard of living rose, gross national product increased, foreign and domestic debts were liquidated, and the national budget was balanced for a period of twenty years. Trujillo wrote: "I had the necessary patience and faith to initiate and carry out a government program which can be described in a single word, 'Build!'"[56]

Freedom.—Perhaps no word, other than "democracy," has been given so many definitions and interpretations in the modern era as "freedom." No other human right has been so often misused and yet so strenuously defended. Trujillo added still another interpretation to the term.

Trujillo felt that freedom could not be defined in abstract or absolute terms and that attempts to do so had contributed to its present-day ambiguity and meaninglessness. In his thinking, order and freedom were inseparable.[57] Freedom, according to Trujillo, was thus based on "prior discernment" and, as such, implied a large measure of restraint.[58] All freedoms were regulated and restrained by pre-determined "norms of general convenience," and their exercise therefore implied an obligation. Only by a just balance of obligation and freedom could order and stability be maintained. Absolute freedom was therefore nonexistent; individual freedom, Trujillo wrote, must be subordinated to the common good.[59]

Freedom was also intimately related to duty to the nation. In the regime's ideology, no individual who isolated himself from

55. Trujillo, *Trujillo Speaks*, p. 18.
56. Trujillo, *Basic Policies*, p. 130.
57. Trujillo, *Position of the Dominican Government*, p. 11.
58. Trujillo, *Basic Policies*, p. 207.
59. *Ibid.*, pp. 111-12.

and existed independently of the state could be really free. Freedom could neither serve as a pretext for individual personal ambition or political anarchy nor be used by a small group to the detriment of the nation as a whole. Freedom had to be harmoniously joined with responsibility so that neither the nation, the collective dignity, nor the individual suffered.[60] Trujillo summarized: "Political freedom cannot be exercised in practice in a completely unrestricted manner, but must rather be conditioned to collective beneficial ends, to national stability and to order and organization, and these can only be defined by an authority that, apart from being legally constituted, bases its actions on deeply sincere ideals of service to, and love of the *Nation, the supreme regulator of all common acts.*"[61] As Vegueriza stated, the Dominican Republic under Trujillo was not "free" in any superficial or shallow sense. It was "truly free."[62]

Democracy.—The contexts of time and place made it almost imperative that Trujillo should couch his system of government in democratic terms. The modern era and the American setting meant that the regime would be more acceptable if it were given a democratic juridical and theoretical basis. Trujillo constantly referred to the Dominican system as "our democracy." All the diverse currents of his political philosophy were lumped together and the term "neodemocracy" applied to the entire ideology.

"Democracy," according to Trujillo, "emerges from prosperity."[63] He stated, "The observance of present-day world events teaches us that political democracy cannot be made workable if it is not founded upon economic democracy."[64] Democracy thus had little to do with elections, constitutional government, competitive political parties, a critical opposition, rule by law, or basic freedoms; it implied, rather, economic development and material progress.

Democracy was also linked to order, stability, and the principle of authority in Trujillo's formulation. Democracy was, like freedom, not an abstract political theory without practical application. Rather, he said, "only by a methodical exercise of freedom, with its consequent rights and obligations, within a logical framework, can true democracy exist."[65] Thus all of Trujillo's earlier concepts—

60. *Ibid.*, p. 116.
61. *Ibid.*, pp. 119-20. The emphasis is Trujillo's.
62. *Acción y doctrina*, p. 331.
63. Balaguer, *El pensamiento*, p. 246.
64. Trujillo, *Discurso pronunciado*, p. 19.
65. Trujillo, *Basic Policies*, p. 124.

his grasp of Dominican reality, nationalism, the organic state, material progress, "true freedom," and peace, order, and stability—went into and were an integral part of his definition of democracy. Trujillo did not conceive of democracy, as he admitted, in any conventional sense. In his system governments were formed and leaders chosen by "public opinion." This principle of the "general will," however, was not further defined nor were its mechanisms worked out.[66] Trujillo's definition of democracy included every realm of man's potential: the enjoyment of rights and the fulfillment of duties, obedience to the law and maintenance of public order, the exercise of personal liberties and respect for those of others, protection of the personal dignity due human beings, man's right to progress and the accord resulting therefrom, elimination of privilege and achievement of a balanced society, social integration, the guiding of national life by a realistic plan for the achievement of maximum benefit, and the glorification of the fatherland as the sum total of all to be attained.

The high-sounding principles were best stated by Trujillo: "I conceived of democracy in all its dimensions: in the exercise of political liberties as well as economic equality; in social justice as well as institutional stability; in absolute autonomy and national sovereignty as well as the safeguarding of personal dignity and all that is encompassed by that term." And further: "Never have I regarded democracy as an agent of misery and retrogression. A hungry, ill-clothed, undernourished, disease-wracked, morally-deficient population does not qualify to reach the goals of democracy—although, theoretically, on paper, that population has given itself that system. Democracy surges from prosperity, physical health, and the moral well-being of the individual and the family. Democracy is something organic, vital, evolutionary that today cannot be founded but on the basis of the better capacity of the Government to make meaningful and valuable the lives of human beings."[67] And finally: "Our political regime has been called anti-democratic because I have imposed respect for the principle of authority. . . . I reject that epithet. . . . Democracy does not infer license to engender hate or to stir up the passions of the masses by every means of propaganda against the legally constituted government, nor to conspire, openly or surreptitiously, not to carry fear into the bosoms of families through terrorism."[68]

66. *Ibid.*, p. 37.   67. *Ibid.*, pp. 97-98.
68. Trujillo, *Address delivered at San Juan de la Maguana*, pp. 10-11.

Trujillo claimed that his democracy was founded upon a basis of popular sovereignty. All Dominicans were invited to participate in helping with his national reconstruction policy, provided that their honesty, intelligence, and morality qualified them. According to Trujillo's definition of democracy, then, power emanated from the people; but, as we have seen earlier, only he knew what the will of the people was. Trujillo stated, "Our regime was born from the people and is maintained by the people. It has given well-being to the people; it works every day to give the people whatever they may need to be prosperous and happy, and it provides Dominicans, irrespective of class or color, with equal education and equal opportunities. This is the type of Democracy I have given Dominicans after eighty years of civil strife that threatened to place the Republic in peril of disappearing from the concert of independent nations."[69]

Trujillo attempted to work into his theory of democracy some of those features which are normally associated with democratic government. He wrote that the rule of law should govern all civic functions, financing, the execution of justice, and "other functions of authority." The individual should be protected from arbitrary abuse by the state or its officials and from any other source of violence, domination, or exploitation.[70] But he stated that "implementation of these principles constitutes the essence and basis of the theory of democracy";[71] and, as this analysis of Trujillo's methods of rule demonstrates, Trujillo's implementation of these principles was far from democratic.

The concept of the organic, corporate state was also an essential part of Trujillo-style democracy. Each group or corporate sector of the society would be represented in decision-making, and all sectors would work for the good of all. In the earliest full-length formulation of his political philosophy Trujillo wrote, "Democracy acts according to the needs and characteristics of each particular group, actuated and governed by the objective structure of each particular society. Democracy is action: economic, religious, political, social human action—in a word, action which evolves and operates in accordance with the traditions, the history, the ethnology and the geography of each group, provided of course it is primarily directed towards the improvement of the community."[72]

69. *Ibid.*, p. 11.   70. Trujillo, *Basic Policies*, pp. 87-88.
71. Trujillo, *Address delivered at San Juan de la Maguana*, p. 11.
72. Trujillo, *Evolution of Democracy*, p. 4.

The state should work to secure maximum community effort, Trujillo continued, by the harmonious activation of all the inert forces of the nation; but it cannot easily achieve this fundamental purpose of organization if it does not enjoy the support of a strong inclination on the part of individuals toward interdependence and a community of mutually supporting interests.[73]

Another bridge was constructed among the varied themes in Trujillo's political philosophy by his statement that the agent of this interdependence and of this community of interests is the principle of authority. No individual would willingly grant power to the state over his person, Trujillo stated, unless in return he received compensation in the form of services, well-being, and peace. In the regime's ideology, it therefore followed that authority could only be achieved when it satisfied the legitimate needs of each individual by working for the common good.[74] As another of Trujillo's apologists stated, "The essence of true democracy is communal obedience freely granted to intelligent or rightful authority."[75]

"Democracy is organic, vital, and progressive," Trujillo stated, "and nowadays can only be based on the maximum capacity of the government to render human life useful and fruitful." The concept of an organic democracy was also tied to the economic programs of the regime since, as Trujillo continued, democracy could not be regarded as the servant of misery and backwardness. Though their constitutions may provide for democratic forms, people who are hungry and undernourished cannot achieve the true goals of democracy. Democracy only emerges, Trujillo argued, where the populace enjoys freedom from want and where the basic needs are assured, so that each individual and group is free from economic restraint.[76]

For Trujillo, the entirety of man's being and his place within the organic national community was thus implicit in his conception of democracy. Democracy signified solidarity and social harmony and eliminated the conflicts which degenerate into class strife and discord. The duty of the democratic leader, as Trujillo saw his own role, was to identify and arrange each social group or interest in the society so that he could better achieve a coordinate

73. Trujillo, *Basic Policies*, p. 16.
74. Trujillo, *Position of the Dominican Government*, p. 6.
75. González-Blanco, *Trujillo*, pp. 45 ff.
76. Trujillo, *Position of the Dominican Government*, p. 7.

and cohesive whole. A nation is democratically governed, he concluded, when its aims are realized, its national values developed in a constructive direction, its solidarity achieved, and, as a result of these prior requirements, its universal accord, spontaneous cooperation, and consolidated public opinion manifested.[77]

Those who did not conceive of democracy in the same way as did Trujillo were labelled pseudodemocrats or Communists. Indeed, Trujillo liked to pose as the "foremost anti-Communist of the hemisphere."[78] He felt that the so-called people's democracies abused the term democracy. He saw an even greater danger, however, in those whom he thought were actually working as unwitting servants of communism, in the name of democracy.[79] These included the foreign journalists who had written disparagingly of the Trujillo era, the domestic politicians who had failed to completely cooperate with the regime, and the growing number of exiles opposed to his rule. All opposition, Communist and non-Communist alike, was branded with the Communist label; only Trujillo's concept of democracy was "true" and no other opinions were allowed.

Conclusions and Implications

What may one validly conclude from this examination of Trujillo's political philosophy? Many of the ideas are incomprehensible, some are contradictory. The most comprehensive of his ideological formulations, *The Basic Policies of a Regime*, is poorly written, poorly translated, and poorly edited. The passages are often unclearly stated; many of them may be dismissed as meaningless nonsense, and it is possible that this author has imposed an artificial order on a collection of thoughts that defy systematization. One reviewer has written that the above-mentioned book is a "collection of fantastic untruths, most of which are unintelligible."[80]

The political philosophy of Trujillo was clearly neither subtle nor profound. It was not a full-fledged ideology of the Communist or national socialist type. Nor was there much more than a half-hearted attempt on the part of the regime to impose the ideology on the Dominican people and to vigorously brainwash or indoctrinate them in the official belief system. Trujillo's political philoso-

77. Trujillo, *Basic Policies*, pp. 99-100.
78. *White Book of Communism in the Dominican Republic*.
79. Trujillo, *Basic Policies*, p. 93.
80. Harry Kantor, Review of Rafael Trujillo, *The Basic Policies of a Regime*.

phy, despite these limitations and shortcomings, nevertheless served several important functions.

The philosophy itself was neither unique nor original. The ideas which were expressed—nationalism, peace, order, and stability, the organic state, national progress, the deification of the leader as the personification of the nation, corporativism, "true" freedom and democracy—had long histories going back into the nineteenth century and earlier. In the twentieth century these ideas were systematized and put into a coherent whole and they became, in varying combinations, the official ideologies of at least two regimes which came to power: the Falange in Spain and fascism in Italy.[81] Trujillo's only original contribution to this "Mediterranean style" philosophy of fascism, the ideas of which he took over practically *en toto*, may have been its rebaptism with the "democratic" label. This rebaptism was necessary in view of the military defeat of the Fascist powers in World War II and the subsequent worldwide discrediting of this ideology combined at the same time with the almost universal, immediate post-war faith in democracy.

Trujillo's political philosophy thus provided a rationale for his regime. Though it was not a full-scale ideology, it did establish a set of principles upon which he could attempt to justify his policies. Particularly in the modern era, when the traditional dictatorial principle of power for its own sake seemed no longer wholly appropriate, these ideas served as a justification and as a rationalization for a dictator who aspired to be considered on a higher plateau. For Trujillo was not merely a traditional Caesar-like caudillo devoid of any political philosophy but a modern caudillo who had to justify his actions with an ideology.

Trujillo's political philosophy also functioned as a rallying point for Dominican patriotism and national aspirations. The elements of nationalism and national independence, of material progress and economic development, of the need for peace, order, and stability after a long history of chaos actually reflected the needs and goals of many Dominicans. Trujillo's ideology thus gave expression to many of these aspirations and helped rally the people to support his regime. There was little doubt that Trujillo, had he so wished, could have won a fair election and that for most of his long rule he had the support of the majority of the people. Many

81. For an interesting comparison of these ideologies see Stanley G. Payne, *Falange*. Linz' distinction between "mentalities" and "ideologies" may also be relevant at this point. See Linz, pp. 301-4.

Dominicans supported the principles on which his regime rested.

Though Trujillo's ideology was not a full-fledged ideology and though the regime did not fully impose its dogma on the entire population, his political philosophy was believed and adhered to by certain sectors of the Dominicans. Trujillo, after all, was in power for thirty-one years and during this long period an entire generation had grown up educated and indoctrinated, as we shall see in the next chapter, only in the official beliefs. In addition, the enforced isolation imposed by Trujillo meant that no conflicting or contrary ideas were allowed to enter the country. Though no figures are available it is certain that, because of the limited educational, travel, and other opportunities in the Dominican Republic, many of its citizens were unaware of other alternative and contrary belief systems. This was particularly true of the less prominent, who never went abroad or were never exposed to the varied ideologies of the modern world. Among such elements, as these, Trujillo's political philosophy was widely accepted and adhered to, even though they had little detailed knowledge or understanding of it. Trujillo's governing principles and system of rule came to be accepted as a matter of form; Trujilloism acquired a certain kind of legitimacy.

In the history of Dominican social and political thought, furthermore, there had always been a powerful strain which made essentially the same arguments as did Trujillo. Some of the country's best known writers—José Ramón López, Américo Lugo, Emiliano Tejera, Francisco Henríquez y Carvajal—had long argued that there was a fatal flaw in the Dominican soul, a congenital defect which rendered the Dominicans incapable of civilized life, of independent existence as a nation, and of democratic government. It is not our purpose here to examine the validity of this thesis, but only to point out that these sentiments are widely shared by Dominicans of all classes—including those who have never read the authors mentioned above. Among Dominicans, there has traditionally been a kind of national inferiority complex, a sense of fatalism and despair, the belief that the country and its people would always be condemned to poverty, chaos, foreign domination, instability, and backwardness. Trujillo clearly recognized and cleverly played upon this sense of inferiority. By grounding his political belief in what was, after all, a powerful national tradition, he was able to identify himself closely with the thinking of his people. What is more, Trujillo promised relief and hope—relief from the ills that always plagued the nation, hope for prosperity, sovereignty, a proud place in the sun after nearly a century of floundering. He satisfied the national longing, subconscious though it may have been, for strong, authoritarian leadership. Trujillo's justifications for his rule were thus firmly grounded in the peculiarly Dominican historical experience; his ideology—expressed initially in speeches, radio broadcasts, and other ways so that oftentimes even the illiterate and unsophisticated received the message—encompassed not only a rejection of the antecedent ways but also a vision of the future, of a changed and reconstructed society.[82]

This political philosophy also helped promote Trujillo's and the regime's image abroad. His propaganda machine, as we shall see, was developed to a high degree of efficiency. Copies of his speeches and works lauding his regime were sent free to libraries all over the world, particularly those in the United States, and full-page advertisements praising Trujillo were run in metropolitan United States newspapers. *The Evolution of Democracy in Santo Domingo* and other books, especially those which stressed democracy and anti-communism, were given to visiting United States dignitaries who then frequently used their influence to support Trujillo. Realizing the large degree of dependence of his government on the United States, Trujillo was particularly clever in employing his political philosophy to build good will there.[83]

Though Trujillo's political philosophy was not at the level of an ideology like communism or national socialism, it did serve several important functions. Though seemingly inconsequential and somewhat meaningless to the enlightened and highly educated outside analysts who simply dismissed it without further analysis, and equally nonsensical to the relatively few Dominicans who had had the opportunity to travel or study abroad, Trujillo's ideology could not be summarily dismissed, especially when considered within the context of a country where the literacy rate was low and the opportunities for education and travel were extremely limited. And when combined with the controls he exercised over the school system, communications, and intellectual life and with the harmonious and mutually supporting working relationship with the Roman Catholic Church in the Dominican Republic considered in the following chapter, Trujillo's political philosophy takes on added importance as an instrument of control.

82. Avelino, *Las Ideas Políticas,* chapter 4.
83. See Hamill, pp. 155-56. This subject is treated in Chapter 7.

7. Thought Control and the Church

Trujillo's political philosophy was not a full-fledged totalitarian ideology. It became of increasing significance, however, when reinforced and buttressed by his control of or monopoly over education, intellectual life, and the communications media, his extensive use of public relations to constantly promote a favorable image, and his mutually beneficial arrangement with the Church. Through these techniques Trujillo maintained nearly absolute thought control, thereby depriving his people of the chance to exercise independent choice or judgment.

Thought control is a new and unique feature of modern totalitarianism, and is intimately linked with twentieth-century developments in the technology of communications. Before the advent of modern communications, it was technologically impossible for an old-style, traditional dictatorship to compel the acceptance of an official dogma, to require the constant and enthusiastic adoration of the regime and its leader, to see that news, culture, teaching, writing, and entertainment all reinforced the dictatorship's control, and to force the cult of the dictator to permeate almost every facet of existence. In all these aspects the Trujillo regime was tending toward modern totalitarianism.

124

Thought Control

The communications media.—The Dominican press was the most reliable guide to official government policy and served as the best index to determine who was in or out of favor. Feature articles, supposedly straight news stories, editorials, advertisements, and the letters-to-the-editor columns were all in strict compliance with the wishes, programs, and subtle modifications as well as complete reversals of policy emanating from the National Palace. The entire press, in short, was completely servile to the regime.

The few daily newspapers in the country were conveyors of *trujillista* propaganda and failed to print anything which might imply a criticism of the government or of Trujillo. Headlines were slanted and articles distorted to conform to the dictates of the regime. Reporters were told when and how to write their stories and independent checks on the supposedly factual information supplied in the official handouts were not condoned. The stories were filled with adulation of Trujillo and became what Ornes called "an endless excursion into hagiography."[1] Writers vied to express his praise in an original manner, prompting Galíndez to remark that "the only difficulty for the Dominican newspaperman is to coin a new adjective."[2]

When Trujillo came to power in 1930, *Listín Diario* and *La Opinión* in the capital city and *La Información* in the country's second largest city of Santiago provided their readers with a variety of political slants. Within the first year of his administration Trujillo was able to coerce, cajole, or bribe much of the journalistic community into collaborating with him or, at the least, remaining silent. Newspaper opposition to his rule could be voiced only at the risk of strong retaliation, and the press soon learned to refrain from any criticism of Trujillo.

In 1939, not satisfied with mere negativism and unable to completely control the existing newspapers, Trujillo launched a new periodical *La Nación* to serve as the official mouthpiece for his regime. The new daily flourished, since government officials were forced to subscribe and advertising was diverted to it from the other papers. Without sufficient advertising, the privately owned *Listín Diario*, which had published continuously since 1889, ceased

1. *Trujillo: Little Caesar*, p. 200.
2. *La era*, p. 320.

publication in 1942. *La Opinión* and *La Información*, also in private hands, continued to publish, although both followed the Trujillo line on most matters and on others remained nonpolitical.[3]

In the face of the democratic wave which surged over Latin America following World War II, Trujillo conceived a maneuver to absolve himself from criticism by creating a "free press" of his own. He proposed that *La Opinión* conduct a "moderate opposition campaign" on the condition that it refrain from attacking him personally or the armed forces. *La Opinión* took its charge seriously and began a crusade in which the newspaper attempted to effect civic reforms, improve labor conditions, lower the cost of living, solve social problems, and eliminate racial discrimination. The crusade inevitably involved Trujillo, however, and the newspaper's criticism of him prompted a retaliatory campaign of villification and slander against its owners and editors. Several months later *La Opinión* was merged with *La Nación*.[4]

By 1947 the capital city had thus become a single-newspaper town with *La Nación* serving as the official mouthpiece for the regime. In April, 1948, *El Caribe* was founded to serve as a second official spokesman. Though at times under private ownership, *El Caribe* did not often deviate from the *trujillista* line; and when it did deviate at one time in 1954, the paper was promptly taken over by the regime. The morning *El Caribe* and the evening *La Nación*, both tightly controlled, provided the dictatorship with a complete blanket of managed news.

Outside the capital city newspapers were not permitted any greater freedom. The only other daily which continued to publish throughout the Trujillo era was Santiago's *La Información*, now wholly subservient to the government. The combined circulation of the three dailies—*La Nación, El Caribe*, and *La Información*—was 45,000.[5] A few newspapers were being published elsewhere in the country, but these were most often weeklies which were concerned exclusively with local news and which occasionally published official handouts. No periodical openly discussed anything of a public nature.

One of the main tasks of the press was to pay homage to Trujillo and to dwell at length on the country's economic prog-

3. *Ibid.*, pp. 317-18.
4. Partido Revolucionario Dominicano y Movimiento Popular Dominicano, *Libertad de Prensa para Santo Domingo.*
5. Ornes, *Trujillo: Little Caesar*, p. 189.

ress, construction programs, health improvements, educational advances, and public works projects.[6] A happy picture of life under the dictatorship was painted while misery, squalor, poverty, calamities, and atrocities were ignored. Editorials and supposedly impartial news stories and features praised Trujillo and denounced those whom he wished to denounce. At times the newspapers were used to create an artificial demand for programs the government had already begun.[7] Similarly, editorials were frequently published on matters which had previously been suppressed so that the readers received heated comments without having any background information. The immortal "Thoughts of Trujillo" column appeared every day, eulogies of the dictator or his regime were reprinted, and unfavorable foreign comments were kept out.[8]

One of Trujillo's favorite devices was the use of the "Foro Público," the letters-to-the-editor column in *El Caribe*, for debasement and character assassination. Those who had failed to mention *el benefactor* in a speech or published work or whose official conduct or private life was displeasing to him were liable to be subject to slanderous villification or calumny in the newspaper. Anonymous letters, originating from the National Palace, usually complained about laziness, graft, alcoholism, sexual deviations, infidelity, or moral turpitude among public officials, businessmen, or the social set.[9] Some of the wrongdoings mentioned in the letters were true and others were fabricated, but almost all of them served as rationalization for the demotion of people who were already marked for other reasons. The accused were obliged to compose elaborate explanations, apologize profusely, and beg forgiveness. As Carleton Beals stated, "reading the Dominican press was an education in the process of the forced debasement of human beings."[10]

Trujillo had other means by which he kept the press under his control. The number of trained, competent journalists was kept purposely small and no journalistic training was provided. No independent news or information service was allowed to come into

6. See, for example, *El Caribe* (January 2, 1959), p. 13.
7. See, for example, *El Caribe* (July 2, 1953), p. 7.
8. See, for example, "Un Gran Discurso" by John McCormack, reprinted in *El Caribe* (March 3, 1957), p. 7, and "Dominican Republic: 28 years of Stability" by David Steinberg.
9. See, for example, the "Foro Público" columns in *El Caribe* (July 1, 1953), p. 7; (November 8, 1955), p. 7; (January 1, 1959), p. 9; and (January 3, 1959), p. 5.
10. "Caesar of the Caribbean," p. 32.

existence, with the result that official handouts provided the only information of national concern. A journalists' association was permitted to organize, but like other organizations in the country, it remained completely under the thumb of the government.[11]

Trujillo monopolized not only the press but also the other mass media. The radio network, "La Voz Dominicana," and the first television station were owned and actively run by brother Arismendi Trujillo. At the height of the dictatorship there were thirty-one radio stations and two television stations in the country broadcasting to fifty thousand radios and two thousand television sets.[12] The control which the Trujillo regime exercised over these media was similar to that exercised over the press.

The propaganda transmitted over radio and television was of the same nature as that which appeared in the newspapers. "Name" entertainers from other Latin American countries were hired to praise Trujillo and thank him for his service to the Dominican Republic.[13] News programs only repeated the official handouts which had previously appeared in the morning press. A well-equipped and technologically proficient communications agency was established to scramble broadcasts from foreign stations. Attacks from Cuba under Carlos Prío Socarrás, from Venezuela under Rómulo Betancourt, and from Costa Rica under José Figueres—all long-time Trujillo foes—were particularly subject to scrambling.[14] In this and other ways, the Dominican Republic was almost completely cut off from the outside world so that only those ideas first censored and approved by the regime were allowed to seep in.

Modern means of communications have, in most countries, expanded the expression of public opinion and the opportunities for the education of the populace in political matters. Under Trujillo, however, this service was turned into a disservice. Opinion groups lacked channels for articulating their interests, for the propagation and education of opinion was monopolized by the regime and it systematically exploited the opportunities which the development of communications made possible for itself.

11. See Dario Flores, *Evolución del periodismo en la era de Trujillo,* and *El 1J4,* I (October 7, 1961), p. 15.
12. These statistics may be found in Rodman, p. 137, and "Report on the Dominican Republic," *Latin American Report,* p. 9. See also United Nations, *Statistical Yearbook,* Table 146.
13. Hicks, *Blood in the Streets,* p. 196.
14. Galíndez, *La era,* p. 321, and Hicks, *Blood in the Streets,* p. 196.

Education and intellectual activity.—Trujillo also tightly controlled the educational system and carefully scrutinized all intellectual activity. The entire educational process, research, writing, and artistic endeavors were transformed into adjuncts to the propaganda of the regime. Teachers were forced to instill the official ideology and to educate the students in the cult of Trujillo, while intellectual life was concentrated primarily on the production of works which glorified the dictator.[15]

The nation's schools were looked upon as the vehicles for *trujillista* indoctrination. Traditional dictators have usually relied on the ignorance of their people to perpetuate their power and have feared the effects of mass education. The experience of twentieth-century totalitarianism, however, has shattered the belief that education necessarily provides immunity against tyranny and dictatorship. Rather, modern totalitarian systems have used education as a political prop and employed it to inculcate a blind acceptance of those in power. While Trujillo was necessarily limited by the high illiteracy rate in his country and by the scanty educational facilities which existed upon his taking power, he applied many of the totalitarian techniques of educational thought control to the Dominican Republic and developed some more refined and novel methods of his own. Those who attended school received what Ornes called "education for tyranny."[16]

The official cult of Trujillo was the most important subject in the school system. Students were steeped in his supposed virtues of wisdom, benevolence, and infallibility. Loyalty to him, the father and benefactor of the country, came before love of family or friends. The authors of school texts had to demonstrate that he was a man of genius and the incarnation of the nation's soul. School children were compelled to read the enormous amount of printed materials which were cranked out glorifying his life and the achievements of his rule. The cult of hero worship, as Ornes remarks, formed the leitmotif of national education.[17]

The basic primer used in the elementary schools, a volume which was most lavish in its praise of the regime, carried Trujillo's name as the author. A few examples from this text illustrate the kind of education Dominican children received. "The President works unceasingly for the happiness of his people,"

---

15. See Friedrich and Brzezinski, Chapter 12.
16. *Trujillo: Little Caesar*, p. 173.
17. *Ibid.*, p. 177.

Trujillo wrote; "he maintains peace, builds roads and schools, favors industry, protects citizens, helps farmers, protects labor, supports hospitals, and encourages learning."[18] The essential elements of Trujillo's ideology were thus incorporated into and became the major subject matter of the educational system as well.

Not only did this basic text glorify Trujillo but it also encouraged school children to report all deviations from the official dogma and to turn in those opposed to the regime, even if this meant reporting one's own parents. "If you should find in your home a man who wishes to disturb order," the textbook stated, "see that he is handed over to the police." And again: "The revolutionary . . . is your worst enemy . . . you should see in every revolutionist an enemy of your life and property." This "civic primer" was used in the schools for almost the entire Trujillo era and was the most widely read book in the country.

Señora Trujillo's *Moral Meditations*, a collection of columns which appeared regularly in the Dominican press, was also made compulsory reading in the schools. One unsympathetic critic stated that it occupied "that empyrean plane side by side with the works of Norman Vincent Peale."[19] But *Moral Meditations* was presented to the school children as a great example of the national literature and as a monumental work of moral philosophy. It too served to reinforce the regime's monopoly over educational life.

The entire system of education was permeated with indoctrination in the cult of the ruling family. On "Books Day," for example, the schools prepared special programs to acquaint the students with the great works of Dominican literary history, primarily those of Trujillo and his wife.[20] On Mother's Day the children were required to compose essays on motherhood with special emphasis on the exemplary virtues of Julia Molina, Trujillo's mother.[21] Hardly any area of learning could escape the official indoctrination.

Indoctrination, however, was not limited to the primary and secondary schools but was continued up through the university level. Ornes wrote that "professors as well as students seem to have been cast in a pattern of silence, subservience, and conformity."[22]

18. These and the following references to the primer are quoted *ibid.*, pp. 177-78. See also Rafael Trujillo, *Patriotismo y educación.*
19. Murray Kempton in the *New York Post*, quoted Ornes, *Trujillo: Little Caesar*, p. 213.
20. See *La Nación* (April 25, 1956), p. 1.
21. Ornes, *Trujillo: Little Caesar*, p. 178.   22. *Ibid.*, p. 179.

Lectures had to be in accordance with the official line, and the rector's office supplied elaborate directions for the teaching of such subjects as history and philosophy.[23] Works about Trujillo and his programs were again the major sources of information, while students' essays reflected their subservience to him. One essay, for example, stated, "The University students will always be at the side of our great and glorious leader."[24] Thus university student education and opinion was also infused with the cult of Trujillo.

The political activities of the university personnel (administrators, teachers, and students) were also closely scrutinized and controlled. Rectors of the single institution of higher learning in the country, the University of Santo Domingo, were political appointees chosen for their loyalty to the regime and not for their intellectual or educational accomplishments. Professors were required to join the official Dominican Party and to submit to their political superiors in intellectual matters. Unlike their counterparts in other Latin American countries, the students were not allowed to organize or engage in political activities; and when they at times forgot these ground rules, immediate and stern reprisals were taken against them. Student spies were planted in the classrooms to ensure that the teachers did not deviate from the established and approved curriculum, and a special corps of the secret police checked the students' political leanings. Recognizing that the universities had often provided the leadership for the overthrow of other Latin American dictatorships, Trujillo refused to allow this potential threat to develop in the Dominican Republic.[25]

A campaign to spread literacy was also instigated by the regime. The success of his educational programs in the existing schools convinced Trujillo that he had nothing to fear from mass education. Though illiteracy was far from wiped out, many schools were built and the education of those who lived in areas where there had previously been no opportunity to learn was encouraged. This education was limited to the primary grades, however, and was therefore not enough to expose the school children to

---

23. *Ibid.*, p. 174.
24. Ruben de Peña Castillo, *Trujillo visto por un estudiante universitario*, p. 8. For a treatment of Trujillo's dealings with the University, see Germán Soriano, *El Liberato de Trujillo en la Universidad*.
25. Armando Hoepelman, "Los estudiantes dominicanos," and Ornes, *Trujillo: Little Caesar*, p. 113.

more complex and possibly conflicting ideas, but only sufficient to further educate them in the official beliefs.[26]

The entire educational system thus proved to be only another arm of the government, designed to teach the glories of Trujillo's rule from books written by him or his collaborators. An entire generation was thus brought up too young to have known anything but life under Trujillo. This generation was educated for subservience to him, indoctrinated by many years of extolling his virtues, and untrained in any conception of democratic rights and responsibilities.

Intellectual activity under Trujillo was characterized by many of the same controls and procedures which existed in the area of education. It was marked by the absence of creative freedom and tolerance and permeated with a stifling dogmatism. Intellectual pursuits such as the social sciences and humanities, which might touch on subjects sensitive to the regime, were largely ignored, and those histories which were written had to laud Trujillo.

The writers and intellectuals were subsidized by the government and forced to write that which was prescribed. Fiction became almost a forgotten genre, and poetry sang the praises of the regime with tedious clichés. Books had to be orthodox within the guidelines set down by the party or by the Ministry of Education and Fine Arts.[27] These controls, coupled with years of censorship, propaganda, and terror, discouraged any creative imagination and produced an intellectual sterility.

Some of the more authoritative works on the country were proscribed. The Spanish version of Sumner Welles' classic history *Naboth's Vineyard: The Dominican Republic, 1844-1924* was banned, reportedly because Trujillo objected to those passages which described the difficulty the United States occupation forces had in securing good officers for the constabulary.[28] Damaging indictments of the regime written by competent foreign newspapermen and scholars, as well as those by exiled Dominicans, were not allowed to circulate.

Awards were bestowed on those who praised the regime and its *jefe*. The Rafael L. Trujillo prize was granted yearly to the author of the best work dealing with any aspect of the "portentous work of government of the illustrious leader of the Dominican

26. See Armando Oscar Pacheco, *La obra educativa de Trujillo*.
27. Galíndez, *La era*, p. 329.
28. Ornes, *Trujillo: Little Caesar*, p. 182.

people."[29] Musicians and painters who lavishly portrayed him were all paid well. In some of their works Trujillo was compared to lightning, the mountaintop, the sun, the eagle, volcanic lava, Pegasus, Plato, and God. Upon the opening of the 1955 international fair in Ciudad Trujillo, Andrés Avelino, a well-known Dominican philosopher, wrote of Trujillo, "He, like God, created from nothing on the seventh day a splendid and brilliant Fair."[30] Again, the list of illustrations could be readily multiplied. This tight control over all education and intellectual activity and the corresponding requirement for the constant adoration of the regime and its leader led to another aspect of Trujillo's system of thought control: public relations and the promotion of a favorable public image.

Megalomania, public relations, and the Trujillo image.—"The politicians and the people," as Austin MacDonald, a prominent student of Latin American politics, wrote, "have been compelled— or thought it wise—to heap extravagant adulation upon the dictator."[31] Like Stalin, Trujillo was the object of such directed, frenetic praise and adoration that it probably verged on megalomania.[32] It is doubtful that any man who had ever lived, Carleton Beals claimed, was so touted as the living superior of every great figure in the history of mankind.[33] The veteran *New York Times* correspondent in the Dominican Republic, Tad Szulc, also stressed this aspect of Trujillo's rule: "It is a world of absolute and mandatory adulation of the nation's master, an adulation that has created a personality cult of Generalissimo Trujillo . . . this ruler . . . lives to the sound of his own name echoing day and night throughout his fief."[34]

Examples of the adulation and worship which Trujillo demanded and received, like his properties, are too numerous to be chronicled in full, but some should be listed to illustrate the

29. *Ibid.,* p. 183.
30. Andrés Avelino, 'Homenaje a Trujillo."
31. *Latin American Politics and Government,* p. 578.
32. It is especially appropriate, at least in this respect, to compare Trujillo with Stalin. Nikita Khrushchev's now-famous "Critique of Stalin's Party Leadership," in which he commented, "Such a man supposedly knows everything, sees everything, thinks for everyone, can do anything, is infallible in his behavior," might just as easily have been said of Trujillo. The Khrushchev critique may be found in William G. Andrews (ed.), *European Political Institutions,* especially p. 170.
33. "Caesar of the Caribbean," p. 32.
34. "Uneasy Year," p. 42.

breadth and variety of this forced acclaim. In addition to renaming the capital city Ciudad Trujillo and the highest mountain in the Antillean chain Pico Trujillo, provinces were now called Trujillo, Benefactor, Libertador, Trujillo Valdez (after his father), and San Rafael. Numerous streets, parks, plazas, bridges, buildings, and children were also named after him or others of the ruling family.[35]

Symbols played a large part in promoting the cult of Trujillo. These symbols gave concrete focus and form to such abstract concepts as "the president," "the nation," or "the leader."[36] While the most famous totalitarian symbols have been the hammer and sickle or the swastika and fasces, in the Dominican situation the symbolic appeal concentrated on the person of Trujillo himself. Instead of swastikas or red stars, his picture was hung prominently in a shrine-like arrangement in nearly all homes. Statues, busts, and monuments were erected throughout the country, constantly reminding Dominicans that *el jefe* oversaw everything and everyone.[37]

Time was measured from his rise to power, and the period of his rule was formally called the "Era of Trujillo." Thus 1955, for example, was the "25th year of the Era of Trujillo," and all published works were required to be dated with the appropriate year corresponding to "The Era."[38] All buildings constructed during the Trujillo era contained a cornerstone with his name engraved, and excerpts from his speeches were carved into the walls.[39] Letters had to be written daily to the newspapers in praise of him, meetings were called to glorify his accomplishments, and parades were staged in his honor. One common way of expressing adulation was to pay for a mass for Trujillo's health. Such a mass in honor of the Generalissimo required the attendance of all the important personalities of the locality regardless of who had actually paid for it.[40]

Trujillo was hailed as the greatest Dominican patriot and his anniversaries became national anniversaries. His name was placed alongside those of the founders of the country in the *Baluarte del Conde* (the national shrine), and in 1938 his Congress declared him the greatest and most outstanding of all Dominican

---

35. See, for example, *El Caribe* (January 1, 1959), p. 1.
36. For a comparative consideration of the use of myths and symbols in totalitarian systems, see Friedrich and Brzezinski, Chapter 10.
37. See, for example, *El Caribe* (March 11, 1957), p. 7.
38. Galíndez, *La era*, p. 343.
39. *Ibid.*, p. 345.
40. *New York Times* (April 5, 1960), p. 18.

presidents.[41] October 24, Trujillo's birthday, was proclaimed the "Day of the Benefactor"; August 16, Dominican independence day and also the date of his inauguration as president in 1930, was celebrated as Trujillo's personal national holiday; and 1955, the twenty-fifth year of his rule, was declared the "Year of the Benefactor."[42] In keeping with his claim to be the personification of the nation, then, Trujillo took over the great national symbols and heroes and used them to further advance his own stature.

Signs were placed throughout the Dominican countryside so that the people could not forget the author of their benefits and good fortune. Signs in the hospitals read "Only Trujillo Cures Us" and those at village pumps "Only Trujillo Gives Us Drink." Other slogans such as "Trujillo Is My Protector" and "Trujillo Always" appeared in academic theses and on plaques hung on public buildings. Two of the signs achieved some notoriety. By the insane asylum on the outskirts of the capital city was a sign which read "All I Have I Owe to Trujillo." The famed neon-lighted sign which proclaimed "God and Trujillo" hung at the entrance to the harbor of Ciudad Trujillo; and some have cynically observed that it was surprising the dictator allowed God's name to appear first.[43]

This comment was not wholly unreasonable since it was becoming clear that Trujillo wished his people to look up to him and see him as a superior being. Thus the picture of the dictator which hung in most homes showed Trujillo's face floating in a mist that appeared cloudy and heavenly. Frequently a candle burned under the picture. San Cristóbal, his birthplace, was now called Blessed City. And when Trujillo appeared in public, Dominicans learned to remove their hats, place them over their hearts, and bow their heads.[44]

Trujillo flaunted the huge number of decorations, honors, and titles which had been bestowed upon him or which he had bestowed upon himself. He was decorated by most Latin American and many European countries, a number of United States organizations, and the Vatican.[45] Trujillo also held honorary de-

41. Vega y Pagan, *Military Biography*, p. 154.
42. Galíndez, *La era*, p. 344.
43. See Ornes, *Trujillo: Little Caesar*, pp. 6-7.
44. *Ibid.*, p. 4.
45. A resolution of the Congress dated January 26, 1947, listed these decorations: Gran Cruz de la Orden de Isabel la Católica (Spain); Gran Cruz de la Orden Jerosolimitana del Santo Sepulcro; Medalla de Oro de la Pan American

grees from the University of Santo Domingo and the University of Pittsburgh.[46] The pageantry of the decorations and awards was always duly described in the Dominican press with much fanfare, and Trujillo, in receiving and bestowing the numerous decorations, impressed upon his people a picture of himself as an international hero and statesman.

Trujillo's list of titles was also lengthy. He was officially referred to as His Excellency, the Generalissimo, Doctor Rafael Leonidas Trujillo Molina, Honorable President of the Republic, Benefactor of the Nation, Restorer of the Financial Independence of the Country, and Commander in Chief of the Armed Forces. In addition to being the "first lawyer" and the "first doctor," Trujillo also claimed to be the "first newspaperman," "first teacher," and "first worker."[47] No one in any field was allowed to occupy a plateau as high as that of the dictator.

The Trujillo cult permeated almost all aspects of Dominican existence. *Merengues,* the national music, proclaimed his infallibility, and songs like "San Rafael" and "San Cristóbal" dominated the Dominican hit parade. One of the most fantastic expressions

Society (New York); Gran Cruz de la Orden de Carlos Manuel de Céspedes (Cuba); Gran Cruz de la Orden Honor y Mérito (Haiti); Gran Crux en brillantes de la Orden del Sol del Peru; Banda de la Orden de la República (Spain); Gran Crux de la Orden de San Gregorio Magno (Holy See); El Collar de la Orden al Mérito (Chile); El Collar de la Orden del Aguila Azteca (Mexico); Gran Cruz Extraordinaria de la Orden de Boyacá (Colombia); Gran Collar de la Orden del Libertador (Venezuela); Gran Cruz de la Orden Nacional del Cóndor de los Andes (Bolivia); Gran Medalla del Mérito Extraordinario Libanés; Gran Cruz de la Orden del Mérito con Banda de Tres Borlas (Ecuador); Gran Cruz de la Orden de Vasco Núñez de Balboa (Panama); Gran Cordon de la Orden Nacional de la Legión de Honor (France); Gran Cordon del Mérito de la Caridad de la Orden Francesa de la Cruz de Sangre; Gran Cruz de la Orden Honor y Mérito de la Cruz Roja Cubana; Gran Cordon Rojo con Bordes Blancos de la Orden China del Brillante Jade; Bailío Gran Cruz de Honor y Devoción de la Soberana Orden de Malta; Orden del Mérito Naval de primera clase (Cuba); Gran Cruz de Medhuia de Marruocos; Gran Cruz de Honor Académico de la Academia Internamericana de Washington; Estrella Abdón Calderón (Ecuador); Gran Cruz de la Orden Nacional Ecuatoriana al Mérito; Gran Cruz de la Orden Nacional de la Cruz del Sur (Brazil); Gran Cruz del Mérito Paraguayo; Gran Cruz del León Nederlandes; Medalla Conmemorativa del Vuelo Panamericano pro-Faro a Colon (Cuba); Medalla Conmemorativa del Primer Centenario de l Muerte del Procer Colombiano General Fc. de Paula de Santander; Collar de la Orden de San Martín (Chile). Trujillo reciprocated by awarding the Order of Trujillo. This list is cited in Galíndez, *La era,* pp. 346-47. Trujillo continued to receive a large number of decorations throughout his rule. See Crassweller, Chapter 18.
46. Almoína, p. 159.
47. Galíndez, *La era,* pp. 341-42.

of Trujillo hero worship was a ten-part symphonic poem, presented as a television spectacular, in which each movement was concerned with different aspects of his rule, ranging from "Public Works" to "Struggle Against Communism."[48] In the public addresses of his partisans he was termed savior, hero, titan, pontiff, messiah, and demi-God.[49]

Trujillo thus presented himself as a superior being, one who was immortal, a chosen instrument of God with a great and noble mission to perform. He did not discourage others from drawing the parallels and certainly paraded himself as a few notches above mere mortals. After a time, the domestic population became used to the ritual of offering adulation to Trujillo and to his big-brother-like countenance watching over their every action. In this way he built up a cult or mystique about his personage, and there is little doubt that after a generation of this kind of indoctrination many Dominicans accepted and believed the myth. Trujillo's entire system of thought control helped maintain his secure grip on his country.

The propagation of the Trujillo myth was not confined to the Dominican Republic, however, but was spread throughout the world. Trujillo was particularly sensitive to criticism and spent lavish amounts on public relations in an attempt to present a favorable, untarnished international image. Because in his part of the world the influence of the United States was so overwhelming economically, politically, and militarily, Trujillo concentrated his efforts on that country.

Fully cognizant of the power of the United States in the Caribbean and of its strategic interest in maintaining stability and in preventing a foreign power from establishing a beachhead in the area, Trujillo constantly strove to impress upon the United States his friendship, the stability which his regime provided, and his opposition to non-American influences. In return, United States money, arms, and moral support, during almost the entire span of the Trujillo era, helped maintain the Dominican regime. If not always positively favorable, United States policy toward Trujillo consistently remained benevolently neutral; and it was not until the last two years of his rule that the traditionally warm relations began to cool. Because of its seemingly longstanding support of Trujillo's government, the United States is still held accountable

48. Szulc, "Uneasy Year," p. 43.
49. Thomson, p. 35.

by many Dominicans for the atrocities, terrorism, and corruption which marked his lengthy tenure.

The United States was not particularly favorable toward Trujillo's candidacy for the presidency in 1930, but once he had taken over power, his government was accepted. Early in his rule, Trujillo began the careful cultivation of the United States which was to help maintain him in office for so many years. He assiduously promoted himself as an efficient, hard-working administrator who could be expected to side with his large North American neighbor on nearly all issues. In 1934, for example, the dictator willingly submitted to a United States-designed solution of the debt question and proved to be very amenable to the demands of the bondholders. In return, Trujillo was permitted to divert a larger percentage of the customs revenues to domestic expenses, such as the improvement and enlargement of his armed forces.[50]

Trujillo's official and unofficial relations with Washington remained harmonious during most of the 1930's. The Haitian slaughter of 1937 produced some concern in the United States, but he easily weathered this storm. Toward the end of the decade he paid a visit to the United States where he was attended by many of that country's officials and diplomats, greeted at the White House by President Franklin D. Roosevelt, and praised by Representative Hamilton Fish of the House Foreign Affairs Committee as "a builder greater than all the Spanish conquistadores together."[51] The year 1940 saw the signing of another United States-conceived treaty settling the debt question; and in 1941 the Dominican declaration of war on the Axis powers, while not significant in terms of a military or strategic contribution to the Allied cause, was warmly welcomed and applauded by United States officials, as was the steady supply of raw materials which the country provided for the war effort.

In the immediate post-World-War-II period Trujillo's Dominican Republic, as well as the rest of Latin America, was largely ignored by the United States, which had to deal with what it conceived to be more important critical areas and problems elsewhere in the world. Thus the increasingly totalitarian nature of the dictatorship was overlooked and relations remained harmonious. A mutual defense treaty provided Trujillo with an even stronger military,

50. See Raymond H. Pulley, "The United States and the Trujillo Dictatorship, 1933-1940," pp. 28-29.
51. Quoted *ibid.*, p. 26.

and foreign aid bolstered his government in other respects. As the Cold War developed, furthermore, the Dominican dictator's opposition to communism and his reputation, fashioned with great care, as a firm friend and warm ally brought him the accolade of many influential United States officials and private citizens. Ambassadors, businessmen, congressmen, supreme court justices, a cardinal, and a vice-president were nearly unanimous in their praise of Trujillo; the opinion, as one congressman expressed it, that what Latin America needed was twenty Trujillos was not an isolated sentiment.[52] Throughout the mid-1950's Trujillo still seemed to be at the height of his power and his relations with the United States appeared to be as close as ever.

A pause for stocktaking is in order at this point, for the question of why United States relations with so brutal a dictatorship remained so harmonious must be considered. Most United States officials, after all, were not inclined to look with sympathy on such a tyranny as Trujillo's. It would seem that from the point of view of what the United States thought to be its more vital interests, however, the undemocratic nature of his regime could be overlooked in favor of its more positive features. Trujillo, in the final analysis, provided three decades of peace, order, and stability in an area considered strategically crucial by the United States but not particularly known in the past for its peaceful, orderly, and stable political processes. In addition, he protected private foreign holdings in his country and proved to be a willing supporter of United States governmental interests and policies in the Caribbean and elsewhere. Though on moral grounds his brutal regime could be, and often was, condemned by many public officials as well as private individuals in the United States, the ability of Trujillo to maintain stability and prevent the country from being dominated by powerful foreign elements took precedence. (After World War II, of course, the Communists rather than the Axis powers constituted the foreign element.) The dictator went to great pains and expense to build and preserve this image.

Mention has previously been made of some of the techniques used by Trujillo to propagate a favorable picture of himself. Writers were hired to tell his life story and his accomplishments,

---

52. See, for example, George S. Long, *El caso Gerry Murphy y la República Dominicana* and *Desenmascarando el comunismo;* William T. Pheiffer, *Address;* and "Un Gran Discurso" by John McCormack, reprinted in *El Caribe* (March 3, 1957), p. 7.

competing only in their use of ever more grandiose superlatives. Editorials, speeches, letters, and other pro-Trujillo literature were printed in several languages and donated to libraries around the world. Entire sections in the United States press were purchased to present a favorable picture of life in the Dominican Republic under its dictator. Posing as the "best friend of the U.S. in Latin America" and as the "foremost anti-communist of the hemisphere," Trujillo won praise from myopic United States political leaders and diplomats.[53]

The methods employed to present a favorable picture of Trujillo were not amateurish. Prestigious law firms, public relations companies in New York, lobbyists in Washington, and large numbers of other paid agents—all professional propagandists—championed his regime and served it in various ways. One of the most famous of these was Igor Cassini, best known for his syndicated, jet-set society column written under the name of Cholly Knickerbocker, whose public relations firm did extensive work for the Trujillo government.[54] Cassini, however, was only one of the more celebrated of the many Trujillo agents.

Public relations was an extensive and high-priced undertaking for Trujillo. The Mutual Broadcasting System, for example, was once paid $750,000 to broadcast pro-Trujillo propaganda in the guise of news.[55] On another occasion the United States Senate Foreign Relations Committee, investigating the influence of lobbyists for foreign interests, revealed that the International News Service (INS, later consolidated with United Press into United Press International) had also prepared dispatches financed by Trujillo's Dominican regime.

When all else failed, Trujillo was not above an outright bribe to help promote his purposes. It was well known that many United States officials received gifts, free vacations in the Dominican Republic, and other favors for their efforts on behalf of Trujillo; but these favors were tiny when compared with the fees paid to some prominent officials and politicians who were active

53. Hicks, *Blood in the Streets*, pp. 132-33, 138.
54. For the highly colorful Cassini story, see Peter Maas, "Boswell of the Jet Set," pp. 28-31, and Igor Cassini, "When the Sweet Life Turns Sour," pp. 94 ff.
55. This colorful story has not been fully told. The story came out when Trujillo, unhappy with the services he was receiving, attempted to sue to recover his money. For one sidelight of the story, see *Miami Herald* (November 3, 1960), p. 12-A. See also "The Foreign Legion of U.S. Public Relations," *The Reporter*.

in various ways on Trujillo's behalf. Four United States senators, several congressmen, and at least two State Department officials reportedly received payments which were large enough to compensate for the obvious risks involved.[56] The Trujillo propaganda machine was all-pervasive; it reached into many still undisclosed corners and further increased the regime's control.

The Church[57]

Prior to Trujillo's assumption of power in 1930, the Roman Catholic Church in the Dominican Republic was not a strong force in the nation's politics.[58] Many clerics, fearing the anticlericalism of the French Revolution, had left Santo Domingo after the area was ceded to France by the Treaty of Basle in 1795, and the Church did not regain strength until modern times. The Church, historically, was not a large property owner or entrepreneur; it could not back up its political pronouncements with economic force. Though several prominent churchmen had in the past held important political posts, including the presidency of the republic, it was not until Trujillo came to power that the Church began to recover its power as an organized unit.[59]

During almost the entire Trujillo era, Church and State in the Dominican Republic were mutually beneficial and mutually supporting institutions; the dictator favored the Church and it, in turn, supported his regime. The Church, however, was the only organization in the country over which Trujillo did not have complete

---

56. The evidence for Trujillo's bribery of the United States officials has not yet surfaced, and it is unlikely that it will come to light at least as long as those involved are still alive and active in politics. The most explicit statement of the charges is in the sometimes reliable and sometimes unreliable Espaillat, Chapter 8. Because much of the necessary evidence has thus far been suppressed, the most reliable sources for these accusations are outside the United States, where the risk of libel is less great.

57. Some of the materials in this section were previously summarized in Howard J. Wiarda, "The Changing Political Orientation of the Church in the Dominican Republic," *A Journal of Church and State*, VII (Spring, 1965), 238-54.

58. In stating that the Church was not a strong force in the nation's politics, we are referring to the Church's strength as a human institution, not as a body of religious beliefs. Thus, while the population of the Dominican Republic was some 98 per cent Catholic, the Church itself was relatively weak.

59. On the historical role of the Church, see Juan F. Pepén, *La Cruz señala el camino*, and William Louis Wipfler, *The Churches of the Dominican Republic in the Light of History*.

control,[60] since an attempt to establish this control would likely have involved the regime in a struggle which it realized could not be won. But, in fact, there was little reason for Trujillo to hold absolute authority over the Church as he did over other groups and institutions. Trujillo and the Church assisted each other in furthering the distinct interests of each, and both benefited from their close association.

Though himself somewhat superstitious, Trujillo sought to project the image of a devout Catholic in whom religiosity was natural. His political philosophy, as we have seen, was couched in moral and religious terms and his belief in God formed the basis of his ideology.[61] The Church, as a result of the many favors he showered upon it, was very pro-Trujillo; Archbishops Carlos Nouel and Ricardo Pittini, especially the latter, as well as a number of other clerics were outspoken in their praise of the Generalissimo. Those priests who, as individuals, held views at variance with those of the Archbishop remained silent.[62]

Some of the measures by which Trujillo favored the Church may be listed briefly. In 1929, a year before he came to power, the Supreme Court had declared the Church nonexistent before the law and a bill was submitted to Congress calling for the liquidation of the Church's small property holdings. This bill was defeated after Trujillo took office, and in 1931 a measure was passed which restored the juridical rights of the Church.[63] In 1936 the Company of Jesus was permitted to return to the country for the first time since Santo Domingo's colonial period. The government financed and the official Dominican Party administered the construction of many churches.[64] Marriage was changed from a civil to a religious institution, and education in the public schools was infused with Catholic teachings.[65] Clerics now became chaplains in the armed forces while representatives of a number of religious orders worked in public hospitals, schools, and other

60. The Church is one of the institutions which all totalitarian systems have had difficulty in completely controlling. For a comparative treatment of this "island of separateness," see Friedrich and Brzezinski, Chapter 23.

61. See especially Balaguer, El pensamiento.

62. Ornes, Trujillo: Little Caesar, p. 296. For the point of view of the Church, see James A. Clark, The Church and the Crisis in the Dominican Republic, Chapter 3.

63. Vetilio J. Alfau Durán, Trujillo and the Roman Catholic Church in Santo Domingo, pp. 11-14.

64. Pensón, El Partido Dominicano, p. 48.

65. Alfau Durán, p. 15.

institutions. Trujillo so favored the growth of the Church that by the end of his era its institutional strength, which during almost all of previous Dominican history had not been especially significant, was equivalent to that of the Church in most of the other Latin American countries.[66]

The most important step Trujillo took to curry the support of the Church was the 1954 concordat which he signed with the Vatican. Despite numerous attempts by previous Dominican presidents, no such concordat had ever been agreed to in the nation's previous 110-year history. Trujillo achieved the long desired agreement by granting vast concessions to the Church. The only "price" the Church paid was apparently to grant Trujillo an annulment of his second marriage and to bestow a papal blessing on his third, to María Martínez.

The Dominican Republic's status as a Catholic nation was affirmed in the first article of the concordat, which stated that "the Catholic Apostolic Roman religion continues to be that of the Dominican nation and will enjoy the rights and privileges that are rightfully hers in conformity with divine and canon law."[67] The accord bound the country to recognize the international legal representation of the Holy See and its perfect character, and guaranteed the full exercise of its jurisdiction and the free and public exercise of worship. The old patronage system was abolished and the Church was given the right to make all episcopal nominations, though these remained subject to a government veto.

The treaty further pledged the State to the full acceptance of Catholic marriage, respect for the Church's holy days, and the right of clerics to minister to the armed forces and in welfare institutions. The Church was guaranteed full freedom to establish and maintain schools at all levels. Students in the public schools were to receive religious instruction and State education was to be "guided by the principles of Catholic doctrine and morals." The Church was granted autonomy in the creation and alteration of parishes, ecclesiastical benefices and offices, as well as appointments to them. All religious institutions and organizations were given the right to acquire, own, and administer real and personal property,

66. For statistics on the number of priests, orders, and so forth in the Dominican Republic, see *Guía Eclesiástica de la República Dominicana*. For comparative figures, see United Nations, *Demographic Yearbook*, Table 4, and World Horizon Reports, *Basic Ecclesiastical Statistics for Latin America*.

67. The text of the concordat is in Zenón Castillo de Aza, *Trujillo y otros benefactores de la iglesia*, pp. 239-57.

which remained tax exempt. Catholic associations having religious, social, or charitable aims were guaranteed freedom to organize and function.

The Church obviously received most of the tangible benefits from the signing of the concordat. All the directives contained in the agreement were implemented by a series of measures subsequently passed by the Congress, thus further adding to the Church's gains.[68] What Trujillo received was less tangible but equally important: an enormous amount of publicity, which he exploited for propagandistic purposes, and the wholehearted support of the Church—the one institution in the country which he could not completely control. Thus, while the Church received many advantages, Trujillo made it appear as though the Church were functioning as an arm of his government. In this fashion Church and State were harmoniously joined in a mutually advantageous arrangement.

After the signing of the concordat, the good will and cooperation which had always existed between the Church and the Trujillo regime reached new heights. When Trujillo's daughter, Angelita, was married, Pope Pius XII bestowed a special blessing on the entire Trujillo family as well as on the newlyweds.[69] In the same vein Archbishop Pittini referred to Trujillo's "resolute protection of the Church" and wrote that: "On the twentieth year of Monsignor Pittini's consecration as a bishop, the Church in the Dominican Republic has reached a degree of spendor it had never known before. It owes its present favorable status to the Catholic-political genius of Generalissimo Dr. Rafael Leonidas Trujillo Molina."[70]

Trujillo then used the Church's praise to further his own political ends. By identifying his rule and programs with the Church and by cloaking his regime in a spiritual and religious mantle, the dictator received additional propagandistic mileage. In his book *Trujillo and the Roman Catholic Church in Santo Domingo*, Vetilio J. Alfau Durán, a prominent Dominican historian and intellectual, wrote: "The Dominican Church has reached a position of splendor as it has never enjoyed before—not even under the Spanish rule—thanks to the Catholic-inspired acumen of an illustrious statesman, Generalissimo Rafael Leonidas Trujillo Molina" (page 14).

68. *Ibid.*, pp. 257-307; and "Dominican Republic Restates Its Catholicity in Concordat," *A Look at the Dominican Republic*, p. 9.

69. Eduardo Ross, "La obra cristiana del Benefactor de la Patria," p. 68.

70. The text is in *A Look at the Dominican Republic*, V (July, 1956), 21.

He continued, "Trujillo has been justly called the *Benefactor of the Church*. Truly, he is the Benefactor of the Church in as high a degree as he is that of the country. For this reason, as well as for his boundless generosity in protecting and promoting the progress of Catholicism in Santo Domingo, the grateful sons of the one and eternal Church who wisely seek to be gathered in one flock under the guidance of one Shepherd, beg that the blessings of heaven be showered upon their illustrious leader" (page 17).

The image of Trujillo as the leader of a holy crusade as well as of a government soon reached proportions which seemed ludicrous to those who had not known only *trujillista* indoctrination. Eventually Trujillo came to be favorably compared with the great Church and State leaders of history. The most fantastic claim was probably contained in Castillo de Aza, *Trujillo y otros benefactores de la iglesia,* in which the "other benefactors" (Constantine, Justinian, and Charlemagne) were dismissed in the first 95 pages and the remaining 242 devoted to the greatest "benefactor," Trujillo. In these ways Trujillo linked the Church with his system of propaganda, thought control, and official ideology to further cement his power.

Church-State relations in the Dominican Republic during almost the entire Trujillo era were most harmonious. Considerably more often than is usual in predominantly Catholic countries, the Archbishop was included in state functions and ceremonies and was frequently pictured with Trujillo, but he did not intervene in the national political life. A Catholic Action group existed but it too remained outside politics. A few clerics served in the Congress and in other governmental positions, but the Church did not actively participate in political decision-making and had little influence, formally or informally, in the deliberations of the regime. At the same time, Trujillo did not interfere in matters that were purely religious.[71]

The result of these policies was that Dominican Church-State relations for twenty-nine of Trujillo's thirty-one years in power were free from the sharp cleavages and lasting antagonisms which had helped precipitate the overthrow of other Latin American dictatorships. Though there was some overlapping of jurisdictions, these possible sources of discord did not blow up into large-scale conflicts; both the Church and the Trujillo government remained sovereign in their respective spheres and only rarely did one

71. Galíndez, *La era,* p. 332.

interfere with the other. Their mutually beneficial arrangement was maintained almost to the end.

It was only in the last two years of his rule, as we shall see in the next chapter, that the Church fell out with Trujillo. The overall relations between the two, however, were summarized upon Trujillo's death by Bishop Francisco Panal in a missive proposing requiem masses for the slain dictator: "The faithful, the clergy, and the bishops acknowledge their debt of charity to Generalissimo Trujillo as a fellow Catholic . . . we have profited abundantly from the immeasurable benefits which he has brought to the nation and to the Holy Church. We owe him a great debt."[72] The Church paid this debt by its support of the dictatorship.[73]

72. The text of Panal's statement and an editorial comment may be found in the official Church paper, *Fides*, III (June 11, 1962), 1-2.

73. Because the Dominican Republic is so overwhelmingly Roman Catholic, Trujillo concentrated his efforts on that Church. But he did not neglect other religious groups. He reaped enormous amounts of favorable publicity in the international realm by providing a haven for approximately a hundred Jewish families, refugees from the anti-Semitism in Europe in the 1930's and 1940's, and by constructing a synagogue for the Jewish community in the capital city. Protestants were also allowed to carry on their religious activities. These favors came at a price. Trujillo did not allow any religious minority to forget that it existed only because of his grace or benevolence and that its continued existence would depend on its subservience to the regime. See, for example, *A Look at the Dominican Republic*, III (November-December, 1954), 10-11.

8. The Overthrow of Trujillo

B
Y THE MID-1950's Trujillo seemed to have reached the height of his power. His control over the armed forces, the government, the economy, communications, education, and thought was nearly absolute and there was no organized opposition or outspoken dissension within the country. Trujillo's position on the international level seemed to be equally secure; he had successfully frustrated two armed assaults by Dominican exiles and had gained the support of many influential political leaders in the United States. Yet, just at the time Trujillo reached his most lofty heights, a number of forces began to undermine his authority. The renewed opposition to his rule began as a result of events outside the Dominican Republic, but eventually came to include many influential elements within the country. In 1961 these two sets of forces—the external and the internal —coalesced and Trujillo was overthrown.

External Forces

The exiles.—The first of the factors outside the Dominican Republic which contributed to the overthrow of Trujillo was psychological: the ground swell of democratic sentiment which swept Latin America during the mid- to late-1950's and which gave new hope to those opposed to dictatorship. Like the wave which flooded the hemisphere immediately following World War II, this new crest of feeling in favor of democracy washed several of Latin America's most imposing dictators out of power. The Bolivian National Revolution of 1952, which swept that country's entrenched oligarchy from power, was the initial sign for pro-democratic hopes. In 1955 Juan Perón was forced from office in Argentina. His overthrow was followed by the ousting of the Gustavo Rojas Pinilla dictatorship in Colombia, the oppressive regime of Marco Pérez Jiménez in Venezuela, and the tyranny of Fulgencio Batista in Cuba. General Manuel Odría of Peru saw the prevailing mood and stepped from office. The success of the liberation movements in these other Latin American countries strengthened the morale of the exiled opposition to Trujillo and stimulated it to new efforts against the dictatorship in the Dominican Republic.[1]

The Dominican exile organizations were less fragmented than, for example, those of the Cuban exiles which formed after Castro took control. Though loosely organized and small in number, they long afforded the only articulate opposition to Trujillo. During the 1950's they steadily increased in size and effectiveness and by 1959 their propaganda had become an important part of the growing anti-Trujillo movement.[2]

Exile colonies existed at one time or another in Caracas, San José, Mexico City, Havana, and elsewhere, depending on the welcome they received from the governments of the host countries. The largest and most active groups were centered in neighboring San Juan, Puerto Rico, and in New York. In New York, especially, the Dominican exiles often found a sympathetic press and help from Norman Thomas and the United States Socialist Party, from Frances Grant and the Inter-American Association for Democracy and Freedom, and from Roger Baldwin and the American Civil Liberties Union.

The Dominican Revolutionary Party (PRD) of future president Juan Bosch was the most important of the exile groups. Organized in the late 1930's and with offices in Venezuela, Cuba, Mexico, Puerto Rico, Costa Rica, and New York, the PRD directed a steady stream of propaganda against the Trujillo regime. The Party

1. See Tad Szulc, *Twilight of the Tyrants*, and Harry Kantor, "The Destruction of Trujillo's Empire" (mimeographed).
2. The best account of the exile groups and their early activities is in Ornes, *Trujillo: Little Caesar*, pp. 300-308.

published several periodicals (such as *Quisqueya Libre, El Dominicano Libre*) as well as a monthly bulletin edited by the New
York section. Bosch, who wielded a vitriolic pen, and Nicolás
Silfa, who headed the branch in New York, became pet hatreds
of Trujillo.[3]

The Dominican Revolutionary Vanguard (VRD) with Miguel A.
Pardo as president and Horacio Ornes as secretary-general, was a
younger and smaller group. Ornes, a veteran of the 1948 Costa
Rican civil war and commander of an ill-fated 1949 invasion of
the Dominican Republic, emerged as the leader of the VRD. It
maintained offices in Puerto Rico, New York, and Mexico City and
published a magazine called *VRD*.[4]

Other exile organizations were smaller, less well organized, and
not so active. These included the Dominican Populist Party under
Francisco Javier Guilliani with its headquarters in Puerto Rico;
the Dominican Liberation Movement under Tulio Arvelo, the
Dominican Patriotic Union under Juan Díaz, the Dominican United
Front under Tobias Cabral—all with their headquarters in New
York; the 27th of February Revolutionary Movement; the "ARDE"
under José Antonio Bonilla Atiles; the Dominican Popular Move-
ment under Máximo López Molina with its offices in Puerto Rico
and later in Havana; and the official Communist organization, the
Popular Socialist Party, which later also came to be centered in
Cuba.[5]

Some Dominican exiles were more important for their individual
opposition to the dictatorship. These included the Basque professor and author of an anti-Trujillo book for which he was killed,
Jesús de Galíndez;[6] the poet Pedro Mir; the military chief of the
unsuccessful Cayo Confites and Luperón invasions General Miguel
Angel Ramírez Alcántara; the intellectual and writer Juan Isidro
Jiménes-Grullón; the journalist and author of an anti-Trujillo book
in English, Germán Ornes; Juan Rodríguez García, Angel Morales,
Horacio Vicioso, Guaroa Velázquez, and others.[7]

3. Galíndez, *La era*, p. 441.
4. Ornes, *Trujillo: Little Caesar*, pp. 305-7.
5. Information on these groups may be found in Galíndez, *La era*, pp.
439-41; Ornes, *Trujillo: Little Caesar*, pp. 307-8; *New York Times* (August 16,
1959), p. 2 and (August 30, 1959), p. 21; and *La República* [Puerto Rico]
(August 16, 1960), p. 39.
6. The Galíndez case is treated in more detail below.
7. See Galíndez, *La era*, pp. 441-43; and Ornes, *Trujillo: Little Caesar*,
p. 308. For a critical consideration of several of the leading exiles see J. A.
Osorio Lizaraza, *Germen y proceso del antitrujillismo en América*.

The activities of the exiles and their organizations were largely confined to the making of propaganda, and in this area the PRD was particularly active and adept. It organized picket lines, political rallies, and patriotic memorial meetings; lobbied success-fully before the International Confederation of Free Trade Unions for the adoption of a condemnation of the regime's oppressive labor policies; filed a complaint with the Pope over the "political activities" of the pro-Trujillo Archbishop of Santo Domingo; asked the inclusion of Trujillo's merchant marine in a worldwide boycott planned by the American Maritime Unions; charged Trujillo with the murder of Galíndez; and appealed to the Organization of American States to have Trujillo's Dominican Republic expelled from the inter-American system.[8] The PRD's pronouncements were usually echoed by the other exile organizations.

For many years the exiles did not pose a very serious threat to Trujillo. Two exile-led invasion attempts had been launched in the late 1940's with the aim of toppling the regime, but both had ended in ignominious failure. And during most of the 1950's the exiles were limited to propaganda attacks on the dictatorship. As the decade ended, however, they were increasingly encouraged by the recent overthrow of other Latin American strongmen and soon began to employ more forceful means. The June 14, 1959, invasion of the Dominican Republic by a group based in Cuba was probably the most important activity in which the reinspired exiles engaged. Landing at Maimon, Estero Hondo, and Constanza, the invaders led Trujillo's armed forces on a long chase for over two weeks until all but a few were killed. This was the first time the Generalissimo had to face what, by Caribbean standards, was a large-scale invasion. The martyrdom of the invaders served as an inspiration to other disenchanted elements and led to the for-mation of the first organized resistance to Trujillo within the country, the clandestine 14th of June Movement. Business and pro-fessional men also began to meet secretly to consider how the re-gime might be overthrown.[9]

The 1959 invasion also stirred the exile groups to a new attempt at unity and a more concentrated drive to overthrow the dictator-

8. See the many issues of the *Official Bulletin of the Partido Revolucio-nario Dominicano,* New York Section.
9. Juan Isidro Jiménes-Grullón, "Sentido Histórico de la Junio de 1959"; Daniel James, "Castro, Trujillo, and Turmoil"; Szulc, "Uneasy Year"; and the dispatches by Szulc from Ciudad Trujillo in *New York Times* (July 2, 1959), p. 6, (July 5, 1959), p. 1, and (July 12, 1959), p. 3.

ship. In Caracas the Dominican Revolutionary Party and the Dominican Revolutionary Vanguard formed a committee to coordinate the diverse exiles and to establish ties with the 14th of June Movement in the Dominican Republic.[10] Sensing that perhaps the end was near for Trujillo, the various exile colonies around the Caribbean and in the United States received new hope and began to increase their opposition activities.

The Galíndez-Murphy case.—At the height of his power in 1956, Trujillo overreached himself by having one of his most articulate critics killed. Jesús de Galíndez had come to the Dominican Republic in 1940 as a loyalist refugee from the Spanish Civil War. He stayed in the country for six years, working in the labor ministry and teaching at the University. He also began to gather materials on the dictatorship. In 1946 Galíndez moved to New York where he served as representative of the Basque government in exile. He began studying and teaching at Columbia University and also wrote a book and many articles on Latin American affairs. In 1956 he presented as his doctoral dissertation at Columbia a work entitled "The Trujillo Era," a thoroughly documented study of the regime.

The proposed publication of the severely critical study represented a threat to the carefully nurtured Trujillo image. The dictator apparently decided to have Galíndez killed to (1) prevent the manuscript from being published and circulated, and (2) serve as an example to others who might be contemplating an attack on the regime. Though the details of Galíndez' disappearance are still uncertain, the general sequence of events has been established. According to the most commonly accepted accounts, on March 12, 1956, Galíndez was kidnapped off the streets of New York, transported to a nearby airport, and flown to the Dominican Republic where he was killed.

The mysterious death of a United States citizen in the Dominican Republic several months later added another explosive ingredient to the already smouldering pot. Gerald Murphy, a twenty-three-year-old pilot and resident of Eugene, Oregon, had been employed by Trujillo to fly several private missions for his government. His death was linked to the disappearance of Galíndez, as evidence accumulated that Murphy was the pilot who flew Galíndez from New York to the Dominican Republic. Murphy

10. *La Prensa Libre* [Caracas] (November 4, 1960), p. 4-B; and Rafael I. Díaz-Balart, *Antitrujillismo y Solidaridad.*

was apparently killed because he knew too much and had a tendency to speak publicly of his activities.[11]

The importance of the Galíndez-Murphy case in contributing to Trujillo's downfall was stressed by a number of students of Latin American politics. Professor Harry Kantor called the case the "great turning point in the career of Trujillo." He argued that since Galíndez was an international figure and a respected writer and scholar, his death created a furor throughout Latin America and the United States which resulted in more and more opposition to the dictator's continued rule.[12] Professor Robert J. Alexander echoed Kantor's statement concerning the importance of the affair in focusing attention on the Dominican dictatorship. Whereas previously Trujillo had been able to carry out his nefarious practices on an isolated island with relatively little fear of the atrocities of his rule becoming public knowledge abroad, Alexander wrote, now the regime came under worldwide scrutiny. The death of Murphy especially, he stated, aroused an "unusual amount of consternation" in the United States; congressmen, senators, and private citizens protested to the State Department and urged the United States government to press for more information on the actions of the Dominican government.[13]

The case indeed focused attention on Trujillo. The respected United States Socialist leader Norman Thomas pointed an accusing finger at the Generalissimo. The Federal Bureau of Investigation was called in to make a probe, and the Inter-American Press Association demanded more information. The affair received the attention of such widely read columnists as Drew Pearson and Marquis Childs, and cBs had a special report on the case. Congressman Charles O. Porter made it a *cause célèbre* in the House of Representatives, and in cooperation with Senator Wayne Morse began an investigation of his own. The Central Intelligence Agency was involved, and the State Department, after long taking no action, also called on the Dominican government to provide further information. A series of spectacular trials and investigations revealed the extensive activities of *trujillista* foreign agents, public relations men, and legal representatives. Such influential news-

11. The Galíndez-Murphy case was the subject of a large number of magazine and newspaper articles in 1956 and 1957 as well as several full-scale investigations. Probably the best brief account is Ornes, *Trujillo: Little Caesar,* pp. 309-38.

12. "The Destruction of Trujillo's Empire," pp. 2-3.

13. "The Trujillo Tyranny."

papers as the *New York Times* and the *Washington Post* launched campaigns to see that justice was served. Even President Eisenhower, who said that he knew nothing about the matter when it was first brought up at a news conference, became aware of the issues involved. Latin American and European newspapers frequently gave the case and Trujillo front page headlines over the course of the following years.[14]

The worldwide attention had a snowballing effect. One result was that Trujillo began to spend even more lavish amounts on public relations in an effort to bolster his fading image. This effort only focused more unfavorable publicity on the dictatorship and started the vicious circle which would soon lead to economic bankruptcy for the previously prosperous Dominican government. Another result of the unfavorable publicity was a sharp decline in the Dominican tourist trade, which further contributed to the economic crisis and began the alienation of the business community. Finally, Trujillo, who was grudgingly admired even by his citics as well as by his fellow dictators as a skillful and talented administrator and ruler, suffered a loss of prestige for his bungling in the Galíndez-Murphy case.[15]

The Organization of American States.—In February, 1959, Rómulo Betancourt took office as the President of Venezuela. Betancourt had long been one of the leading spokesmen for democratic government in Latin America and had been strongly critical of dictatorships, especially that of Trujillo. As president he con-

14. The thesis that the Galíndez-Murphy affair focused the attention of the world, particularly that of the United States, on the Dominican Republic may be empirically supported by the use of two handy indices. By measuring the space devoted to the country in the monthly review of Latin American affairs, the *Hispanic American Report* (Vol. IX), it was found that during January and February, 1956, the number of inches was 5 and 6 respectively; in March when Galíndez disappeared, and April, when the case received additional attention, the inches of space had more than doubled to 12 and 14 respectively. The amount of space concerning the Dominican Republic stayed at this high level until 1959 when, as opposition to Trujillo became more intense, it jumped again. The *New York Times Index* shows a similar pattern. In the two years prior to the Galíndez case, 1954 and 1955, the number of column inches devoted to the Dominican Republic were 3 and 4½ respectively, while in 1956 and 1957 Dominican events rated 12 and 11 column inches respectively. It is again interesting that in 1959 and 1960 the number of column inches increased to 31 and 52 respectively. See also Crassweller, Chapter 21.

15. See *New York Times* (June 10, 1957), p. 10; and also Rafael Molina Morillo, "La Verdad Sobre la Muerte de Trujillo," in which it is reported that Pedro Livio Cedeño, one of the participants in Trujillo's assassination, pointed, just before his own assassination by Trujillo's heirs, to the "shadow of Galíndez" in the affair.

tinued his criticism of the Dominican regime. In retaliation, Trujillo attempted to have Betancourt overthrown and even assassinated. For these attempts against Betancourt the Organization of American States, for the first time in its history, voted diplomatic and economic sanctions against a member state. The sanctions further contributed to the economic crisis in the Dominican Republic and hurt most those who were in a position to overthrow the dictatorship.

Venezuela broke relations with the Trujillo regime on June 12, 1959, two days before the 14th of June invasion of the Dominican Republic, and Betancourt persisted in his verbal attacks on the dictatorship. In retaliation for these activities and for alleged Venezuelan assistance to the 14th of June invasion force, Trujillo sought to topple the Betancourt government. The first of his efforts made Trujillo appear foolish. On November 19, 1959, a plane was loaded with propaganda leaflets attacking Betancourt and urging his overthrow. But rather than dropping them over the intended target, Caracas, the confused pilot dumped them on the Dutch island of Curaçao off the Venezuelan coast and landed his plane on another Dutch island, Aruba, when he ran out of gas.

The second attempt against Betancourt's government was more serious. In April, 1960, an ex-Venezuelan general, Jesús María Castro León, along with a group of co-conspirators who had entered neighboring Colombia on Dominican passports, launched an invasion of Venezuela. The invaders captured the border town of San Cristóbal, announced over the radio that they had overthrown Betancourt, and appealed to Venezuelans to support the new government headed by Castro León. But the invaders were driven out within a few days by loyal armed forces units.

The third attempt against Betancourt nearly succeeded. Using equipment supplied by the Dominican government, a group of assassins came very close to killing the Venezuelan president on June 24, 1960. A charge of explosives was placed in a parked car along a route the Betancourt car was traveling. The charge was detonated at precisely the right time, killing the president's military aid and seriously injuring Betancourt's driver. Betancourt himself escaped with severe burns. Those involved in the assassination attempt were soon discovered, along with other propaganda materials and sabotage equipment prepared in the Dominican Republic.[16]

16. These three cases are documented in Organization of American States,

The issues were clear and the evidence overwhelming, and Venezuela began to press its case before the oas. On June 8, 1960, the Inter-American Peace Committee made public a study, initiated previously at the request of Venezuela, which accused the Dominican Republic of "flagrant and widespread violation of human rights," including the "denial of free assembly and of free speech, arbitrary arrests, cruel and inhuman treatment of political prisoners, and the use of terror and intimidation as political weapons." In the view of the committee these violations aggravated tensions in the Caribbean, and it advised that steps be taken by the Dominican government to remedy the situation.[17]

This resolution had little effect on Trujillo. The condemnation was published, it will be noted, approximately two weeks before Trujillo attempted to have Betancourt assassinated, and, when this attempt occurred, the Dominican case was brought up again. The specific charge this time was not that the Trujillo government was a dictatorship which had suppressed human rights (a charge which seemed to many hemispheric delegates, regardless of their dislike of Trujillo, to imply intervention in strictly internal affairs) but that the Dominican Republic had committed an act of aggression against Venezuela. A committee was appointed to investigate the charge of aggression brought by Venezuela against the Dominican Republic. The investigating committee's findings proved beyond any doubt that the Trujillo government was involved in the plot against Betancourt's life and was hence guilty of aggression against Venezuela. The oas then voted for a consultative meeting of the foreign ministers in San José, Costa Rica, to determine what action to take.

The United States, represented by Secretary of State Christian Herter, felt that instead of immediately applying sanctions against the Dominican Republic, the oas should try to persuade Trujillo to democratize his regime. Fearing that the overthrow of Trujillo might lead to a Communist or Castro-like takeover, the United States argued that getting rid of the dictator would not ensure the establishment of democracy in the country and that the transition to representative democracy could best be achieved by resort to orderly and peaceful methods. The United States proposal thus

Report Submitted to the Committee of the Council. See also Kantor, "The Destruction of Trujillo's Empire," pp. 3-5.

17. Organization of American States, *Report of the Inter-American Peace Committee on the Case Presented by Venezuela.*

called for free elections under the supervision of an international commission.[18]

The United States proposal, labelled as "soft on Trujillo," was rejected by the meeting. Most of the Latin American delegations favored a strong condemnation of the Dominican regime and the imposing of such severe sanctions as to ensure the collapse of the dictatorship. Since it was clear that the other nations were determined to punish Trujillo, Herter joined them, apparently hoping that the United States would thereby gain their support for a condemnation of Castro's Cuba in a forthcoming meeting.

On August 20, by a vote of 19-0 (with the Dominican Republic and Venezuela abstaining), the OAS Council of Foreign Ministers condemned the Trujillo government for intervention and acts of aggression against Venezuela. It was agreed that the following sanctions would be imposed: (1) The breaking of diplomatic relations of all OAS member states with the Dominican Republic; (2) The partial interruption of economic relations of all the member states with the Dominican Republic, beginning with the immediate suspension of trade in arms and implements of war of every kind.[19] The Council was also empowered to lift the sanctions "at such time as the Government of the Dominican Republic should cease to constitute a danger to the peace and security of the hemisphere." It became apparent, however, that the Dominican government continued to disregard OAS admonitions and resolutions, and additional sanctions were voted against the regime. The suspension of trade was extended to include (1) petroleum and petroleum products, and (2) trucks and spare parts.[20]

The strong action taken by the OAS was another serious blow to the long secure Trujillo regime and further intensified the economic and political crisis which had been developing in the country and which led ultimately to the collapse of the dictatorship. Fearing that the next step would be an armed invasion of the Dominican Republic, Trujillo began to spend vast quantities of money in Europe for larger arms and redoubled his propaganda campaign in the United States. The sanctions, combined with

18. *Department of State Bulletin,* XLIII (September 5, 1960), 357.
19. Organization of American States, *Sixth Meeting of Consultation of Ministers of Foreign Affairs,* pp. 4-5.
20. Organization of American States, *Special Committee to Carry Out the Mandate Received by the Council.* The report was made on December 21, 1960, and the additional sanctions were voted at the January 4, 1961, meeting.

Trujillo's wild spending, severely taxed those middle- and upper-class Dominicans who had long collaborated with or at best retained some neutrality toward the regime. Realizing that their interest could no longer be served by his continued rule, some elements in the armed forces, the government service, and the business-professional-landholding elite began to turn against Trujillo. When the United States and the oas threatened to impose still further crippling sanctions on the country, these same elements organized the plot and formed the group which assassinated Trujillo.[21]

The United States.—The role played by the United States, apart from its activities as a member of the oas, in the overthrow of the Trujillo regime was also considerable. Because of its numerous prior activities in support of the Trujillo dictatorship, the United States government had been severely criticized by many of its own citizens as well as by many Latin Americans. In the late 1950's, however, United States policy began to change; its longstanding warm *abrazo* for dictators such as Trujillo now frequently turned into only a lukewarm handshake.

The argument for United States support of Trujillo began to lose relevance during the last two years of his rule. The trips of Vice-President Richard Nixon and of President Dwight D. Eisenhower to Latin America were instrumental in awakening the United States to the degree of resentment and hatred which many Latin Americans had for the "Colossus of the North." The coming to power of Fidel Castro and the Communists in Cuba, furthermore, revealed that the hemisphere was no longer to be considered "safe" from communism and that it could not any more be ignored. At least part of the Latin American resentment toward the United States stemmed from its seeming longtime support for dictators like Trujillo; and it was in response to this resentment, coupled with the fear that dictators like Cuba's Fulgencio Batista and Trujillo might actually make conditions ripe

21. For treatments of the important role played by the oas in the overthrow of Trujillo, see John C. Dreier, *The Organization of American States and the Hemisphere Crisis*, pp. 97-101; Kantor, "The Destruction of Trujillo's Empire," pp. 5-6; J. Lloyd Mecham, *The United States and Inter-American Security, 1889-1960*, pp. 419-21; Frances R. Grant, "Hemisphere Repudiates Trujillo"; de Lesseps S. Morrison, *Latin American Mission: An Adventure in Hemispheric Diplomacy*; Serafino Romualdi, "Trujillo on the Carpet"; Jerome Slater, "The United States, the Organization of American States, and the Dominican Republic, 1961-1963"; Slater, *The OAS and United States Foreign Policy*; and Gonzalo J. Facio, "Sanciones al régimen de Trujillo."

for communism, that the United States began to re-evaluate its stand with regard to the Dominican dictatorship.[22] The inauguration of the Kennedy administration in January, 1961, furthermore, implied increased influence for those who were manifestly opposed to the tacit acquiescence of the United States in the continuation of the Trujillo dictatorship and who favored the policy of pushing for democratic social and political reform in the Dominican Republic and in Latin America generally.

The Dominican dictatorship, however, presented a special dilemma for Washington policy-makers. From the days of the "Good Neighbor Policy" the United States had generally adhered to the principle of nonintervention in the domestic affairs of the Latin American nations. At the same time the United States was criticized for the inconsistency of proclaiming the establishment of democracy as one of the aims of the struggle against the Fascist or Nazi countries in the 1930's and 1940's and of the Cold War in the post-World-War-II period while at the same time supporting the dictatorship of a close neighbor and ally. The United States had justified support of Trujillo and provided military and economic aid to him on the apparent assumptions that he provided stability and prevented communism and that alternative policies might lead to Soviet control. Though the United States had been long committed to preserving as much peace and stability as possible in the greater Caribbean area, which dictatorships usually assured, Trujillo's constant tussles with his neighbors tended to diminish the strength of that argument. Further, the ease with which the similar dictatorship of Batista in neighboring Cuba had collapsed and Castro and the Communists gained power undoubtedly served as a lurid and immediate example for the makers of policy in Washington. There were, thus, not two but several horns to the dilemma.[23]

The Dominican dilemma, moreover, could not be separated from the Cuban problem, also emerging during this period, and the convergence of the two issues raised further complications. It has already been stated that the United States began to take more interest in Latin America at least partly as a response to the fact that the Cuban example had demonstrated that the continent could no longer be assumed safe from communism,

22. See Milton S. Eisenhower, *The Wine Is Bitter.*
23. Theodore P. Wright, Jr., "The United States and Latin American Dictatorship."

went along with a "tough" OAS condemnation of Trujillo apparently because it hoped to secure Latin American support for a condemnation of Castro, and feared that the Batista example might be repeated in the Dominican Republic. It soon became clear, in addition, at least during the last months of the Eisenhower administration, that the United States was more interested in condemning a dictatorship of the Left than an at least equally oppressive dictatorship of the Right. Many Latin Americans concluded that the United States began to oppose the Trujillo dictatorship only because its opposition to the Castro regime alone would have placed it in an embarrassingly hypocritical position and it would not have been able to secure the required votes to condemn the Cuban regime.[24]

A further complicating factor was Trujillo's own changed international stance. Whereas previously Trujillo had always sided with and supported the United States and had presented an image of himself as an implacable foe of communism, he now began an open and highly vocal flirtation with the Soviet Union. He began to affect a pro-Communist pose, and the use of Tass news releases gave his government-controlled press a Russian slant. And, after a short but bitter conflict with the new Cuban regime, highlighted by the June 14, 1959, invasion of the Dominican Republic by a group of exiles based on the neighboring island, Trujillo and Castro reached a mutually advantageous accord based on their common interests in survival and opposition to the United States. Further, after June, 1959, a clandestine *fidelista*-oriented group and the Communist Dominican Popular Movement (MPD) also began functioning within the Dominican Republic. Though there is little concrete evidence to support the suggestion, Trujillo's flirtation with Moscow, accord with Castro's Cuba, and permissive nod to Communist groups in his own country may have further spurred the United States to reassess its policies.[25]

The United States thus began to oppose Trujillo, but it did so with mixed and uncertain motives and a two-edged policy. In accord with the OAS resolution the United States suspended diplomatic relations (though maintaining a political section and a Cen-

24. Dreier, pp. 97-98; and J. Lloyd Mecham, *A Survey of United States-Latin American Relations,* p. 291.
25. See James, pp. 63 ff.; Espaillat, Chapter 14; and Irving P. Pflaum, *Area of Decision,* Chapters 22-23.

tral Intelligence Agency nucleus in its consulate) and cut off trade in petroleum and petroleum products, arms and implements of war, and trucks and spare parts. But while the sanctions were being formally complied with, the spirit of the OAS resolution was broken; the Dominican Republic's share of the United States sugar quota was quadrupled as a result of the recently suspended Cuban quota. This sugar windfall was strongly criticized because it was well known that the Trujillo family personally owned some 60 to 70 per cent of the country's major product and industry. As a partial attempt to live up to the spirit of the OAS resolutions, the Republican administration responded to the criticism by later imposing a special tax of 2 cents per pound on Dominican sugar.[26]

Only in 1961, the year Trujillo was killed, did Secretary of State Dean Rusk obtain authority to cut off the Dominican Republic's special sugar quota. Though the cutoff came late, it nevertheless added to the regime's economic woes and provided a powerful psychological lift to those already opposing Trujillo. Because the Dominican Republic was so dependent on the United States (economically as well as in other ways) the cutting off of sugar importation, particularly when combined with the other economic sanctions, was the proverbial final straw which broke the back of the Trujillo regime. And, as we shall see shortly, United States opposition to Trujillo was by this time no longer only limited to diplomatic and economic sanctions.

Internal Forces

As the external opposition to Trujillo's rule increased, internal opposition began to emerge as well. The mounting external and internal opposition forces reflected and reinforced each other, as illustrated particularly by the increasingly grave economic crisis.

The economic crisis.—The financially ruinous 1955 International Peace Fair, on which the Dominican government spent some $50 million and reaped almost nothing in return, was probably the initial cause of the previously prosperous Trujillo regime's spiraling economic decline. Economic difficulties accelerated following the Galíndez case. The unfavorable publicity which the Dominican Republic received beginning in 1956, as mentioned previously, kept the tourists away, and the three luxury hotels which Trujillo had built remained nearly empty. Tourism was not the only

26. Douglas Cater and Walter Pincus, "Our Sugar Diplomacy." See also Crassweller, Chapter 29.

industry to suffer; in the last five years of Trujillo's rule almost every Dominican business—agricultural, commercial, and industrial—suffered a decline. Official government statistics reveal that after the peak years of the mid-1950's, production and revenues dipped sharply. The earnings from the export of the three main crops, sugar, coffee, and cacao, dropped from $98 million at their height to $78 million in 1959, and with the impact of the sanctions and of falling market prices, 1960 was an even worse year for Dominican revenues. Similar losses were evident in other commodities and in industrial production.[27]

The economic decline was accelerated still more after the June, 1959, invasion attempt forced the government to take extra defense measures. Because the OAS resolutions prohibited the sale of arms or weapons of war to the Dominican Republic by any member state, Trujillo had to buy the materials from European producers, often at higher costs. The government announced an extra appropriation of $50 million for weapons in addition to the $38 million already budgeted to the armed forces. (The amounts were comparatively huge, particularly considering that the total national budget for that year was in the neighborhood of $130 million.) In his anxiety to arm himself against any possible future invasions, Trujillo dealt another blow to the staggering economy.[28]

The large expenditures for weapons forced the regime to seek up to $40 million in loans, mostly from Canadian banks, to help cover the costs. Using sugar as collateral, the Royal Bank of Canada and the Bank of Nova Scotia, both of which had branches in the Dominican Republic, granted the loans. This marked the first time in twelve years that Trujillo, known since 1947 as the "Financial Emancipator of the Nation" for having wiped out the foreign debts which had plagued the country for over half a century, had been forced to contract a foreign loan.[29]

The country's economic plight steadily worsened. Under pressure from the International Confederation of Free Trade Unions and its member seamen's and longshoremen's unions, several shipping lines, such as the Alcoa Steamship Company, cancelled their calls at Ciudad Trujillo.[30] Dominicans, accepting discounts of 5 to

27. See Dirección General de Estadísticas y Censos, *República Dominicana en Cifras* (Santo Domingo: Sección de Publicaciones, 1964).
28. *New York Times* (March 6, 1960), p. 2.
29. *New York Times* (October 27, 1959), p. 1.
30. *Hispanic American Report*, XII (November, 1959), 490-91, and (February, 1960), p. 668.

15 per cent below normal par value, began to pour pesos into the market at the rate of $100,000 per week until New York's leading foreign exchange dealer, Perera and Company, no longer considered the peso a freely convertible currency.[31] Agricultural and industrial declines, foreign debts, and fleeing currency combined to produce a dangerous deficit in the Dominican balance of payments.

Merchants soon felt the effects and reported that the tourist trade and other businesses were being hit even harder. Because of the deterioration of the government's finances and the retrenchment in business activities after the 1959 invasion, the cost of living, which had been stable for years, rose 20 per cent between July and October, 1959. There was practically no construction being done and little investment with the result that the unemployment rate climbed to 50 per cent, starvation ensued, and business practically came to a halt.[32]

In the face of the spiraling economic crisis, Trujillo overtaxed those groups which were already chafing at the uncertainties and barriers to advancement and wealth under the shaking dictatorship. He announced that the government's traditional Christmas bonus, equal to a full month's pay, would have to be shouldered by private employers. The 10 per cent commission which businessmen had been obligated to pay to high officials or to Trujillo himself in order to carry on transactions was now raised to 20 to 25 per cent, thus further strangling the already tightly squeezed commercial interests.[33]

Although the OAS sanctions had not had the devastating effect that was envisioned at the time they were adopted, when coupled with the Dominican Republic's own economic misfortune, they were probably sufficient to tip the balance. While the regime could probably have coped with another exile invasion, the collapse of economic prosperity, which had been the main source of pride for Trujillo, helped to push the growing middle-to-upper sectors into opposition and thus led to the increased shaking of the entire edifice. The climate was unpropitious for business and the interests of the regime no longer coincided with those of the business-professional-landowning elements, several members of which now began to conspire against the government.[34]

31. *Foreign Commerce Weekly*, LXI (March 9, 1959), 7.
32. Morrison, pp. 129-30.   33. *New York Times* (July 12, 1959), pp. 1 ff.
34. Ramón Grullón, "Antecedentes y perspectivas del Momento Político

The business-professional-landowning sectors.—Few of the middle- and upper-class elements now opposed to Trujillo were willing to jump from passive to active resistance. Many feared that a violent revolution would lead to a Castro-like takeover and additional measures inimical to their interests. While some businessmen and professionals began to hold secret meetings of small, select groups, few joined the now-flourishing underground, though many of their sons became members of the clandestine 14th of June Movement.

The opposition to his continued rule gradually built up during the last half of 1959 and early 1960 until Trujillo was forced to take drastic action against it. In January, 1960, some forty-four leading members of the business-professional-landowning community were arrested for plotting against the regime. Those arrested included seven well-known physicians and medical specialists, six leading members of the Dominican bar, five prominent businessmen, and five engineers. Many of the others were sons of some of the country's most prominent families.[35]

During the following month, forty of those arrested were sentenced to thirty-year prison terms at hard labor and were held responsible for damages to the state set at $600,000. The mass trial was one of the largest in the history of the regime. But this number was insignificant compared to the reported hundreds, and possibly thousands, seized in a government crackdown on what it called "subversive elements," who continued in prison without trial.[36] The mass arrests gave credence to the contention that Trujillo was facing the greatest wave of oppposition of his career, mostly from the relatively small prosperous and educated sectors. Guido D'Alessandro, a businessman who turned rebel and escaped to Puerto Rico after two months of hiding during the early 1960 crackdown, reported that the underground by that time numbered between 30,000 and 40,000 persons.[37]

The government workers.—The economic crisis also had an adverse effect on another increasingly significant group in Dominican

Dominicano," pp. 234-38; and Carleton Beals, "Gunboat Diplomacy and the Dominican Crisis," p. 4.

35. *New York Times* (January 30, 1960), p. 1; and Crassweller, Chapter 25.

36. *New York Times* (February 6, 1960), p. 8.

37. See the series of three articles by Edward C. Burks in the *New York Times* (April 4-6, 1960); and also Germán Ornes, "El Inminente Ocaso de Trujillo."

politics, the government workers. Measures used to keep the budget balanced in the face of frenetic spending on arms included slashes in the salaries of public service employees on a scale ranging from 4 per cent for those earning up to $300 per month to upwards of 25 per cent for the higher paid officials. The pay cuts at the top meant that those aides who had long been loyal to the regime were alienated.[38]

In addition to the salary reductions, the country's critical financial situation forced the government to suspend the 1959 Christmas bonus, which was annually given to government employees as well as to those employed by private employers. As an attempt to alleviate the ill feeling generated by this measure, Trujillo offered to contribute $1 million from his own funds toward reinstating the bonus and Lieutenant General Rafael Trujillo, Jr., announced that he would forego his $3,000 monthly salary; but the promises reportedly went unfulfilled and the government workers went without their bonuses. These actions turned Trujillo's closest collaborators as well as lower-ranking public employees against him.[39]

When the mass arrests began in mid-January, 1960, many government officials or their sons were in the roundup. Those arrested included diplomatic personnel, several high ranking public employees, Dominican Party officials, and former congressmen and members of their families. Others who were close to the regime but whose names or positions were not made public were also among those jailed.[40]

The Church.—During the last two years of his rule, Trujillo lost the support of another influential group in Dominican politics, the Church. The wave of indiscriminate terror unleashed following the 1959 invasion attempt had led to the jailing of many of the country's most prominent citizens, including a priest and three seminarians. It was this resurgence of terror, the jailing of churchmen, and probably the realization that the regime would not last much longer which prompted the Church to repudiate the harmonious arrangement under which it had cooperated with Trujillo for many years.

The personnel of the Church also underwent a change at this time. At the top level Archbishop Pittini (ultra-conservative,

38. *New York Times* (October 31, 1959), p. 13.
39. See *Hispanic American Report*, XII (January, 1960), 603, and *New York Times* (October 27, 1959), p. 1.
40. *New York Times* (February 6, 1960), p. 8.

Italian-born, eighty years old, and a staunch Trujillo supporter) was replaced by Octavio Beras (moderate, Dominican-born, fifty-four years old, and unenthusiastic about the regime). In addition, new men were assigned to the country's four bishoprics in the late 1950's. All were relatively young (average age, forty-nine), more committed to social reform, and less inclined to favor dictatorships. These shifts in Church leadership from conservatism to the middle of the road or even to liberalism, from foreign-born to Dominican nationals, and from old age to relative youth reflected the change which was taking place in the Church with regard to the Trujillo regime.[41]

The Papal Nuncio, Lino Zanini, also began to play an increasingly important role in the attempt to curtail the power of the regime. It had been Zanini who in 1958 arranged for the breakup of the archdiocese of Santo Domingo into five dioceses, thus decentralizing authority and weakening Trujillo's hold. Foreigners were put in charge of two of the dioceses apparently so that their families would be less subject to recriminations. The Nuncio, who was eventually expelled by Trujillo, took the lead in rallying the Church into opposition to the dictatorship.[42]

The first open break between Trujillo and the Church came in the form of a pastoral letter dated January 25, 1960. The letter was read in all the Roman Catholic churches in the country and indicated that the Church was at the point of cutting its ties with the government. The hierarchy declared their solidarity with the many families bereaved by the arrest of loved ones. A long section was devoted to an assertion of human rights which, the letter said, had priority over the rights of any state. These rights did not exist in the Dominican Republic, the bishops warned, and to suppress them was a "grave offense against God."[43]

Trujillo's immediate public response to the pastoral letter was a humble letter in return, in which he promised the release of all women who had been arrested and guaranteed full respect for the legal rights of all others. But he would not, Trujillo's letter concluded, allow peace, order, and stability to be upset; "communism" would not be permitted to cause anarchy and disintegra-

41. Statistics on the personnel of the Church may be found in *Guía Eclesiástica de la República Dominicana.*
42. James A. Clark, "The Church and the Dominican Crisis," p. 127.
43. The text is in *New York Times* (February 3, 1960), p. 16. The letter was not published in the Dominican Republic and the regime tried unsuccessfully to keep its issuance a secret.

tion. To this end, he argued, Church and State must continue to carry out their noble task in the same spirit of harmony and solidarity that had existed since the signing of the 1954 concordat.[44]

The dictator's reply, in which he appeared to have complied with the bishops' suggestions, was calculated to woo back the Church to the support which it had traditionally given his government. In this attempt he was only partially successful. Though the Church soon refrained from attacking him officially, individual clerics continued their unofficial opposition. The rift between Trujillo and the Church became an open secret; there could be no going back to the shared harmony of previous years.

Attacks on the part of individual priests, even at the hierarchy level, therefore continued. Bishop Thomas F. Reilly reiterated the charges which the pastoral letter had leveled against Trujillo and called for an end to the "excesses" of the regime. Bishop Francisco Panal excommunicated provincial authorities, including the governor, who were holding a pro-Trujillo and anti-Church rally in the town square opposite his church in La Vega.[45] At a special service in the national cathedral, Archbishop Beras spoke of the nation's history but failed to mention Trujillo's name. To omit speaking of the Generalissimo in any speech had long been considered a grave offense, and many believed that its omission by Beras was deliberate. Other clerics began to criticize the regime from their pulpits.[46]

Whereas Trujillo's response to the Church's criticism in the pastoral letter had been conciliatory, the continued and increasing denunciation of his regime by churchmen prompted him to take more drastic measures. Some sixty priests were soon expelled from the country. Bishop Reilly then accused the dictator of having engaged in "acts of intimidation and persecution" against the Church and its organizations, including the expulsion of a Spanish missionary from Reilly's district of San Juan de la Maguana, the kidnapping and mistreatment of another, police intimidation of Catholic Action groups, and the setting on fire of the doors of his cathedral.[47]

44. The text is in *New York Times* (March 4, 1960), p. 8.
45. On the role of both Reilly and Panal in the anti-Trujillo movement, see "La Iglesia en la cruzada redentora," *Ahora*.
46. *New York Times* (February 28, 1960), p. 33, and (February 29, 1960), p. 2.
47. "Otra vez desafía la iglesia dominicana la furia homicida de Rafael Trujillo," *El Dominicano Libre,* and Crassweller, Chapter 26.

It should be kept in mind that these attacks on the regime were made by individual churchmen. After its initial criticism in the pastoral letter of January, 1960, the official Church policy had been to seek a reconciliation. Behind-the-scenes fence-mending took place so that by January, 1961, the Church newspaper, published at the archbishop's office, could editorialize that with a spirit of good will on both sides the friction which had existed had been erased. Church and State, the editorial concluded, were in "just harmony."[48]

The Church was thus attempting to gain the favor of the opposition but at the same time trying to maintain good working relations with Trujillo. While certain individual clerics, such as Bishop Reilly and Monsignor Eliseo Pérez Sánchez, were outspoken in their ciriticism of and opposition to the regime, the Church, realizing that the Trujillo government might remain in power for some time, refused to formally break with it and was careful not to give its official sanction to the opposition. For attempting to play both sides of the question, the Church was severely criticized by at least one leader of the anti-Trujillo movement, who called its noninvolvement a dishonor and a forsaking of Christ's injunctions. The bishops, he wrote, have gone back to collaborating with the tyranny.[49]

Though the Church's position remained ambiguous, it became apparent from the number of the attacks that a large percentage of clerics, including those at the top of the hierarchy, were thoroughly disenchanted with the regime. Many priests who failed to speak out publicly were nevertheless equally opposed to the dictator. In a country so overwhelmingly Catholic, where the Church had become one of the strongest voices politically as well as spiritually, these criticisms were powerful blows to the once monolithic and absolute Trujillo regime and served notice that another influential force was no longer unequivocally supporting the government. The result was that many people of the middle and upper classes, who had been disillusioned by the Church's long support of the dictatorship, again turned to the Church for guidance and leadership. It was these same middle- to upper-class elements who assassinated Trujillo.

The armed forces.—The ultimate source of Trujillo's power had

48. *Fides*, III (January 22, 1961), 2.
49. Eduardo Sánchez Cabral, *De la Clandestinidad* (Santo Domingo, n.p., 1962).

always been the armed forces. Without the continuous support of the military, the elaborate controls which he had established over the governmental machinery, the national economy, socioeconomic and political groups, and educational and intellectual life would have made little difference. It was especially significant, therefore, that during the last two years of his rule, some elements in the armed forces joined the anti-Trujillo movement.[50]

As early as 1957 it had become clear that within the armed forces there existed diverse points of view and potentially clashing interests. Germán Ornes' statement of the differences in the military seems, particularly when considered in retrospect, to be remarkably prophetic: "Still if there is a faint ray of hope, it must be looked for in the Armed Forces. Of course nothing can be expected from the generals (of which the Dominican Army has a larger number comparatively than any other army in the world); they are so enamored of their wealth and property, and too involved to be trusted. Moreover they are so afraid of popular vengeance that they dare not risk any change.

"However, not all the officers, especially the younger ones, are seasoned hoodlums or illiterate underworld characters, haunted by fears and burdened with crimes. Among the newer promotions are men who, under other circumstances, would have behaved as decent human beings. They cannot feel proud of themselves. It is our hope that whenever the country as a whole turns against the regime, as is bound to happen, these younger elements will meet the challenge and help with an orderly transition to a popular, representative form of government."[51]

It is thus significant that the initial impetus to opposition to Trujillo within the armed forces came from a nucleus of thirty to forty younger and better educated air force officers. In 1958, the year Ornes' book was published, these young men were sent to the Panama Canal Zone to pursue technical studies at military training schools run by the United States. Prior to this Trujillo had sought to keep the armed forces isolated on Dominican soil and had allowed its officers to establish few contacts with outsiders. In the Canal Zone, however, the air force personnel exchanged ideas with military colleagues from more democratically governed Latin American countries, had access to books and periodicals which provided more factual information on Trujillo's Dominican

50. See Murray Kempton, "The Vault Cracks."
51. *Trujillo: Little Caesar*, pp. 147-48.

Republic, and apparently learned how other dictatorships had been overthrown.[52]

The fall of the Batista dictatorship in Cuba gave an additional stimulus to those air force officers who were becoming disenchanted with the Trujillo regime. The ease with which Batista was removed from power when the Cuban armed forces refused any longer to defend his tyranny provided an example for the younger Dominican officers. After Castro had assumed power, nightly radio broadcasts were beamed at the Dominican Republic—at least for a time—calling for the similar liberation of its people, and members of the armed forces began to meet clandestinely to listen to these programs and discuss political questions.[53]

Anti-Trujillo sentiment soon spread to other branches of the armed forces. A group of six former members of the National Police formed an organization to kill the Generalissimo. The plot failed, largely because in the disarmed Dominican Republic they were unable to acquire arms and ammunition; those involved were later found out and sentenced to lengthy jail terms.[54] The fact that such a plot had been worked out and grown to serious proportions, however, was significant. Other anti-Trujillo sentiments and activities began to take place in the navy and the army.[55]

When the June 14, 1959, invasion attempt was launched against the Dominican Republic, the armed forces were sent out to crush the invaders. Instead of attacking them, however, some military men joined the rebels. Others attempted to sabotage the effort against the guerrillas by slowing up or canceling orders and supplies of arms and men. The invasion was eventually crushed and, though Trujillo attempted to keep the insubordination a secret, it became well known that he no longer could take for granted the loyalty of the armed forces.[56]

Opposition within the armed forces continued to grow. The fact that a well-coordinated plan to overthrow the regime had been formulated by the business-professional-landowning community,

52. Raymundo Cuevas Sena, "Gesta contra la tiranía: complot de los sargentos técnicos A.S.D.," *El 1J4*, I (February 28, 1962), 4.

53. *Ibid.*

54. Eladio Guaroa Pepén Soto, "Gestas contra la tiranía: complot de los expolicías de tránsito," *El 1J4*, I (March 17, 1962), 7.

55. Kempton.

56. See Carlos M. Nolasco, "Gestas contra la tiranía: complot de los sargentos técnicos A. S. D.," *El 1J4*, I (March 7, 1962), 2.

high-ranking government workers, and some armed forces officers became widespread public knowledge. Trujillo's crackdown on those involved in January, 1960, included the arrest of forty-seven officers and an unknown number of enlisted men.[57] These arrests did not result in the curtailment of anti-Trujillo activities, however; as late as May 13, 1961, only two and one-half weeks before Trujillo was assassinated, it was reported that there was unusual activity in Ciudad Trujillo and that there were persistent rumors that underground groups, in cooperation with military elements, were planning a coup.[58]

The Assassination of Trujillo

The external and the internal forces which were opposed to Trujillo gradually increased in strength starting in the mid-1950's; they began to interact and reinforce each other as the decade came to an end and the 1960's dawned, and finally coalesced to produce a movement which overthrew his dictatorship.

On the night of May 30, 1961, Rafael Leonidas Trujillo Molina was assassinated on a lonely stretch of highway leading along the Dominican Republic's south coast, just outside the capital city. The assassination was carried out by those who had long been his closest collaborators but who had turned against the regime in its last years—representatives of the armed forces, the business-professional-landowning community, and government officials. Those implicated in the plot included former Brigadier General Juan Tomás Díaz, forced into early retirement by Trujillo; General José Román Fernández, secretary of the armed forces; Lieutenant Amado García Guerrero, formerly on Trujillo's personal staff; Antonio de la Maza, a businessman and lumber magnate; Luis Amiama Tió, a former mayor of Ciudad Trujillo who had extensive banana and transportation holdings; Antonio Imbert, an ex-governor of Puerto Plata; Robert Reid Cabral, a physician; Modesto Díaz, a senator; and other middle- to upper-class citizens.[59]

---

57. *New York Times* (January 31, 1960), p. 9, and Brigadier General Fernando A. Sánchez, hijo, "Gestas contra la tiranía: complot de los sargentos técnicos AMD."
58. *New York Times* (May 14, 1961), p. 27.
59. See Rodman, pp. 152-58; Gustavo Guerrero Pichardo, *La Muerte de 2 Dictadores y la del Presidente Cáceres;* Eduardo Sánchez Cabral, *Los Mártires de Hacienda María;* Teodoro Tejeda Díaz, *Yo investigué la muerte de Trujillo;* and Espaillat, p. 13.

The assassination of Trujillo was apparently carried out with the knowledge, and most probably the sympathy and actual assistance, of United States officials.[60] According to the more reliable accounts, the United States Central Intelligence Agency (CIA) assisted in bringing together the conspirators and, in later stages, may even have provided encouragement and even arms to the assassins. According to these accounts, the aid in providing weapons was particularly important because (1) it demonstrated in concrete terms United States support for the project, and (2) it allowed the plot to develop without arousing the suspicion which the removal of arms from the closely scrutinized arsenals would have aroused.[61]

The CIA apparently began the shipments of weapons to the conspirators in late 1960 following a series of talks between Amiama Tió and United States diplomatic representatives. Once the initial discussions had taken place with these consulate officials, contact was then established between Amiama and a CIA representative. Another link between the CIA and the assassins, reportedly, was a longtime United States resident of the Dominican Republic who had excellent contacts with both the United States colony and the middle- to upper-class Dominicans who were part of the conspiracy.

The assassination of Trujillo was being planned at the same time that plans for the Bay of Pigs invasion of Cuba were being mapped out. It seems that when the assault on the Castro regime failed in April, 1961, the United States requested a postponement of the attempt on Trujillo's life, fearing that another possible failure would be too damaging to its prestige. This hesitancy was perhaps bolstered by erroneous reports reaching President Kennedy that the Dominican Republic was about to explode in a Castro-like revolution. The weapons were already in the hands of the conspirators, however, and they refused the appeals of United States officials to delay the assassination.

60. The evidence for this assertion is, admittedly, not complete. The most reliable account is Norman Gall, "How Trujillo Died." Other aspects of the story may be gleaned from Beals, "Gunboat Diplomacy," p. 4; Rafael Cesar Hoepelman, "Las Armas para Ajusticiar a Trujillo Fueron Proporcionadas Por Wimpy"; Espaillat, pp. 7-22; Maas, "Boswell of the Jet Set"; Cassini; Rodman, pp. 152-58, Nathaniel Weyl, "Yanqui Corruption," *National Review;* and Sam Halper, "The Dominican Upheaval," *The New Leader.* Additional evidence has been collected by the author.

61. According to some of those involved, the psychological factor of United States assistance was most important.

On the night of May 30, Trujillo set out for a rendezvous at his San Cristóbal estate, La Fundación, with his latest mistress. Around 10:30 P.M. two carloads of gunmen converged on Trujillo's unescorted Chevrolet (the reason he was alone, save for his chauffeur, is obscure), pumped round after round of shots into the dictator's body, and dumped the riddled corpse into the trunk of one of the assassins' cars.

The original plan of the conspirators, apparently, had been to assassinate Trujillo, form a provisional government which would be speedily recognized by the United States, and hold elections which the assassins would win because of their exploitation of the roles they played in ridding the country of the hated tyrant. The plan went awry, seemingly, for several reasons. The assignment of General Román Fernández was to summon the rest of the Trujillo family in the country to a military base, tell them of the dictator's death, and have them killed as well. He was unable to carry out this plan, however, because on the afternoon of the assassination he had been sent out of the capital city on a mission by Trujillo himself. Román Fernández complied with his instructions rather than give his *jefe* cause for last-minute suspicions. The other members of the ruling family thus went unmolested. Moreover, Trujillo's eldest son and heir apparent, Ramfis, was in Paris and instructions had been given to the airlines to have him held up. But he chartered a private plane and hurriedly returned home. These small hitches in the plans enabled the Trujillo family dictatorship under puppet president Joaquín Balaguer and, more importantly, Rafael, Jr., who assumed control of the armed forces, to linger on for several months. The failure of the entire conspiracy also helped pave the way for the chaos of succeeding years rather than for a possible peaceful and orderly transfer of power.

The role of the CIA or the Department of State in the plot is seldom mentioned, either in the Dominican Republic or in the United States. When the exiled Arturo Espaillat, former head of Trujillo's Military Intelligence Service, gave his version of these events at a press conference in Canada, the United States categorically denied the story. State Department press officer Lincoln White, when asked about the Espaillat story, said "I've checked this out, and I'm told these allegations are completely without foundation."[62] For nationalistic reasons, the role of the United States in the conspiracy is seldom mentioned in the Dominican Republic

62. Quoted in *New York Times* (September 21, 1962), p. 1.

either. In the three books written by Dominicans about Trujillo's assassination, for example, the national heroes are glorified and the United States is never mentioned.[63] One suspects that the CIA prefers to keep its participation quiet, though there remains little doubt that the role of the United States in the anti-Trujillo movement and in the ultimate assassination plot was considerable.[64] These events, furthermore, foreshadowed the later, even greater United States involvement in Dominican affairs.

63. See footnote 59 for citations.

64. The actual extent of the active participation of the United States in the conspiracy against Trujillo is still a moot point and open to discussion. While the degree of United States involvement is debatable, there is little doubt that the United States was fully informed about the conspiracy in advance, did nothing to prevent it, and most likely collaborated with the conspirators and actively participated in the plot. United States involvement can no longer be open to question, even though the borderline between acquiescence and active participation is still somewhat obscure. See Tad Szulc, *The Winds of Revolution: Latin America Today—and Tomorrow,* pp. 219-23.

9. Dictatorship and Development
The Implications of the Trujillo Regime

THE TRUJILLO REGIME, 1930-61, was clearly an extremely severe and absolute kind of dictatorship. For thirty-one years Trujillo governed his country in an imperious fashion that has seldom been equaled; only in the last two years of his lengthy rule did the elaborate web of dictatorial controls which he had carefully fashioned and maintained for so long begin to come unraveled. It remains for us in this chapter to summarize the methods and techniques of his control, to recapitulate briefly the theoretical presentation of the introductory chapter and to see where the Trujillo dictatorship might fit within this conceptual framework, and to attempt to arrive at some conclusions as to the implications of the Trujillo regime both for the theory of dictatorship and for the Dominican Republic.

Summary

The Dominican Republic, prior to Trujillo's seizure of power, had remained essentially a traditional, semifeudal land. Poverty was widespread and the illiteracy rate was high. The economy was almost exclusively agricultural; the early stages of industrialization had hardly begun. The society was divided into two widely

174

separated classes and consisted of a small group at the top, a large number at the bottom, and only a few in between. Modern kinds of organizations such as political parties, a bureaucracy, a professional armed force, and associational interest groups were nonexistent or still in their infancy, and political power was determined most often by competing caudillos, in alliance with rival first family groups, who sought to muster enough force to take office.

Trujillo's own upbringing reflected the society in which he was born. Without much formal education, raised in a poverty-ridden agricultural village, of middle-class parents, Trujillo desired a more important rank both for himself and his nation. Employing his considerable talents as an administrator and organizer, he rose to power through the only channel open to ambitious youths who were outside the dominant elite but who sought to rise in prominence—the military. In 1930 he seized the presidency and during his lengthy tenure exercised dictatorial control over his country.

The primary pillar of Trujillo's control over the Dominican Republic was the armed forces. It was through the Marine-created constabulary that he had risen to prominence, with the backing of the army that he had seized the presidency, and by armed forces might that he remained in power. Under Trujillo the military became a huge, powerful, and well-organized force at the service of the dictatorship. The dictator never allowed the reins of control over the armed forces to slip from his own hands and used this juggernaut not so much for purposes of national defense but to impose a technologically advanced, all-pervasive terror over the domestic population.

The second major pillar of the Trujillo regime was his control over the entire governmental apparatus. With his army's help he gained the presidency and thereafter controlled absolutely the institutional and political machinery of the state. Not withstanding the façade of constitutionalism and democracy, the constitution, the Congress, the courts, elections, the legal system, local and provincial administration, and the national bureaucracy were manipulated at Trujillo's whim. A single official party functioned as the political arm of the regime fulfilling certain special services for it. The entire system was a constitutional and democratic parody in which, despite appearances, Trujillo alone exercised authority.

The near-monopoly which Trujillo had over the national economy further cemented his hold over the country. The regime not only manipulated the economy for its own enrichment but used its predomiance in agriculture, commerce, and industry to destroy or control real or potential opposition. In addition to his conversion of the country into a private fief or corporation, Trujillo kept all socioeconomic groups (the rural peasantry, the rural-urban workers, the middle sectors, and the elite) under his control. No group or association of interests was allowed an independent existence; no organized nucleus could be formed to rival or perhaps compete with the dictator's personal rule.

Trujillo's political philosophy was perhaps not a full-fledged ideology, as is Marxism, for example; and there were only limited efforts on the part of the regime to vigorously indoctrinate the mass of the population in an official set of beliefs. Despite these limitations, Trujillo's ideology did serve some purpose, the importance of which should not be underestimated. The principal ideas—nationalism, the need for peace, order, and stability, the organic state, material progress, corporativism, the deification of the leader and the personification of him as the essence of the nation, "true" freedom and democracy—provided not just a rationale for his own practices but also a set of goals and aspirations which rallied Dominican nationalism and patriotism. Furthermore, his ideology was believed by wide sectors of the population to embody all that was worth knowing, and proved an effective propaganda device for bettering the Trujillo image abroad as well.

The ideology took on added importance when considered in the light of his highly developed system of thought control. Through his monopoly over education, intellectual life, and the communications media, through his extensive use of public relations, particularly concentrated on the United States, and through his mutually supporting arrangement with the Church, Trujillo deprived his people of free choice, forced the cult of the leader to permeate almost all aspects of existence, and maintained nearly absolute control over all aspects of thought. In these respects the Trujillo regime was tending more and more toward modern totalitarianism.

The Trujillo system was, however, eventually overthrown. The string of fallen Latin American strong men tended to make the Dominican dictatorship an anachronism in the late 1950's. The exile organizations increased in strength, and the Galíndez-Murphy affair resulted in a barrage of unfavorable publicity for Trujillo. The sanctions voted by the Organization of American States and the actions eventually taken by the United States further increased the pressure. As the external opposition to Trujillo increased, internal opposition grew as well. Important sectors in the business-professional-landowning elite, middle-sector merchants, elements in the government service, in the Church, and in the armed forces became disenchanted with the regime and began to plot its overthrow. When the external and internal opposition coalesced, the dictator fell; on the night of May 30, 1961, he was brutally assassinated.

The Trujillo regime, as hardly needs re-emphasis, was a very tightly knit dictatorship. The personal power of the dictator was nearly absolute. The elaborate controls which were established over the armed forces, the governmental machinery, the national economy, communications, education, intellectual life, and thought processes, together with the longtime harmonious and beneficial arrangement with the Church, meant that no group, institution, or individual could effectively function independent of Trujillo's controls. The extensiveness of these controls helps explain the longevity of his rule.

Trujillo's total system of control, however, was considerably greater than merely the sum of its parts. Trujillo's own considerable talents as a leader and organizer enabled him to weld together the military, political-governmental, economic, communications, educational-intellectual, religious, and ideological aspects of his era into a tightly knit, interlocking pattern which was probably as absolute and as unbreakable as the world had ever seen. Trujillo's dictatorship was, in the words of Robert D. Crassweller, based upon a "honeycomb of power," with all the cells joined together and harmonized and each buttressing the others. The strength and endurance of the various components were as nothing compared with the structure as a whole. The entire system remained under the absolute personal control of Trujillo.

While Trujillo's regime was clearly a very strong dictatorship, could it be classified as a dictatorship of a particular kind or type? Was it a traditional dictatorship of the caudillo variety, a modern totalitarian system, or a peculiar hybrid of the two? Can the Trujillo dictatorship, in other words, be placed in some sort of comparative perspective and can any implications be drawn from this case study which will help students of politics to better understand the nature of different kinds of dictatorship and the relationship of these to socioeconomic and political change? These questions call for a brief recapitulation of the theoretical formulations presented in Chapter 1 and for a reconsideration of the Trujillo regime, then, in the light of this conceptual framework.

A Theoretical Recapitulation

In traditional kinds of dictatorships, as we have stated, the rule which the dictator exercises is of necessity limited to military, political, and perhaps one or two other areas of control. While the traditional dictator may monopolize armed might and the machinery of the state, he does not ordinarily control other areas of man's existence, such as his family life, religion, friendships, or personal beliefs. The authoritarian systems of history remained limited in their means and effectiveness by mutual contractual obligations, by weak lines of communications, by archaic forms of organization, and, in general, by the impossibility of exercising "total" control in societies which had not yet experienced twentieth-century technological innovations. In these respects, classic nineteenth century Latin American caudilloism was not wholly different from other traditional kinds of dictatorship.

Modern totalitarianism seems to be an historically unique form of dictatorship, a type peculiar to the age of advanced technology and mass society. By its very nature, the controls in a totalitarian system are no longer limited but total; no facet of existence can be allowed to remain outside the regime's control. Totalitarianism may perhaps best be understood as a syndrome of interrelated and reinforcing traits, such as a powerful dictator, an official ideology, a single official party, a system of terroristic police control, a technologically conditioned monopoly of effective mass communications, a similarly technologically conditioned monopoly of all means of armed combat, a centrally directed and controlled national economy and the corresponding coordination and control of all associational and group activities. Given these requirements, totalitarianism would be most likely to develop in a highly advanced, modern, industrial society.

The differences between traditional dictatorships and modern totalitarian systems should not, however, be thought of (as they often have) in terms of either/or, dichotomous categories. Many of the transitional systems of the developing world, in their effort to rapidly modernize, are employing the various techniques associated with totalitarian models (single mass parties, official ideologies, deification of the leader, mass mobilization, and so forth). In addition, the very factors which are at the heart of the developmental process, such as improved communications, expanding technological knowledge, and large-scale organizations, may, at the same time that they are breaking down the traditional order, make the society susceptible to more totalitarian domination.

While in pre-industrial, agrarian societies there were both no necessity and no possibility of organizing a fully totalitarian system, in modernizing nations both the need and the possibilities for the formation of such a system may become possible. Totalitarian-like dictatorships—those in which all seven of the characteristics designated as being required for a full-fledged totalitarian system may be present though in varying degrees—may arise in transitional societies out of the felt need to use coercive means to achieve development, out of the attempt to prevent the growth of the newer and possibly conflicting political and social organizations and values which normally accompany the industrialization and economic development processes, or out of a desire to suppress these organizations and values in countries where they have already begun to emerge. The Trujillo regime would thus seem to fit this transitional pattern.

The Trujillo Dictatorship in Perspective

The Trujillo regime was probably the strongest and most absolute dictatorship ever to be established in Latin America and perhaps the most personal dictatorship in the world. Trujillo did not share power with anyone but maintained nearly absolute authority in his own hands. It would not be accurate to label his system either Left or Right, Nazi or Fascist, for the Trujillo regime was essentially the story of a single individual and his personal power. As Herbert Matthews wrote, it was "a personal tyranny to a degree surely unparalleled on either side of the Iron Curtain."[1]

Trujillo's dictatorship was not, furthermore, a Caribbean version of oriental despotism, as Robert D. Crassweller maintains,[2] nor was it simply a form of Caesarism, as Ornes, Espaillat, and others assert,[3] for these categorizations ignore the dynamics of

1. *New York Times* (March 28, 1953), p. 7.
2. Crassweller, *Trujillo: The Life and Times of a Caribbean Dictator.*
3. Ornes, *Trujillo: Little Caesar;* Espaillat, *Trujillo: The Last Caesar.*

social and political change which were occurring in the Dominican Republic during this period and hence fail to account for what was new, unique, and "modern" in Trujillo's rule. Nor does the Trujillo dictatorship fully conform to Linz' model of an authoritarian regime.[4] In Trujillo's Dominican Republic the political pluralism and general looseness or relaxation of dictatorial controls, found to be present in Franco's Spain and other more or less authoritarian systems, did not exist. Trujillo maintained as absolute and as monolithic a dictatorship as possible.

Under Trujillo's control the Dominican Republic was also, at least until the Cuba of Fidel Castro and the Communists, probably the most totalitarian regime in the history of the hemisphere. The Latin American countries had often been subjected to arbitrary and dictatorial rule, but the controls these dictators of the past exercised were not total. Dictatorship in Latin America had traditionally been formless rather than systematic. Only in the mid-twentieth century, as the industrial and technological revolution accelerated in the area, has systematic totalitarianism come to Latin America. The totalitarian techniques only became possible with ever improving organizational structures and lines of communications and transportation, and they awaited a dictator of Trujillo's ability and ilk to put them into operation.[5]

The Trujillo regime was not wholly a traditional or Caesaristic dictatorship nor was it wholly totalitarian. Coming to power in 1930 in an unindustrialized and largely pre-modern nation, Trujillo began his rule in much the same way as had other traditional Latin American dictators. His power initially rested almost exclusively on armed might, which provided a base for him to take over the machinery of government. During the 1930's and early 1940's, then, the Trujillo regime was not unlike those of similarly based and similarly oriented caudillos. It corresponded closely to the models of traditional dictatorships described previously by Gómez, Pierson and Gil, and others; it exhibited almost none of the features of modern totalitarianism.

Trujillo indeed began his lengthy rule as a rather typical man on horseback, but his regime eventually went far beyond the models of traditional dictatorships. In maintaining himself in power for thirty-one years and following the examples of previous sys-

4. Linz, "An Authoritarian Regime."
5. See Robin A. Humphreys, *The Evolution of Modern Latin America*, pp. 82-83.

tems, Trujillo employed techniques and a system of control which became increasingly more like modern totalitarianism. This transition was suggested by Germán Ornes: "To Trujillo politics is not a system—it is a great and contradictory panorama providing an outlet for his acute megalomania, his lust for power, his demagogic talents as well as his sharp ability for maneuver. At its best Trujillo's is totalitarianism at the service of the absolute and untrammeled personal will of one man."[6]

The Trujillo regime may thus most accurately be considered as a blend of traditional, nineteenth-century caudillo dictatorship, transitional authoritarianism (in the sense this term is used by Linz), and modern, twentieth-century totalitarianism. In the case of the Trujillo system these models may be neatly combined chronologically. Trujillo had first gained power by enlisting in the national constabulary and by rising to a position of influence as commander in chief of the National Army. With military backing he assumed the presidency. Once in control of the government, he systematically eliminated all opposition and brought the entire state apparatus under his direct control. In these techniques and controls, his regime did not differ significantly from those of other Latin American caudillos.

What made the Trujillo regime unique in Latin America, however, was its transition to increased totalitarianism. Control over the armed forces and the governmental machinery enabled Trujillo to convert the national economy into his personal fief and to coordinate the economic system into an almost corporate structure owned by the ruling family. Greatly improved and expanded communications and transportation systems enabled the regime to eliminate provincialism and regionalism and to build up, correspondingly, the power of the central state. These and other technological advances made it possible for Trujillo to gain control over intellectual and educational life and to impose a system of thought control. A single official political party served as an additional apparatus of political control, and the terroristic police control became technologically more proficient. All intermediate organizations, such as interest associations, societal sectors, formal and informal groups, and even families, were subjected to Trujillo's centralized control and direction.

Why did this transformation from caudilloism to a more modern form of dictatorship take place? The primary reasons center

6. *Trujillo: Little Caesar*, p. 88.

around economic development, industrialization, and technological improvements and their accompanying social and political effects. In the early years of the Trujillo era, the Dominican Republic remained, for the most part, an agrarian, pre-industrial, semifeudal society. In this type of society not only was totalitarianism not possible but there was no need for it. The vast majority of the population remained atomized, inarticulate, isolated, and unorganized and, as such, constituted little potential threat to Trujillo's rule. The traditional aristocracy, by the same token, among whom political power had been rotated during most of Dominican independent history, was unable to replace or remove Trujillo because the only well-organized group in the country, the armed forces, was loyal to and under the control of the dictator. The elite had been deprived of its traditional military allies.

More rapid economic development, industrialization, and technological advancements, stimulated by the demand for Dominican products during World War II and in the postwar years, sparked the set of interrelated processes of change that ultimately led the regime to become more totalitarian. Trujillo took great pride in the economic achievements of his regime, and, despite the notorious inaccuracy of official statistics, there is little doubt that the economy boomed during his rule. To cite only a few of many possible indices, between 1939 and 1942, 297 new industries were registered with the Ministry of Finance and Commerce; and from 1945 until Trujillo's death in 1961, capital investment and national production tripled.[7] In addition, the Trujillo era meant stability, and stability encouraged private investment and the growth of small businesses. Widespread public works projects also created new jobs, stimulated urban growth, and led to the enlargement of the government service.

All the economic changes gave rise to new social classes, and new ideas concerning the way society should be organized and run filtered in.[8] Industrialization, though still not extensive, gave rise to trade unions and other kinds of associational groups whose members became conscious of their diverging interests and of their collective strengths—a development which potentially threatened the survival of Trujillo. Not only did economic development create new

7. See González Blanco, *Trujillo: The Rebirth of a Nation*, p. 45; *El Caribe* (March 12, 1966), p. 6-A; Augelli, pp. 2-5; and Crassweller, p. 205.
8. This analysis relies heavily on the theoretical presentation of Kautsky, pp. 91-94.

societal sectors and organizations which might have threatened the regime, but it also made the regime increasingly dependent on these same groups, hence making the threat even greater. Trujillo was skillfully able to balance and juggle these forces and control this set of developments for many years, but eventually the entire edifice collapsed.

Trujillo was clearly not a conscious revolutionary. As part of his ideology he had rejected the antecedent system because it had led to instability, chaos, and national humiliation, and he had proposed a new order based on authority, order, stability, and material progress. However, he desired no social revolution, no societal-wide upheaval. Trujillo had no wish to overthrow the social order, only to command it. He sought to resurrect the system of Heureaux and to use it more skillfully than had his notorious predecessor for his own personal power and aggrandizement—not to topple the old order or effect fundamental changes in it. At least initially, Trujillo was unaware of the great social forces which were set loose by his desire to industrialize and spur economic growth. Nor was he fully cognizant of the revolutionary changes implied in the entire modernization process. Trujillo wanted his country to industrialize, to develop economically, and to modernize; but he wanted all these things under his absolute hegemony and he wanted none of the social and political side effects (increased pluralism, a greater awareness on the part of lower-class people and a desire for a better life, potentially subversive ideologies, popular demands for change and a share in decision-making, and so forth) which ordinarily accompany these changes. Trujillo sought to dominate the social-political forces he had unleashed, and he was thus forced to use ever more stringent measures of control. He used the modern propaganda and control techniques of this century to help maintain his own power, but he sought to bottle up popular aspirations and hold back the tide of revolutionary social and political change.[9] The inevitable explosion came only after Trujillo had passed from the scene.

It does not seem to be pure coincidence, then, that the beginnings of the widespread use of more totalitarian techniques corresponded almost exactly with the beginnings of the transition to a more modern, industrialized society. To cite only a few of many possible examples, the industrialization which was stimulated by

9. See Crassweller, pp. 84-85.

World War II gave rise to a labor movement which felt strong enough to call a full-scale strike in 1946. Trujillo saw sufficient potential danger in this uprising to quickly crush the movement and subject the trade unions to strict official control. It was also during this period of the later 1940's and early 1950's that the dictator first began to formulate an official ideology. Though the official Partido Dominicano had already been founded in 1931, its usefulness as a device of control was limited until the postwar years when its mass branches were established and its activities vastly expanded.[10] As the government service mushroomed as a result of the increasing activities of the state, finally, elaborate security checks, eavesdropping techniques, and the like were employed for the first time to assure the absolute loyalty of the bureaucracy.

Increased totalitarianism in the Dominican Republic grew out of Trujillo's attempt to maintain his absolute personal power while, at one and the same time, making rapid economic development and the acceleration of industrialization compatible with the prevention of the growth of groups, organizations, and possibly conflicting ideologies which industrialization tended to spawn or suppressing them where they had already grown. The totalitarian techniques which he employed served to break up and destroy the units which tend to emerge in a modernizing, rapidly developing society (political parties, labor organizations, professional and trade associations, communications media, bureaucracy) as potential centers of diverse and conflicting interests and hence possible resistance. Essentially the post-World-War-II Trujillo regime involved one strong man's attempt to harness and control the great revolutionary wave of social, economic, political, and ideological changes which during this period were occurring not only in Latin America but in many areas of the world.

The Trujillo regime was not, however, fully totalitarian. Indeed, there have been pockets of resistance and groups largely untouched by the dictatorial controls in all systems which have been generally referred to as totalitarian. No totalitarian system has ever been "total" in the absolute sense of the word. In the Dominican Republic the rural peasantry was never subjected to the same kinds

10. La Palombara and Weiner maintain that these kinds of mass organizations come into existence at a point of time when the mass public must either participate or be controlled. See Joseph La Palombara and Myron Weiner (eds.), *Political Parties and Political Development*, pp. 3, 23, 433.

of totalitarian controls as were other sectors of the population simply because this group constituted no potential threat; Trujillo allowed the peasantry to remain, for the most part, in an unintegrated state. For the 40 to 50 per cent or so of the population that was integrated into the national existence, however, Trujillo's Dominican Republic was about as totalitarian as the level of its development and technology would allow. At the same time, the Trujillo regime represented the liquidation of Dominican caudilloism in the classic, pre-modern sense of the word.[11]

A number of other unrelated factors contributed to the growth of a more modern and more absolute form of dictatorship in this Caribbean nation. One of these was simply the time factor: Trujillo remained in power so long that he had sufficient time to fully impose a wide gamut of totalitarian controls. An entire generation grew up knowing only life under Trujillo, educated and formed in the cult of his personality. Indeed, those born during the thirty-one-year Trujillo era constituted the majority of the Dominican population. Less long-lived regimes have had difficulty in securing more total control if for no other reason than that they were not in power long enough to completely reshape their citizenries.

The second important variable was the size of Trujillo's laboratory. The Dominican Republic is geographically a very small nation, not much larger than a city-state, which made the lines of control comparatively easy to develop and keep in hand. The establishment of a similar system in a country at roughly the same level of development but of greater size with a more diverse and scattered population would have proved more complicated, simply because of greater communications and transportation difficulties.

Third, Trujillo had the advantage of ruling on an island isolated and cut off from the main currents of modern life. It was thus relatively easy for him to keep other and possibly conflicting ideas out and also to keep his own people in, and to prevent the real nature of his regime from becoming public knowledge abroad.

All three of these factors—longevity of rule, the city-state size of the country, and natural isolation—enabled Trujillo to establish a more nearly totalitarian system in the Dominican Republic (given its relatively low level of industrial-technological development as compared with technologically more advanced but less long-lived, more spread out, and non-isolated totalitarian states)

11. Juan Isidro Jiménes-Grullón, *La República Dominicana*, p. 87.

than would ordinarily have been the case. What, then, are the implications of his regime for both the theory of dictatorship and for the Dominican Republic?

Implications

For the theory of dictatorship.—Trujillo's control over his country was thus, it may be argued, more nearly totalitarian than that of other recent Latin American strong men. Juan Vicente Gómez of Venezuela, Anastasio Somoza of Nicaragua, Tiburcio Carías Andino of Honduras, and Jorge Ubico of Guatemala remained essentially traditional caudillo dictators. Marcos Pérez Jiménez of Venezuela, Manuel Odría of Peru, and Gustavo Rojas Pinilla of Colombia were military guardians who employed some totalitarian techniques but never gained near-total control. The rule of Getulio Vargas in Brazil was on the whole a mild authoritarianism in keeping with the traditionally more easygoing approach which Brazilians have to politics. Juan Perón in Argentina succeeded in "coordinating" many sectors with his regime but he never succeeded in establishing ascendancy over all groups. Among the Latin American nations, only in Castro-Communist Cuba have the full controls of the totalitarian state approached the level reached by Trujillo.[12]

Outside the Americas, regimes which fall somewhere on the transitional scale between traditional authoritarianism and modern totalitarianism have become prominent. What variations, similarities, and patterns can be discerned between the Latin American dictatorships and Nkrumah's Ghana, Sukarno's Indonesia, and Nasser's Egypt? Would it be possible to construct a set of rough indices by which these and other regimes could be more systematically compared?

It will likely be some time, if ever, before we could possibly begin to have a full and complete empirical theory of dictatorship. There are, on the one hand, too many dictatorships which have not been fully analyzed. What is required, then, are numerous case studies of different types of regimes. On the other hand, there are still too many variables whose relationships are still not fully known to construct an all-encompassing model for the study of dictatorship.

It has not been the purpose of this study to construct such a

12. See Martin C. Needler, *Latin American Politics in Perspective*, pp. 145-46.

complete theory, but rather to suggest a number of directions in which future research concerning dictatorship and development might go. What has been suggested is that the commonly used dichotomy between traditional dictatorship and modern totalitarianism is of limited utility in dealing with the large number of transitional systems. The approach here employed sees social systems as indeed that—systems in which the various parts are interrelated and in which change in one sphere usually is accompanied by changes in other spheres. For the analysis of dictatorship, this approach implies that we need not only information concerning the political aspects of control but also comparative data concerning social structure, level of development, literacy rates, and so forth. In short, what is required for a full theory of dictatorship is complete and accurate information on a wide variety of political systems and also systematic explanations of their similarities and differences. Clearly this goal is still a long way off and will not shortly or easily be reached.[13]

This study has attempted to analyze in some detail a single dictatorial system which falls somewhere in between the traditional and the modern. The Trujillo regime was a hybrid, a complex and dynamic mixture of traditional dictatorship, transitional authoritarianism, and modern totalitarianism. In the course of the study it has been demonstrated that concepts of socioeconomic and political development and modernization might be fruitfully combined with models of different kinds of dictatorships. It remains for us to link these conceptions, at least in a tentative and preliminary way.

In many ways the Trujillo regime reflected and was a product of its particular times and circumstances. These times and circumstances were not of course limited to the Dominican Republic, nor was the Trujillo dictatorship, thus, entirely unique. Trujillo's rule was longer and his dictatorship tighter, but in a number of

13. For an excellent early formulation of a typology which relates civil-military relations and types of regimes in Latin America to the particular situations of the different countries, see Gino Germani and Kalman Silvert, "Politics, Social Structure, and Military Intervention in Latin America." Linz' model of a transitional "authoritarian regime" is also useful in this regard. His model, however, appears to be rather static without adequately or fully accounting for the dynamics of change and is limited by the difficulty of generalizing from a single case. And though the Latin American experience is mentioned in only two brief footnotes, a path-breaking study in this connection is Barrington Moore, Jr., *Social Origins of Dictatorship and Democracy.*

areas there were significant parallels between the Trujillo, Somoza, Gómez, Vargas, and probably other regimes of the present century. This is not to deny the distinct aspects of any of these regimes or of the countries where they came to power, but the similarities seem to be equally striking and perhaps of greater significance. It should not be wholly surprising, given certain common underlying conditions characteristic throughout much of Latin America during this as well as other epochs, that in the evolution of their political, social, and economic development, a number of common patterns and shared tendencies should emerge. These common features override to a considerable extent the differences of various kinds that distinguish one country from another.[14] It may well be that Sukarno's Indonesia, Nasser's Egypt, and Nkrumah's Ghana may also find their place within this broad framework.

Traditional dictatorships, be they of the caudillo or other subtypes, tend to reflect the societies in which they appear. These societies are most often characterized by widespread illiteracy, mass inertia, rigid class-caste lines, lack of functioning representative institutions, particularism, lack of differentiated roles, ascriptive behavioral patterns, and so forth.[15] They tend to be agrarian, pre-industrial, and pre-modern. The dictatorships themselves which may arise in these systems are limited by and reflective of the traditional environment.

More modern totalitarian dictatorships also reflect the social systems in which they appear, but these societies are fundamentally different from the traditional societies. The more modern systems tend to be highly urbanized, to have high literacy rates, and to be more industrialized. They are mass societies which have been mobilized and are organized more around principles and behavioral patterns of universalism, role differentiation, specialized division of labor, and so on. The dictatorships which come to power in these systems may be able to employ for their own ends all the technology of the modern state and may thus become "total."

Dictatorships such as Trujillo's appear to be products of the transition from tradition to modernity. They tend to appear at a

14. Wise, p. ix.
15. Many of these terms follow the familiar "pattern variables," as employed by Talcott Parsons. See Parsons and Edward Shils (eds.), *Toward a General Theory of Action*. For their use in the political development field see, for example, Gabriel A. Almond and James S. Coleman (eds.), *The Politics of the Developing Areas*.

time of breakdown in the old order and at a time when no new order has been firmly implanted. They emerge in a legitimacy vacuum when the traditional ways are no longer relevant, appropriate, or fully acceptable, and in systems characterized by the absence of well-established institutional structures. The transitional dictator is a product of the societal cleavages and discontinuities which ordinarily accompany the early stirrings of modernization and industrialization. He usually rules in a deeply divided society where new demands and new conflicts are becoming rampant. He may come to the fore in societies which are not fully integrated, which are experiencing accelerated economic and social changes, where local autonomy is beginning to give way to centralism, and where a sense of nationhood has begun to appear. The transitional dictator may thus be an embryonic nation-builder, unifying his country behind a new ideology or his own person, playing on nationalism, building communications and transportation systems, and centralizing authority.

This classification is clearly related to Weber's familiar three forms of legitimacy: traditional, charismatic, and rational. A progression is implied in these forms of legitimacy. Thus in the traditional form, authority is legitimized by the established, immutable ways of the society. This is the oldest form of authority, and most systems in past history have been based upon it. Examples of this traditional form of legitimacy would include patriarchal orders, oriental dynasties, monarchies, feudal systems, and so forth. In the second pattern legitimacy is based on the charismatic ruler or leader who is seen as a deliverer, great teacher, symbol of popular aspirations, and man of destiny. In the rational form, authority is based more on impersonal, recognized legal norms, laws, and regularized bureaucratic procedures. Legitimacy is conceived in terms of functions and rules that are "rationally" devised and established. Various combinations of these forms may also exist.

Neither the first (traditional) nor the third (rational) forms of authority are especially appropriate for looking at transitional kinds of regimes. The transitional ruler, such as Trujillo, does not come to power through the immutable or established ways; indeed, it is characteristic of such a ruler that he usually represents a sharp break with the past. Nor is his authority based wholly upon law, established norms, or bureaucratized procedures. Rather, his legitimacy must revolve around his own person, his own charisma, his own magnetism, and his own power. He emerges as a deliverer and savior, as a symbol of the aspirations of his people, and as their incarnation. He is endowed with extraordinary abilities and also powers, a man of destiny who will lead his humble people. The grounds of his legitimacy tend to be shaky which means he may have to compensate for it by using arbitrary methods and by imposing a system of tight control. The ideology he employs may be only nascent and he may come to rule by force. If he rules as long and as absolutely as Trujillo did, he may bridge two or more epochs and combine two or more forms of legitimacy; and his rule may be characterized by a combination of traditional and modern forms and practices. Though useful for analytical purposes, however, none of the Weberian categories —or, indeed, any combination of them—are really sufficient to shed much light on and explain the complexities of a dynamic, rapidly changing transitional system like Trujillo's, some new concepts, and a new theoretical framework, which take into account the dynamics and complexities of the present era, are needed.

The fact that dictatorships like Trujillo's reflect and are products of a particular time and set of circumstances means that this form of dictatorship may tend to disappear as the social and political conditions that give rise to it disappear. Dictatorship in other forms may of course appear, but it will not be of the same genre. The particular kind of transitional dictatorships of the Trujillo sort are characteristic of the transitional period when the old order is fading away but has not yet disappeared and when the new order is rising but has not yet been firmly established. As the Latin American countries continue to develop economically and modernize socially, to be sure at different speeds and in different forms in the separate countries, their political systems are changing as well. Oligarchic and caudillo rule is giving way to more modern kinds of rule. The Trujillo regime provides a particularly vivid example of these kinds of transformations.[16]

What seems to be required now are more case studies of individual regimes and, concurrently, a considerable refinement of the conceptual tools. We need to know a great deal more about these transitional systems and about the processes of change. Only by continued contributions in both empirical and theoretical areas can a better understanding of this increasingly important subject be achieved.

16. Wise, p. 176.

For the Dominican Republic.—The implications of the thirty-one-year Trujillo regime for the Dominican Republic merit brief mention, though a full exposition of the legacy of his dictatorship is reserved for a planned subsequent volume.

From 1930 to 1961 Trujillo had exercised absolute control over almost all aspects of the Dominican Republic's social, political, economic, military, educational, and intellectual life. Because near-total control had been concentrated in his hands, Trujillo's death produced a near-total vacuum. Few Dominicans knew anything but life under Trujillo and all were inexperienced in democratic methods and procedures. The political institutions that might have facilitated a peaceful and orderly transition after 1961 were almost wholly lacking. At the time of Trujillo's assassination Max Frankel wrote: "The 69-year-old Generalissimo, who ruled for thirty-one years, left more than a power vacuum in his capital. In the Dominican Republic he has left an ideological void, a people unaccustomed to governing themselves and unschooled in any political doctrine except the jungle doctrine that the strongest shall rule."[17]

The armed forces emerged as the strongest force in the country following the death of Trujillo. The comparatively huge military had been the ultimate pillar of the dictatorship and maintained many of its old habits in the post-Trujillo period. Trained in the corrupt and oppressive tactics of the Trujillo era, the armed forces remained largely immune from the various reforms attempted and frustrated the early attempts to reconstruct Dominican society along more democratic lines.

Government and politics in the post-Trujillo era also illustrated the legacy left by the dictatorship. Nepotism and corruption remained prevalent and few competent and trained administrators could be found to man the many government posts. Inexperienced in genuine elections, in the practice of local self-government, in government by constitution, in the rule of law, in the functions of political parties, and in a wide range of other governmental institutions and political processes, the Dominicans stood little chance of building a functioning and stable political system.

Trujillo's exploitation of the national economy for the enrichment of himself, his family, and his friends also presented grave problems for a succession of post-Trujillo governments. Much of the wealth of the country had been drained off or wastefully used,

17. *New York Times,* Sec. 4 (June 4, 1961), p. 4.

and the efforts to promote rapid economic development following the Generalissimo's death were largely unsuccessful. The future of the vast former-Trujillo properties remained uncertain, and in the agricultural, commercial, and industrial spheres the sluggish economy could not fully recover from the enormous problems bequeathed by the fallen regime.

Socioeconomic groups were more deeply divided and highly fragmented, making the integration of the nation and the building of consensus nearly impossible, while the state of atomization in which all elements in the society had been kept made the newly emerging groups weak, fluid, and amorphous. The rural peasantry remained inarticulate, isolated, and unorganized. Frequently the trade unions and the labor federations which emerged after Trujillo's demise worked at cross-purposes, both with employers and among themselves. The growing middle sectors developed little self-identity, while the business-professional-landholding elite sought at all costs to regain and preserve the power it had lost during Trujillo's rule. The degree of atomization remained so high and divisions between social groups, economic classes, and different interests so deep and bitter that the entire nation exhibited almost no solidarity and seemed at times on the verge of complete disintegration.[18]

An entirely new system of values and beliefs had to be created to replace the Trujillo ideology and to serve as substitutes for the cult of the dictator. But this required a complete reform of the educational system from the grade schools to the University, as well as a total changeover in the formerly Trujillo-controlled mass communications media. The Church had difficulty overcoming the legacy of its close association with the dictatorship; and its attempts to fill the moral, spiritual, and ethical void were not wholly successful.

For the Marine-created constabulary through which Trujillo rose to power, for the praise which congressmen, clerics, ambassadors, and other high officials showered upon him, for the aid given him, and for the close and friendly relationship which long existed between the two countries, the United States was often considered by many Dominicans to bear responsibility for the entire Trujillo era. The Communists were able to exploit this apparent long-standing alliance between Trujillo and the United States and thus gain a measure of popular support by making the choice for the

18. See Wiarda, "From Fragmentation to Disintegration," *América Latina.*

country seem to be either United States-backed Trujilloism on the one hand or communism on the other. United Statese efforts in the post-Trujillo years to find a middle way, to convert the Dominican Republic into a "Showcase for the Alliance for Progress," were made more difficult by its earlier relations with the dictatorship.

If Trujillo had been only another in the long line of Dominican caudillos, the legacy of his rule would not have raised so many difficulties. But Trujillo's rule was a watershed in Dominican history; in many ways his era, however undemocratic, signaled the beginning of the transition to modernity. At the same time the Trujillo regime represented the end of the country's semifeudal, pre-modern order. In his effort to promote economic development, the traditional, agrarian-based order was broken down. Roads were built, radios acquired, and overall transportation and communications improved. Concurrently, previously isolated elements were beginning to be uprooted, mobilized, organized, and imbued with new ideological and value systems. The entire society became much more complex. While many of these developments constitute the essence of the political modernization process, they also provide the base for the growth of more totalitarian controls.[19] Trujillo destroyed much of the old order, but the new groups and organizations which began to rise were also methodically crushed. Trujillo's absolute personal control meant that upon the death of the dictator, no group, individual, or institution could begin to fill the void.

Trujillo's rule provided the Dominican Republic with a period of peace, order, stability, and material progress, but these benefits came at a huge cost. Not only were liberal and democratic ideals and institutions completely snuffed out or kept from emerging in the first place, but his regime left a pervasive legacy of problems which contributed in a major way to the disorder, frustration, and chaos of the post-Trujillo period and ultimately, to the 1965 breakdown of the system into revolution and civil war. In recent years successive Dominican governments have struggled, in varying ways but without great success, to overcome the enormous difficulties which grew out of the collapse of Trujillo's absolute and monolithic regime. It is unlikely that many of these complex and difficult problems, which were the heritage of his system of repression and control, may ever be adequately or satisfactorily solved.

19. Eckstein and Apter, pp. 433-40.

While Trujillo's dictatorship thus provided peace, order, stability, and material progress in the short run, in any longer range perspective his type of rule was bound to produce conflict, disorder, instability, and decay.

Since the revolution and United States intervention of 1965, there has been a growing tendency in certain circles, both in the Dominican Republic and in the United States, to affirm that Trujillo's regime was not so bad after all and that extremely authoritarian strong-man rule may be the best alternative in countries going through the transition from tradition to modernity. Trujillo, this essentially Stalinist argument runs, maintained stability and built up much of the basic infrastructure of the nation— roads, public works, a communications network, and so forth— and, besides, his successors have been far worse. Apart from any humanistic considerations, what these arguments fail to take into account is that Trujillo-style economic development was immensely costly and that the society at large derived almost no benefits from it. His suppression of or control over all the opportunities for political education and development and all the practices and institutions of democratic government left his successors with a host of nearly unsolvable problems and no organizational structures with which to begin to solve them. The disruptive consequences of Trujillo's rule will likely be felt for a long time in the Dominican Republic.[20]

The nearly total control which Trujillo exercised thus helps explain the weakness of the fledgling political groups and institutions and the dysfunctional nature of the political process in the post-Trujillo years. Political parties and interest associations were too weak to serve as effective channels of demands. The various societal sectors were highly fragmented and stratified, both vertically and horizontally, while the entire society was in a condition of *anomie*—that is, a state in which diversity and division became so complete that it made for a disintegrated social order with no apparent common purpose.[21] The traditional sectors, attempting to reassert their dominance following the interruption of the Trujillo era, felt threatened by the newer groups and trends, while the newer, modernizing groups found accessibility to deci-

20. See Samuel P. Huntington, "Political Development and Political Decay."
21. The concept of *anomie* is used here in the sense that it was developed by Emile Durkheim and applied to contemporary politics by Sebastian de Grazia, *The Political Community*.

sion-making limited. Deep cleavages and ineffective governments brought on a succession of legitimacy crises.[22] There was no sharing of or consensus on primary values. The political system was imbalanced with certain groups having a decided advantage, and conflicts between the noncommunicating sectors became so extreme that the system eventually polarized and broke down. The Trujillo dictatorship bequeathed to the Dominican Republic a legacy which, in almost every aspect of national life (the political system, the social structure, the economy, the value system), rendered the rebuilding of the nation along other lines nearly impossible. Practically none of the minimum institutional and other requirements for a stable, functioning, viable system—be it democratic or any other kind—were present in the post-Trujillo Dominican Republic.[23]

The political development and modernization of the country was also interrupted, rechanneled, and perhaps permanently impaired by the imposition of the Trujillo dictatorship. At precisely the same time that many of the Latin American countries were, in varying degrees and fashions, beginning to develop or accelerating the development of more pluralistic and more democratic systems, the Dominican Republic remained under the control of perhaps the most monolithic and most nearly totalitarian dictatorship to have been formed in previous hemispheric history. Trujillo's rule left a deeply ingrained, all-pervasive, negative heritage which led directly to the bitter and bloody revolution and civil war of 1965 and which rendered the prospects for democratic development tenuous at best.

22. Seymour M. Lipset, "Some Social Requisites of Democracy," pp. 86-87.
23. These post-Trujillo developments are explored in greater detail in Wiarda, *The Aftermath of the Trujillo Dictatorship.*

Bibliography

THERE IS a dearth of sound, scholarly studies dealing with the government, politics, and indeed with most aspects of the Dominican Republic. The nature of the Trujillo dictatorship made unbiased research nearly impossible for a period of thirty-one years; and it is only in the post-Trujillo period that a growing number of studies have begun to appear.

Research on the Trujillo era is difficult not only because of the lack of many sources but also because of the extremely biased nature of the works which were published. Generally, those works written outside the Dominican Republic are critical of the regime while those published in the country are uniformly favorable. In addition, the Trujillo dictatorship frequently doctored official statistics, such as census returns, to suit its purposes.

Extreme care must thus be used when studying the Trujillo period. Perhaps the best and most comprehensive studies of the dictatorship are Germán Ornes, *Trujillo: Little Caesar of the Caribbean*; Jesús de Galíndez, *La era de Trujillo*; and Robert D. Crassweller, *Trujillo: The Life and Times of a Caribbean Dictator*. Many of the volumes published officially, primarily those mentioned in the footnotes, may also provide useful information.

In the preparation of this study, the published sources consulted were supplemented by hundreds of interviews, structured and unstructured, conducted over a period of some six years of research interest in the Dominican political system. These interviews were conducted with Dominicans and non-Dominicans of widely varied political views and orientations and provided a large storehouse of information and lore not always found in published accounts. Pre-interview promises of complete anonymity prevent the listing of these invaluable sources, however, so that only the published materials are included in the bibliography.

Articles

Alexander, Robert J. "Dictatorship in the Caribbean," *Canadian Forum,* XXVIII (May, 1948), 35.
————. "The Trujillo Tyranny: The Dominican Dictatorship in Crisis," *The Socialist Call,* XXV (March, 1957), 12-14.
Almond, Gabriel A. "Comparative Political Systems," *Journal of Politics,* XVIII (August, 1956), 391-409.
Arredondo, Alberto, and Carlos M. Campos. "Las condiciones de vida del campesino dominicano," *Panoramas,* No. 4 (July-August, 1964), pp. 81-110.
Augelli, John P. "The Dominican Republic," *Focus,* X (February, 1960), 1-6.
Avelino, Andrés. "Homenaje a Trujillo," *El Caribe* (November 8, 1955), p. 14.
Beals, Carleton. "Caesar of the Caribbean," *Current History,* XLVIII (January, 1938), 31-34.
————. "Fountain of Light," *The Nation,* CLXXXII (January 14, 1956), 25-27.
————. "Gunboat Diplomacy and the Dominican Crisis," *National Guardian,* XIV (December 11, 1961), 1 ff.
Bell, Daniel. "Ten Theories in Search of Reality: The Prediction of Soviet Behavior in the Social Sciences," *World Politics,* X (April, 1958), 327-65.
Bocca, Geoffrey. "A Dictator's Legacy," *This Week* (September 19, 1965), pp. 3 ff.
Bosch, Juan. "Trujillo: Problema de América," *Combate,* I (March-April, 1959), 9-13.
————. "Trujillo y su ambición de poder," *El Dominicano Libre* (November, 1959), pp. 2 ff.
Brzezinski, Zbigniew. "The Politics of Underdevelopment," *World Politics,* IX (October, 1956), 55-75.
Carsley, C. F. "Generalissimo Trujillo and Santo Domingo," *The Tablet* [Brooklyn]. Reprinted as "Why Dominicans Call Him El Benefactor," *The Herald of the Dominican Republic* [Ciudad Trujillo], 1959.
Cassinelli, C. W. "The Totalitarian Party," *Journal of Politics,* XXIV (February, 1962), 111-41.
Cassini, Igor. "When the Sweet Life Turns Sour: A Farewell to Scandal," *Esquire,* LXI (April, 1964), 94 ff.
Cater, Douglas, and Walter Pincus. "Our Sugar Diplomacy," *The Reporter,* XXIV (April 13, 1961), 24-28.
Chapman, Charles E. "The Age of the Caudillos: A Chapter in Hispanic American History," *Hispanic American Historical Review,* XII (August, 1932), 281-300.
Clark, James A. "The Church and the Dominican Crisis," *Thought,* XLI (Spring, 1966), 117-31.

Clements, R. J. "Events That Judge Us," *The New Republic,* CXXXV (July 2, 1956), 9-12.

Crist, Raymond E. "Cultural Dichotomy on the Island of Hispaniola," *Economic Geography,* XXVIII (April, 1952), 105-21.

Cuevas Sena, Raymundo. "Gesta contra la tiranía: complot de los sargentos técnicos A.S.D.," *El 1J4,* I (February 28, 1962), 4.

Díaz Valdeperes, Julián. "La cuestión de 'El Caribe,'" *El Caribe* (December 29, 1961), p. 5.

"Dominican Republic: Chamber of Horrors," *Time,* LXXIX (April 13, 1962), 41.

"Dominican Republic Restates Its Catholicity in Concordat," *A Look at the Dominican Republic,* III (November-December, 1954), 9.

Drake, St. Clair. "Traditional Authority and Social Action in Former British West Africa," *Human Organization,* XIX (Fall, 1960), 150-58.

Draper, Theodore. "Trujillo's Dynasty," *The Reporter,* V (November 27, 1951), 20-26.

Dyer, Donald R. "Distribution of Population on Hispaniola," *Economic Geography,* XXX (October, 1954), 337-46.

Ebenstein, William. "The Study of Totalitarianism," *World Politics,* X (January, 1958), 274-88.

Epstein, Klaus. "A New Study of Fascism," *World Politics,* XVI (January, 1964), 302-21.

Facio, Gonzalo J. "Sanciones al régimen de Trujillo," *La República* [Costa Rica] (August 13, 1960), p. 3.

Fererabend, Ivo K. "Expansionist and Isolationist Tendencies of Totalitarian Political Systems," *Journal of Politics,* XXIV (November, 1962), 733-42.

"The Foreign Legion of U.S. Public Relations," *The Reporter* (December 22, 1960), pp. 15 ff.

Fournier, Fernando. "Trujillo: Dictador Tropical y Folklórico," *Combate,* IV (November-December, 1962), 27-31.

Galíndez, Jesús de. "Un reportaje sobre Santo Domingo," *Cuadernos Americanos,* LXXX (March-April, 1955), 37-56.

Gall, Norman. "How Trujillo Died," *The New Republic,* CXLVIII (April 13, 1963), 19-20.

Germani, Gino, and Kalman Silvert. "Politics, Social Structure, and Military Intervention in Latin America," *Archives Europeénes de Sociologie,* II (1961), 62-81.

Grant, Frances R. "Hemisphere Repudiates Trujillo," *Hemispherica,* IX (October, 1960), 1-2.

Growth, Alexander J. "The 'Isms' in Totalitarianism," *American Political Science Review,* LVIII (December, 1964), 888-901.

Gruening, Ernest. "Dictatorship in Santo Domingo: A Joint Concern," *The Nation,* CXXXVIII (May 23, 1934), 583-85.

Grullón, Ramón. "Antecedentes y perspectivas del Momento Político Dominicano," *Cuadernos Americanos,* CXX (January-February, 1962), 221-52.

Haigh, Roger M. "The Creation and Control of a Caudillo," *Hispanic American Historical Review,* XLIV (November, 1964), 481-90.

Halper, Sam. "The Dominican Upheaval," *The New Leader,* XLVIII (May 10, 1965), 3-4.

Hardy, Osgood. "Rafael Leonidas Trujillo Molina," *Pacific Historical Review,* XV (1946), 409-16.

Herrera Billini, Hipólito. "La era de Trujillo y la Jurisprudencia Dominicana," *Renovación,* No. 28 (January-February-March, 1961), pp. 66 ff.

Herring, Hubert. "Scandal of the Caribbean: The Dominican Republic,

Achievements and the Savagery of the Trujillo Dictatorship," *Current History*, XXXVIII (March, 1960), 140-43.

Hicks, Albert C. "Election Day in Santo Domingo," *The Nation*, CLXIV (May 10, 1947), 543-44.

Hoepelman, Armando. "Los estudiantes dominicanos: una juventud en peligro," *Combate*, IV (November-December, 1961), 65-71.

Hoepelman, Rafael César. "Las Armas para Ajusticiar a Trujillo Fueron Proporcionadas Por Wimpy," *La Nación* (December 7, 1961), p. 4.

Hook, Sidney. "The Hero in History" in Betty B. Burch (ed.), *Dictatorship and Totalitarianism* (Princeton: D. Van Nostrand, 1964).

"How One-man Rule Works on Doorstep of U.S.," *U.S. News and World Report*, XL (June 15, 1956), 76-80.

Humphreys, R. A. "Latin America: The Caudillo Tradition" in Michael Howard (ed.), *Soldiers and Governments* (Bloomington: Indiana University Press, 1959).

Huntington, Samuel P. "Political Development & Political Decay," *World Politics*, XVII (April, 1965), 386-430.

"La Iglesia en la cruzada redentora," *Ahora*, I (January 15, 1962), 18-19.

James, Daniel. "Castro, Trujillo, and Turmoil," *Saturday Evening Post*, CCXXXIX (January 16, 1960), 63 ff.

Jiménes-Grullón, Juan Isidro. "Estructura de Nuestra Oligarquía," *Listín Diario* (December 12, 1964), p. 7.

————. "Sentido Histórico de la Junio de 1959," *Listín Diario* (June 14, 1964).

————. "Trujillo: More Croesus than Caesar," *The Nation*, CLXXXIX (December 26, 1959), 485-86.

Kautsky, John H. "An Essay in the Politics of Development" in Kautsky (ed.), *Change in Underdeveloped Countries: Nationalism and Communism* (New York: John Wiley and Sons, 1962), pp. 3-119.

Kempton, Murray. "The Vault Cracks," *New York Post* (February 10, 1960). Reprinted in *New York Times* (February 11, 1960), p. 29.

Kent, George. "God and Trujillo: The Dominican Republic's Dictator," *Inter-American*, V (March, 1946), 14-16.

Kilson, Martin L. "Authoritarian and Single Party Tendencies in African Politics," *World Politics*, XVI (July, 1964), 558-75.

Linz, Juan J. "An Authoritarian Regime: Spain" in Erik Allardt and Yrjö Littunen (eds.), *Cleavages, Ideologies and Party Systems: Contributions to Comparative Political Sociology* (Helsinki: Transactions of the Westermarck Society, X, 1964), 291-342.

Lipset, Seymour M. "Some Social Requisites of Democracy: Economic Development and Political Legitimacy," *American Political Science Review*, LIII (March, 1960), 69-105.

Maas, Peter. "Boswell of the Jet Set," *Saturday Evening Post*, CCXXXVI (January 19, 1963), 28-31.

Molina Morillo, Rafael. "La Verdad Sobre la Muerte de Trujillo," *Unión Cívica*, I (December 9, 1961), 3.

Moore, Barrington, Jr. "Totalitarian Elements in Pre-Industrial Societies" in Moore (ed.), *Political Power and Social Theory* (Cambridge: Harvard University Press, 1958), pp. 30-88.

Mörner, Magnus. "Caudillos y Militares en la evolución hispanoamericana," *Journal of Inter-American Studies*, II (July, 1960), 295-310.

Nolasco, Carlos M. "Gesta contra la tiranía: complot de los sargentos técnicos A.S.D.," *El 1J4*, I (March 7, 1962), 2.

Ornes, Germán E. "El Imminente Ocaso de Trujillo," *La Prensa Libre* (April 21, 1961), p. 2-B.

Ornes, Germán E., and John McCarten. "Trujillo: Little Caesar on Our Own Front Porch," *Harper's Magazine,* CCXIII (December, 1956), 67-72.

"Otra vez desafía la iglesia dominicana la furia homicida de Rafael Trujillo," *El Dominicano Libre,* I (May, 1961), 1 ff.

Pepén Soto, Eladio Guaroa. "Gestas contra la tiranía: complot de los ex-policías de tránsito," *El 1J4,* I (March 17, 1962), 7.

Pulley, Raymond. "The United States and the Dominican Republic, 1933-1940: The High Price of Caribbean Stability," *Caribbean Studies,* V (October, 1965), 22-31.

"El régimen de Trujillo y los sindicatos," *Combate,* I (July-August, 1958), 53-54.

"Report on the Dominican Republic," *Latin American Report,* V (September, 1963), 2-23.

Rippy, J. Fred. "Dictatorship in Spanish America" in Guy Stanton Ford (ed.), *Dictatorship in the Modern World* (Minneapolis: University of Minnesota Press, 1935).

Romualdi, Serafino. "Trujillo on the Carpet," *Inter-American Labor Bulletin,* XI (March, 1960), 1.

Ross, Eduardo. "La obra cristiana del Benefactor de la Patria," *Renovación* (January-February-March, 1959), pp. 68 ff.

Sánchez, Fernando A., hijo. "Gesta contra la tiranía: complot de los sargentos técnicos A.M.D.," *El 1J4,* I (March 10, 1962), 6-7.

Shaw, Roger. "Ye Big Negrocrat," *Review of Reviews,* XCIII (June, 1936), 49-50.

Sinks, A. H. "Trujillo: Caribbean Dictator," *American Mercury,* V (October, 1940), 164-71.

Skilling, H. Gordon. "Interest Groups and Communist Politics," *World Politics,* XVIII (April, 1966), 435-51.

Slater, Jerome. "The United States, the Organization of American States, and the Dominican Republic, 1961-1963," *International Organization,* XVIII (Spring, 1964), 208-91.

"Sobre el Sindicato," *Unión Cívica,* I (November 15, 1961), 3.

Steinberg, David. "Dominican Republic: 28 Years of Stability," reprinted from the *New York Herald Tribune* in *A Look at the Dominican Republic,* III (June, 1958), 12-14.

"Swarthy Autocrat," *The Literary Digest,* CXXII (July 4, 1936), 13-14.

Szulc, Tad. "Uneasy Year 29 of the Trujillo Era," *New York Times Magazine* (August 29, 1959), pp. 9 ff.

Thomson, C. A. "Dictatorship in the Dominican Republic," *Foreign Policy Reports,* XII (April 15, 1936), 30-40.

Thorning, J. F. "The Dominican Republic: Twenty-five Years of Peace and Prosperity," *World Affairs,* CXVIII (Summer, 1955), 45-47.

Toribio Piantini, Pascasio A. "El progreso médico en la era de Trujillo," *Renovación,* No. 22 (July-August-September, 1959), pp. 71 ff.

Troncoso de la Concha, Manuel de J. "La clase media en Santo Domingo" in *Materiales para el estudio de la clase media en América Latina,* IV, (Washington: Unión Panamericana, 1950).

Trujillo, Flor de Oro. "My Life as Trujillo's Daughter," as told to Laura Berquist, *Look,* Parts I and II, XXIX (June 15, 1965), 44 ff. (June 29, 1965), 52 ff.

Tucker, Robert C. "The Dictator and Totalitarianism," *World Politics,* XVII (July, 1965), 555-83.

———. "Towards a Comparative Politics of Movement Regimes," *American Political Science Review,* LV (June, 1961), 281-89.

Villard, Oswald Garrison. "Men and Issues—Santo Domingo, 1937," *The Nation,* CXLIV (March 3, 1937), 323-24.

Weyl, Nathaniel. "Yanqui Corruption," *National Review,* XV (December 17, 1963), 530-31.

Whitney, Thomas P. "The U.S. and the Dominicans: What Will Be Done with the Trujillo Properties?" *The New Republic,* CXLVI (February 12, 1962), 13-14.

Wiarda, Howard J. "The Changing Political Orientation of the Church in the Dominican Republic," *A Journal of Church and State,* VII (Spring, 1965), 238-54.

————. "The Development of the Labor Movement in the Dominican Republic," *Inter-American Economic Affairs,* XX (Summer, 1966), 41-63.

————. "Dictatorship and Development: The Trujillo Regime and Its Implications," *Southwestern Social Science Quarterly,* XLVIII (March, 1968), 548-57.

————. "From Fragmentation to Disintegration: The Social and Political Effects of the Dominican Revolution," *América Latina,* X (April-June, 1967), 55-71.

————. "The Politics of Civil-Military Relations in the Dominican Republic," *Journal of Inter-American Studies,* VII (October, 1965), 465-84.

Wiles, Peter. "Comments on Tucker's 'Movement Regimes,'" *American Political Science Review,* LV (June, 1961), 290-93.

Wolfe, Bertram D. "The Durability of Soviet Despotism," *Commentary,* XXIV (August, 1957), 93-104.

Wright, Theodore P., Jr. "The United States and Latin American Dictatorship: The Case of the Dominican Republic," *Journal of International Affairs,* XIV (1960), 152-57.

Ziegler, Jean. "Santo Domingo: Feudo de Trujillo," *Cuadernos,* No. 46 [Paris] (January-February, 1961), pp. 98-102.

Books, Pamphlets, Reports, and Published Speeches

Adorno, T. W. *et al. The Authoritarian Personality* (New York: Harper, 1950).

Aiken, George D. *Report of a Study Mission to the Caribbean in December, 1957, to Committee on Foreign Relations, United States Senate* (Washington: Government Printing Office, 1958).

Alfau Durán, Vetilio J. *Trujillo and the Roman Catholic Church in Santo Domingo* (Ciudad Trujillo: Editora Handicap, 1960).

Almoína, José. *Yo fuí secretario de Trujillo* (Buenos Aires: Editora y Distribuidora del Plata, 1950).

Almond, Gabriel A., and James S. Coleman (eds.). *The Politics of the Developing Areas* (Princeton: Princeton University Press, 1960).

Alvárez Aybar, Ambrosio. *La política social de Trujillo* (Ciudad Trujillo: Impresora Dominicana, 1955).

Andrews, William G. (ed.). *European Political Institutions* (Princeton: D. Van Nostrand, 1962).

Arbaje Ramírez, Elías, and Luis Emilio Jourdain Heredia. *Gran desfile nacional, 16 agosto, 1958* (Ciudad Trujillo: Editora del Caribe, 1958).

Arendt, Hannah. *The Origins of Totalitarianism* (New York: Harcourt, Brace and Co., 1951).

Ariza, Sander. *Trujillo: The Man and His Country* (New York: Orlin Tremaine Company, 1939).

El atentado contra el señor presidente de la república de Venezuela, Rómulo Betancourt (Caracas: Grabados Nacionales, 1960).

Avelino, F. A. *Las Ideas Políticas en Santo Domingo* (Santo Domingo: Ed. Arte y Cine, 1966).

Aybar Mella, Salvador. *Génesis y evolución del estado* (Ciudad Trujillo: Editora Pol Hermanos, 1953).

Balaguer, Joaquín (ed.). *Discursos: panegíricos, política y educación, política internacional* (Madrid: Ediciones Acies, 1957).

————— (ed.). *El pensamiento vivo de Trujillo* (Ciudad Trujillo: Impresora Dominicana, 1955).

—————. *La realidad dominicana: semblanza de un país y de un régimen* (Buenos Aires: Imprenta Ferrari Hermanos, 1947).

Baquero, Gastón. *Cuban-Dominican Relations* (Ciudad Trujillo: Diario de la Marina, 1956).

Barbu, Zevedei. *Democracy and Dictatorship: Their Psychology and Patterns of Life* (New York: Grove Press, 1956).

Beras, Francisco Elpidio. *La autodeterminación del pueblo dominicano, extremo irreductible de la política exterior de Trujillo* (Ciudad Trujillo: Editora del Caribe, 1954).

Besault, Lawrence de. *President Trujillo: His Work and the Dominican Republic* (Washington: The Washington Publishing Company, 1936).

Bishop, Crawford M., and Anyda Marchant. *A Guide to the Law and Legal Literature of Cuba, the Dominican Republic, and Haiti* (Washington: Library of Congress, 1944).

Blandford, John B. *Public Administration in Latin America* (Washington: Pan American Union, 1955).

Bonet, Father Antonio. *La verdad sobre la era de Trujillo: refutación de "la Era" de Galíndez* (Managua, Nicaragua: n.p., 1957).

Bosch, Juan. *Crisis de la Democracia de América en la República Dominicana* (Mexico: B. Costa-Amic, 1964). Published in English as *The Unfinished Experiment: Democracy in the Dominican Republic* (New York: Praeger, 1965).

—————. *Trujillo: Causas de una tiranía sin ejemplo* (Caracas: Grabados Nacionales, 1959).

Brown, Bernard E. *New Directions in Comparative Politics* (Bombay: Asia Publishing House, 1962).

Burch, Betty B. (ed.). *Dictatorship and Totalitarianism: Selected Readings* (Princeton: D. Van Nostrand, 1964).

Castillo de Aza, Zenón. *Trujillo: benefactor de la iglesia* (Ciudad Trujillo: Editora del Caribe, 1955).

—————. *Trujillo y otros benefactores de la iglesia* (Ciudad Trujillo: Editora Handicap, 1961).

Castillo S., Benigno del. *Trujillo y su obra* (Ciudad Trujillo: Impresora Arte y Cine, 1955).

Castro, Donald S. *et al.* (eds.). *Statistical Abstract of Latin America: 1963* (University of California at Los Angeles: Center of Latin American Studies, 1964).

Castro Noboa, H. B. (ed.). *Antología poética trujillista* (Santiago: Editorial El Diario, 1946).

Cestero Burgos, Tulio. *Filosofía de un régimen* (Ciudad Trujillo: Editora Montalvo, 1951).

—————. *Trujillo y el cristianismo* (Ciudad Trujillo: Editorial Ateneo, n.d.).

Clark, James A. *The Church and the Crisis in the Dominican Republic* (Westminster, Md.: Newman Press, 1966).

Cooper, Page. *Sambumbia: A Discovery of the Dominican Republic: The Modern Hispaniola* (New York: The Caribbean Library, 1947).

204 BIBLIOGRAPHY

Crassweller, Robert D. *Trujillo: The Life and Times of a Caribbean Dictator* (New York: Macmillan, 1966).

Cruz y Berges, Frank. *Trujillo, gobierno y pueblo dominicano frente al comunismo internacional* (Ciudad Trujillo: Editora Babeque, 1957).

Cuatro Conferencias, Sentido y justificación de la resolución del Congreso Nacional que confirió el título de Benefactor de la Patria al Generalísimo Trujillo (Ciudad Trujillo: Impresora Dominicana, 1958).

Damiron, Rafael. *Nosotros: volumen publicado como contribución a la celebración del 25 aniversario de la era de Trujillo* (Ciudad Trujillo: Impresora Dominicana, 1955).

Davis, H. P. *Black Democracy: The Story of Haiti* (New York: Dodge Publishing Co., 1936).

De Grazia, Sebastian. *The Political Community: A Study of Anomie* (Chicago: University of Chicago Press, 1948).

Díaz-Balart, Rafael I. *Antitrujillismo y Solidaridad* (New York: n.p., 1959).

Díaz Ordónez, Virgilio. *In Praise of an Era* (Ciudad Trujillo: Editora del Caribe, 1955).

———. *La política exterior de Trujillo* (Ciudad Trujillo: Impresora Dominicana, 1955).

Dirección General de Estadística y Censos. *República Dominicana en Cifras* (Santo Domingo: Sección de Publicaciones, 1964).

Dominican Constitution of 1955 (Washington: Pan American Union, 1958).

Dreier, John C. *The Organization of American States and the Hemisphere Crisis* (New York: Harper and Row, 1962).

Ebenstein, William. *Totalitarianism: New Perspectives* (New York: Holt, Rinehart and Winston, Inc., 1962).

Eckstein, Harry, and David E. Apter. *Comparative Politics: A Reader* (New York: Free Press, 1963).

Eisenhower, Milton S. *The Wine Is Bitter: The United States in Latin America* (Garden City, N.Y.: Doubleday and Co., Inc., 1963).

Emerson, Rupert. *From Empire to Nation* (Cambridge: Harvard University Press, 1960).

Espaillat, Arturo. *Trujillo: The Last Caesar* (Chicago: Henry Regnery, 1963).

Finer, Samuel E. *The Man on Horseback* (London: Pall Mall Press, 1962).

Flores, Dario. *Evolución del periodismo en la era de Trujillo* (Santiago: Imprenta La Información, 1956).

Franco, Franklin J. *Republica Dominicana: Clases, Crisis y Comandos* (Havana: Casa de las Américas, 1966).

Friedrich, Carl J., and Zbigniew Brzezinski. *Totalitarian Dictatorship and Autocracy* (New York: Praeger, 1962).

Galíndez, Jesús de. *La era de Trujillo* (Santiago de Chile: Editorial del Pacífico, 1956).

Gallegos, Gerardo. *Trujillo en la historia: Veinticinco años en la ruta de un glorioso destino* (Ciudad Trujillo: Editora del Caribe, 1956).

García Bonnelly, Juan Elises. *Las obras públicas en la era de Trujillo* (Ciudad Trujillo: Impresora Dominicana, 1955).

García Godoy, Emilio. *Glimpses of our Democracy* (Ciudad Trujillo: Editora del Caribe, 1951).

Garrido, Víctor. *Trujillo: Patron of Sports* (Ciudad Trujillo: Official publication, 1959).

Goldwert, Marvin. *The Constabulary in the Dominican Republic: Progeny and Legacy of United States Intervention* (Gainesville: University of Florida Press, 1962).

Gómez, R. A. *Government and Politics in Latin America* (New York: Random House, 1960).

González Blanco, Pedro. *Algunas observaciones sobre la política del Generalísimo Trujillo* (Madrid: Impresora Gráficas Uguina, 1936).

————. *Decadencia y liberación de la economía dominicana* (Mexico: Ediciones Rex, 1946).

————. *La era de Trujillo* (Ciudad Trujillo: Editora del Caribe, 1955).

————. *Trujillo: The Rebirth of a Nation* (Ciudad Trujillo: Editora del Caribe, 1953).

González Herrer, Julio. *Trujillo: genio político* (Ciudad Trujillo: Editora del Caribe, 1956).

Guardia Universitaria, "Presidente Trujillo," *Proclamación del Partido Trujillista por la Guardia Universitaria, en la noche del 14 de Noviembre de 1940* (Ciudad Trujillo: Imprenta La Opinión, 1940).

Guerard, Albert J. *The Exiles* (New York: Macmillan, 1962).

Guerrero Pichardo, Gustavo. *La Muerte de 2 Dictadores y la del Presidente Cáceres* (Santo Domingo: Editorial La Nación, 1962).

Guía Eclesiástica de la República Dominicana (Santo Domingo: Escuela Salesiana de Artes y Oficios "María Auxiliadora," 1963).

Hamill, Hugh M., Jr. (ed.). *Dictatorship in Spanish America* (New York: Knopf, 1965).

Hanke, Lewis. *The First Social Experiments in America* (Cambridge: Harvard University Press, 1935).

Harding, Bertita. *The Land Columbus Loved: The Dominican Republic* (New York: Coward-McCann, 1949).

Henríquez, Enrique Apolinar. *Episodios Imperialistas* (Ciudad Trujillo: Editora Montalvo, 1958).

Henríquez, Noel. *La verdad sobre Trujillo: Capítulos que se le olvidaron a Galíndez* (Havana: Imprenta Económica en General, S.A., 1959).

Henríquez Ureña, Max. *Los Estados Unidos y la República Dominicana: la verdad de los hechos conprobada por datos y documentos oficiales* (Havana: Imprenta "El Siglo XX," 1919).

Here Is Our Answer. A summary of the comments of the Government of the Dominican Republic on the June 6, 1960 Report of the Inter-American Peace Committee (Ciudad Trujillo: Official publication, 1960).

Herraiz, Ismael. *Trujillo dentro de la historia* (Madrid: Ediciones Acies, 1957).

Herrera Báez, Porfirio. *Discurso pronunciado por el presidente del Senado y de la Assamblea Nacional Lcdo. Porfirio Herrera, el 16 de agosto de 1957, en el acto de recibir el juramento de sus excelencias, el general Héctor B. Trujillo Molina y Dr. Joaquín Balaguer, como presidente y vicepresidente de la República Dominicana respectivamente, para el período de gobierno de 1957 a 1962.* (Ciudad Trujillo: Editora Arte y Cine, 1957).

————. *A Tribute to Generalissimo Dr. Rafael L. Trujillo Molina by the City of New Orleans.* Address delivered on the dedication of the "Trujillo Drive" and "Trujillo Park" in New Orleans (Ciudad Trujillo: Official publication, 1956).

Herring, Hubert. *A History of Latin America: From the Beginnings to the Present* (New York: Knopf, 1957).

Hicks, Albert C. *Blood in the Streets: The Life and Rule of Trujillo* (New York: Creative Age Press, 1956).

Hoepelman, Antonio. *Era y obra de Trujillo* (Ciudad Trujillo: Impresora Dominicana, 1954).

Hoepelman, Antonio. *Páginas Dominicanas de historia contemporánea* (Ciudad Trujillo: Impresora Dominicana, 1951).

Homenaje de los estudiantes universitarios al Generalísimo Trujillo (Ciudad Trujillo: Editora del Caribe, 1957).

Horowitz, Irving Louis. *Three Worlds of Development: The Theory and Practice of International Stratification* (New York: Oxford University Press, 1966).

Humphreys, Robin A. *The Evolution of Modern Latin America* (New York: Oxford University Press, 1964).

Incháustegui Cabral, Joaquín Marino. *La República Dominicana de hoy* (Ciudad Trujillo: Impresora y Grabados "Cosmopolita," 1938).

Instituto Trujilloiano. *Mensaje a los intelectuales del mundo libre* (Ciudad Trujillo: Official publication, 1955).

Jane's Fighting Ships (London: Jane's Fighting Ships Publishing Co., 1958).

Jiménes-Grullón, Juan Isidro. *Una Gestapo en América* (La Habana: Editorial LEX, 1946).

————. *La República Dominicana: Una Ficción* (Mérida, Venezeula: Talleres Gráficos Universitarios, 1965).

Jiménez, Ramón Emilio. *Biografía de Trujillo* (Ciudad Trujillo: Editora del Caribe, 1955).

————. *Trujillo y la paz* (Ciudad Trujillo: Impresora Dominicana, 1952).

Johnson, John J. *Political Change in Latin America: The Emergence of the Middle Sectors* (Stanford: Stanford University Press, 1958).

Jorrín, Miguel. *Governments of Latin America* (New York: D. Van Nostrand, 1953).

Knight, Melvin Moses. *The Americans in Santo Domingo* (New York: Vanguard Press, 1928).

Kornhauser, William. *The Politics of Mass Society* (New York: Free Press of Glencoe, 1959).

Krehm, William. *Democracias y tiranías en el Caribe* (Havana: Editora Popular de Cuba y del Caribe, 1960).

Kurzman, Dan. *Santo Domingo: Revolt of the Damned* (New York: Putnam, 1965).

Lacay Polanco, Ramón. *Perfiles de Trujillo* (Ciudad Trujillo: Editorial Atenas, 1956).

Lamarche, Carlos M. *La democracia en función de éxito: la democracia frente al comunismo* (Ciudad Trujillo: Editora del Caribe, 1951).

Langa Mota, Luis. *Trujillo ante los representantes diplomáticos* (Ciudad Trujillo: Editora del Caribe, 1957).

La Palombara, Joseph, and Myron Weiner (eds.). *Political Parties and Political Development* (Princeton: Princeton University Press, 1966).

Lieuwen, Edwin. *Arms and Politics in Latin America* (New York: Praeger, 1960).

Lipset, Seymour M. *Political Man: The Social Basis of Politics* (Garden City, New York: Doubleday, 1960).

Loewenstein, Karl. *Political Power and the Governmental Process* (Chicago: University of Chicago Press, 1957).

Long, George S. *El caso Gerry Murphy y la República Dominicana* (Ciudad Trujillo: Official publication, 1957).

————. *Desenmascarando el comunismo*. Nueva interpretación del honorable George S. Long de Louisiana, en la Cámara de Representantes de los Estados Unidos (Ciudad Trujillo: Official publication, 1957).

López, Nicolás F. *Algo sobre la República Dominicana* (Quito, Ecuador: Editorial Colon, 1948).

Lowenthal, Abraham. *Hydraulic Resource Development in the Dominican Republic: An Historical Review* (Santiago de los Caballeros, Dominican Republic: Asociación para el Desarrollo, Inc., 1965).

McAlister, L. N. *The "Fuero Militar" in New Spain, 1764-1800* (Gainesville: University of Florida Press, 1957).

MacDonald, Austin. *Latin American Politics and Government* (New York: Thomas Y. Crowell, 1949).

Machado Báez, Manuel Arturo. *La dominicanización fronteriza* (Ciudad Trujillo: Impresora Dominicana, 1955).

Marion, Georges. *For the Reestablishment of Truth: The Dominican Republic Today* (Ciudad Trujillo: Official publication, 1956).

Marrero Aristy, Ramón. *Trujillo: síntesis de su vida y de su obra* (Ciudad Trujillo: Impresora Dominicana, 1953).

Martin, John Bartlow. *Overtaken by Events: The Dominican Republic From the Fall of Trujillo to the Civil War* (Garden City, New Jersey: Doubleday, 1966).

Martínez, Servio Tulio. *Un Trujillo sigue la grandiosa obra de Trujillo* (Ciudad Trujillo: Imprenta Hernández, 1957).

Martínez H., Ignacio. *El pueblo dominicano: el fervor católico que alienta su alma, y su protección que la Era de Trujillo le ha dado a la Iglesia dominicana* (Ciudad Trujillo: Editora del Caribe, 1957).

Mecham, J. Lloyd. *Church and State in Latin America: A History of Politico-Ecclesiastical Relations* (Chapel Hill: University of North Carolina Press, 1934).

―――. *A Survey of United States-Latin American Relations* (Boston: Houghton-Mifflin, 1965).

―――. *The United States and Inter-American Security: 1889-1960* (Austin: University of Texas Press, 1961).

Mejía, Luis, F. *De Lilís a Trujillo: Historia Contemporánea de la República Dominicana* (Caracas: Editorial Elite, 1944).

Mejía Ricart, Marcio Antonio. *Las clases sociales en Santo Domingo* (Ciudad Trujillo: Libería Dominicana, 1953).

Meyreles Soler, Rafael. *De pies sobre la cumbre enhiesta de la gloria: vida y verdad de un patriotismo inmaculado* (Ciudad Trujillo: n.p., 1955).

Miolán, Angel. *La Revolución Social Frente a la Tiranía de Trujillo* (Mexico, 1938).

Monclús, Miguel Angel. *El Caudillismo en la República Dominicana* (Ciudad Trujillo: Impresora Dominicana, 1948).

Moore, Barrington, Jr. *Social Origins of Dictatorship and Democracy: Lord and Peasant in the Making of the Modern World* (Boston: Beacon Press, 1966).

Morales Castillo, Antonio. *Me encontrarán de pie* (Ciudad Trujillo: Editora Montalvo, 1953).

Morrison, de Lesseps S. *Latin American Mission: An Adventure in Hemispheric Diplomacy* (New York: Simon and Schuster, 1965).

Mota, Fabio A. *Un estadista de América: obra socio-política de Trujillo— filosofía, historia, estadística* (Ciudad Trujillo: Editora Montalvo, 1945).

Nanita, Abelardo R. *La era de Trujillo* (Ciudad Trujillo: Impresora Dominicana, 1955).

―――. *Trujillo* (Ciudad Trujillo: Impresora Dominicana, 5th ed., 1951).

―――. *Trujillo: A Full-Size Portrait*, trans. M. A. Moore (Santiago: Editorial El Diario, 1939).

National Congress. *Declaration by the National Congress of the Dominican Republic in Joint Session, March 16, 1960* (Ciudad Trujillo: n.p., 1960).

Needler, Martin C. *Latin American Politics in Perspective* (New York: D. Van Nostrand, 1963).

Neumann, Sigmund. *Permanent Revolution: The Total State in a World at War* (New York: Harper, 1942).

Nolte, Ernst. *Der Faschismus in seiner Epoche* (Munich: Piper Verlag, 1963). Republished in English as *Three Faces of Fascism* (New York: Holt, Rinehart, and Winston, 1966).

Ojeda, José. *Ayer y hoy* (Ciudad Trujillo: Official publication, 1956).

Organization of American States. *Report of the Inter-American Peace Committee on the Case Presented by Venezuela* (Washington: Pan American Union, June 7, 1960).

———. *Report on the Situation Regarding Human Rights in the Dominican Republic* (Washington: Pan American Union, 1962).

———. *Report Submitted to the Committee of the Council, Acting Provisionally as Organ of Consultation in the Case Presented by Venezuela, to Comply with the Provisions of the Third Paragraph of the Resolution of July 8, 1960* (Washington: Pan American Union, 1960).

———. *Report of the Technical Assistance Mission of the Organization of American States to the Dominican Republic on Electoral Matters* (Washington: Pan American Union, 1961).

———. *Sixth Meeting of Consultation of Ministers of Foreign Affairs Serving as Organ of Consultation in Application of the Inter-American Treaty of Reciprocal Assistance, San José, Costa Rica, August 16-21, 1960. Final Act* (Washington: Pan American Union, 1960).

———. *Special Committee to Carry Out the Mandate Received By the Council Pursuant to Resolution I of the Sixth Meeting of Consultation of Ministers of Foreign Affairs.* First Report of the Special Committee (Washington: Pan American Union, 1960).

Ornes, Germán. *The Other Side of the Coin: A Collection of Articles* (Washington: Embassy of the Dominican Republic, 1958).

———. *Trujillo, Brownell, and Braden* (Ciudad Trujillo: n.p. 1953).

———. *Trujillo Buys—He Does Not Despoil* (Ciudad Trujillo: Editora del Caribe, 1955).

———. *Trujillo: Little Caesar of the Caribbean* (New York: Thomas Nelson and Sons, 1958).

Ortiz, S. Salvador. *Dominican Taxation During the Trujillo Era* (Ciudad Trujillo: Editora del Caribe, 1953).

Ortiz Alvárez, Horacio. *Nuestra abecedario de año nuevo: era del benefactor de la patria y padre de la patria nueva* (Ciudad Trujillo: Imprenta Compostela, 1959).

———. *La obra del Generalisimo Doctor Trujillo en el Ejército Nacional: Observaciones Militares* (Ciudad Trujillo: Tipografía Cambier, 1937).

Osorio Lizaraza, José Antonio. *Así es Trujillo* (Buenos Aires: Artes Gráficas, 1958).

———. *El bacilo de Marx* (Ciudad Trujillo: Editora La Nación, 1959).

———. *Germen y proceso del antitrujillismo en América* (Santiago de Chile: Imprenta Colombia, 1956).

———. *The Illumined Island*, trans. James I. Nolan (Mexico: Ediciones Offset Continente, 1947).

Pacheco, Armando Oscar. *La obra educativa de Trujillo* (Ciudad Trujillo: Impresora Dominicana, 1955).

Pagán Perdomo, Dato. *Por qué lucha el pueblo dominicano: análisis del fenómeno dictatorial en América Latina* (Caracas: Imprenta Caribe, 1959).

Palmer, Bruce. *Hecatomb* (New York: Simon and Schuster, 1965).

Parsons, Talcott, and Edward Shils (eds.). *Toward a General Theory of Action* (New York: Harper, 1962).

Partido Dominicano. *Acción y obra del Partido Dominicano* (Ciudad Trujillo: sus publicaciones, 1956).

———. *Declaración de Principios y Estatutos del Partido Dominicano* (Ciudad Trujillo: Editora Montalvo, 1945).

Partido Revolucionario Dominicano y Movimiento Popular Dominicano. *Libertad de Prensa para Santo Domingo* (Havana: Editorial La Verdad, 1956).

Patin Maceo, Manuel Antonio. *Dominicanismo* (Ciudad Trujillo: Librería Dominicana, 1947).

Pavia Franco, Alberto. *Two Letters to Mr. Charles O. Porter* (Mexico: n.p., 1960).

Payne, Stanley G. *Falange: A History of Spanish Fascism* (Stanford: Stanford University Press, 1961).

Peña Batlle, Manuel Arturo. *Contribución a una campaña* (Cuatro discursos políticos) (Santiago: Editorial El Diario, 1942).

———. *Política de Trujillo* (Ciudad Trujillo: Impresora Dominicana, 1954).

Peña Castillo, Ruben de. *Trujillo visto por un estudiante universitario* (Ciudad Trujillo: Impresora Arte y Cine, 1959).

Peña Roulet, Rafael. *Raiz y escencia del Partido Dominicano* (Ciudad Trujillo: Impresora Dominicana, 1954).

Peña Santander, Santiago de. *Canto de fe universal al benefactor de la patria* (Ciudad Trujillo: Editora del Caribe, 1955).

———. *Trujillo: adalid de la construcción social en Santo Domingo, 1844-1952* (Ciudad Trujillo: Editorial Babeque, 1957).

Penson, José F. *El Partido Dominicano* (Ciudad Trujillo: Imprenta Arte y Cine, 1958).

Ponzini Hernández, Juan. *Las acusaciones contra Trujillo: Assault by Slander* (Ciudad Trujillo: Sociedad Dominicana de Prensa, 1956).

Pepén, Juan F. *La Cruz señala el camino: influencia de la iglesia en la formación y conservación de la nacionalidad dominicana* (Ciudad Trujillo: Editorial Duarte, 1954).

Pérez, Carlos Federico. *Transcendencia histórica de una fecha* (Ciudad Trujillo: Editora del Caribe, 1957).

Pérez, Manuel Ramón. *Decimas sobre la era de Trujillo* (Ciudad Trujillo: Editora Montalvo, 1955).

Pérez Ortiz, R. *Gestas Heróicas* (Ciudad Trujillo: Imprenta Rincón, 1952).

Perkins, Dexter. *La Cuestión de Santo Domingo, 1849-1865* (Ciudad Trujillo: Editora Montalvo, 1955).

Pflaum, Irving P. *Area of Decision: Latin America in Crisis* (Englewood Cliffs, N.J.: Prentice Hall, 1964).

Pheiffer, William T. *Address of Hon. William T. Pheiffer, Ambassador of the United States of America to the Dominican Republic, at the Luncheon Meeting of the Miami Beach Rotary Club on March 6, 1956* (Ciudad Trujillo: Impresora Dominicana, 1956).

Pierson, William W., and Federico G. Gil. *Government and Politics of Latin America* (New York: McGraw Hill, 1957).

Porter, Charles, and Robert J. Alexander. *The Struggle for Democracy in Latin America* (New York: Macmillan, 1960).

Puigsubira-Menino, Juan Enrique. *Pensamientos en la lucha contra la tiranía* (Santo Domingo: Editora Montalvo, 1963).

Pye, Lucian W. *Aspects of Political Development* (Boston: Little, Brown and Co., 1965).

Resolución del claustro universitario de la Universidad de Santo Domingo (Ciudad Trujillo: Official publication, 1959).

Rivista diplomática. Edición extraordinaria dedicada a la juramentación del Excmo. Sr. General Héctor B. Trujillo Molina, Presidente de la Republica Dominicana (Havana: Official publication, 1957).

Roberts, T. D., *et al. Area Handbook for the Dominican Republic* (Washington: Foreign Area Studies, American University, 1966).

Rodman, Selden. *Quisqueya: A History of the Dominican Republic* (Seattle: University of Washington Press, 1964).

Rodríquez Demorizi, Emilio. *Cronología de Trujillo* (Ciudad Trujillo: Impresora Dominicana, 1955).

————. *La dificultad de gobernar* (Ciudad Trujillo: Impresora Dominicana, 1955).

————. *De política dominicana-americana: discurso ante la estatua de Cordell Hull* (Ciudad Trujillo: Editora Montalvo, 1957).

————. *Trujillo and Cordell Hull* (Ciudad Trujillo: Editora del Caribe, 1956).

————. *Trujillo y las aspiraciones dominicanas: discurso en Santiago* (Ciudad Trujillo: Editora Montalvo, 1957).

————. *United States Military Intervention* (Ciudad Trujillo: Official publication, 1958).

Román, Miguel Alberto. *Trujillo: el libertador dominicano* (Ciudad Trujillo: Editora del Caribe, 1956).

Ross, Eduardo. *La obra cristiana del benefactor de la patria* (Ciudad Trujillo: Editora del Caribe, 1959).

Rymer K., Roberto. *La excelsitud del verbo: algo de lo que me enseña mi maestro* (Ciudad Trujillo: Imprenta Hernandez, 1958).

Sánchez Cabral, Eduardo. *De la clandestinidad* (Santo Domingo: n.p. 1962).

————. *Los Mártires de Hacienda María* (Santo Domingo: Editora del Caribe, 1962).

Santana, Julio Cesar. *La mujer dominicana en la "Era de Trujillo"* (San Pedro de Macorís, Dominican Republic: Impresora La Orla, 1956).

Schoenrich, Otto. *Santo Domingo: A Country with a Future* (New York: Macmillan, 1918).

Secretaría de Educación Pública y Bellas Artes. *Trujillo: restaurador de la independencia financiera de la República Dominicana.* Breve historia politica-financiera de la República (Ciudad Trujillo: Official publication, 1941).

Secretaría de Estado de la Presidencia. *The political-economical and financial work of his Excellency, President Trujillo.* Brief summary description of the external and internal debts of the country, from 1930-46, and of the execution of the national budget at the same time (Ciudad Trujillo: Official publication, 1947).

Secretaría de Relaciones Exteriores. *Nuestra actitud* (Ciudad Trujillo: Official publication, 1944).

Slater, Jerome. *The OAS and United States Foreign Policy* (Columbus: Ohio State University Press, 1967).

Sociedad Dominicana de Prensa. *The American People Condemn a Move Against a Caribbean Friend* (Ciudad Trujillo: Official publication, 1960).

————. *Germán Ornes: A Self Portrait* (Ciudad Trujillo: Official publication, 1958).

————. *Timesman Edward C. Burks—Deliberate Misrepresentation* (Ciudad Trujillo: Official publication, 1960).

————. *La traición de Germán Ornes* (Ciudad Trujillo: Official publication, 1956).

————. *Trujillo and the Communist Threat* (Ciudad Trujillo: Official publication, 1956).

Soriano, Germán. *El Liberato de Trujillo en la Universidad* (Ciudad Trujillo: Impresora Dominicana, 1953).

————. *Trujillo y el mundo en que vivimos* (Ciudad Trujillo: Impresora Dominicana, 1954).

Sosa, Andres Nicolas. *Enfoques de la obra de Trujillo* (Ciudad Trujillo: n.p., 1958).

Stefanich, Blas. *Comunismo sin máscaro* (Ciudad Trujillo: Official publication, 1957).

Steinberg, S. H. (ed.). *The Statesman's Year Book, 1961-1962* (New York: St. Martin's Press, 1961).

Stokes, William S. *Latin American Politics* (New York: Thomas Y. Crowell, 1959).

Suárez Vásquez, Ramón. *Anecdotario épico del Generalísimo Trujillo* (Ciudad Trujillo: Secretaría del Estado de Educación y Bellas Artes, 1957).

Suncar Chevalier. Manuel E. (ed.). *Album simbólico*. Homenaje de los poetas dominicanos al generalísimo Dr. Rafael L. Trujillo Molina, padre de la patria nueva en la vigesimoquinto aniversario de la era de Trujillo (Ciudad Trujillo: Ateneo Dominicano, 1957).

Szulc, Tad. *Twilight of the Tyrants* (New York: Henry Holt, 1959).

————. *The Winds of Revolution: Latin America Today—and Tomorrow* (New York: Praeger, 1965).

Tapia Brea, Manuel. *Reseña de un viaje trinfal* (Ciudad Trujillo: Editora del Caribe, 1954).

Tejeda Díaz, Teodoro. *Yo investigue la muerte de Trujillo* (Barcelona: Plaze and Janes, S.A., 1964).

Tolentino Rojas, Vicente. *This Is the Dominican Republic* (New York: Consulate General of the Dominican Republic, 1954).

Trujillo, Hector B. *Discursos y mensajes, 1952-1957* (Madrid: n.p., 1957).

————. *Strengthening Relations Between the Dominican Republic and the United States* (Washington: Embajada de la República Dominicana, 1958).

Trujillo, Rafael. *Address at St. John the Baptist Fair* (Ciudad Trujillo: Editora Handicap, 1960).

————. *Address by Generalissimo Rafael L.. Trujillo at the Cathedral of Santiago de los Caballeros, May 17, 1960* (Ciudad Trujillo: Dominican Press Society, 1960).

————. *Address delivered at San Juan de la Maguana on the 22nd December 1959 on occasion of the 104th anniversary of the Battle of Santomé* (Ciudad Trujillo: Official publication, 1960).

————. *Address to the Congress of the Dominican Republic*, trans. Otto Vega (Ciudad Trujillo: Official publication, 1952).

————. *The Basic Policies of a Regime* (Ciudad Trujillo: Editora del Caribe, 1960).

————. *Discurso pronunciado por el Excmo. Sr. Pres. de la República Dr. Rafael L. Trujillo Molina al inaugurar el Barrio de Mejoramiento Social el dia 20 de abril de 1946* (Ciudad Trujillo: Editora Montalvo, 1946).

————. *Discurso pronunciado por el Generalísimo Dr. Rafael Leonidas Trujillo Molina, Benefactor de la patria y padre de la patria nueva, declinando su postulación como candidato del partido dominicano a la presidencia de la república en los comicios del 1957* (Ciudad Trujillo: Impresora Dominicana, 1956).

————. *Discurso pronunciado por Rafael Trujillo en el acto de inauguración del banco agricola e hipotecario* (Ciudad Trujillo: Editora Luis Sánchez Adujar, 1945).

———. *Discurso pronunciado por Su Excelencia El Generalísimo Doctor Rafael L. Trujillo M. al recibir el Diploma de Honor conferidole por la Asociación Médica Panamericana* (Ciudad Trujillo: Official publication, 1954).

———. *Discursos, Mensajes y Proclamas* (Ciudad Trujillo: Official publication, 1938).

———. *Discursos, Mensajes y Proclamas* (Santiago: Editorial El Diario, 1946).

———. *Discursos, Mensajes y Proclamas: Seleciones 1952-1957.* (Madrid: Ediciones Acies, 1957).

———. *Dos discursos transcendentales sobre política exterior* (Ciudad Trujillo: Editora del Caribe, 1954).

———. *The Evolution of Democracy in Santo Domingo*, trans. Otto Vega (Ciudad Trujillo: Official publication, 1950).

———. *Latin Unity: Two Momentous Addresses* (Ciudad Trujillo: Editora del Caribe, 1955).

———. *Message Declining to be a Candidate for President* (Ciudad Trujillo: Editora del Caribe, 1951).

———. *La nueva patria dominicana.* Recopilación de discursos, mensajes, y memorias del Generalísimo Rafael Trujillo Molina, Presidente de la República Dominicana, Benefactor de la Patria, durante el cuatriceneo de 1930 a 1934 (Santo Domingo: Official publication, 1934).

———. *Obras* (Ciudad Trujillo: Editora Montalvo, 1956).

———. *The Other Side of the Galíndez Case* (New York: Dominican Republic Cultural Society of New York, 1956).

———. *Patriotismo y educación* (Ciudad Trujillo: Editora del Caribe, 1960).

———. *Position of the Dominican Government.* Two letters and some declarations (Ciudad Trujillo: Editora La Nacion, 1945).

———. *President Trujillo Molina Declines to be a Candidate for Reelection* (Ciudad Trujillo: Official publication, January 8, 1938).

———. *Reajuste de la deuda externa* (Santiago: Editorial El Diario, 1937).

———. *Reajuste de la deuda externa* (Ciudad Trujillo: Editora del Caribe, 1959).

———. *Trujillo Speaks.* A series of four articles expressly written for and published by the *Miami Herald* on April 3-6, 1960 (Ciudad Trujillo: Official publication, 1960).

Trujillo and the Church. Statements by Prominent Roman Catholics (Ciudad Trujillo: Official publication, 1956).

Trujillo, un viaje de reafirmaciones. La fe en el vaticano, La hispanidad en la madre patria (Ciudad Trujillo: Editora del Caribe, 1954).

United Nations. *Demographic Yearbook* (1961).

———. *Statistical Yearbook* (1960).

Ureña, Buenaventura. *Cosas de Antaño* (Ciudad Trujillo: Editora del Caribe, 1955).

Uribe, Max. *Función del Partido Dominicano en la era de Trujillo* (Ciudad Trujillo: Impresora Dominicana, 1961).

Valldeperes, Manuel. *Acción y pensamiento de Trujillo* (Ciudad Trujillo: Editora del Caribe, 1955).

Varney, Harold Lord. *La conjura comunista en el Caribe* (Ciudad Trujillo: Official publication, 1957).

———. *Señales de peligro en el Caribe* (New York: Centro Informativo de la República Dominicana, 1956).

Vega, Augusto. *Civismo y decisión, ensayo político-internacional: anticomu-*

nismo y doctrina económica de Trujillo triunfan en el exterior (Ciudad Trujillo: Impresora Dominicana, 1955).

Vega y Pagan, Ernesto. *Historia de las Fuerzas Armadas.* 2 vols. (Ciudad Trujillo: Impresora Dominicana, 1955).

————. *Military Biography of Generalissimo Rafael Leonidad Trujillo Molina, Commander in Chief of the Armed Forces,* trans. Ida Espaillat (Ciudad Trujillo: Editorial Atenas, 1956).

————. *Sintesis Histórica de la Guardia Dominicana* (Ciudad Trujillo: Editorial Atenas, 1953).

Vegueriza, Teodoro. *Acción y doctrina de un régimen político,* 2nd ed. (Ciudad Trujillo: Editora del Caribe, 1959).

————. *Permanencia trujillista en el continente americano* (Ciudad Trujillo: Editora del Caribe, 1957).

Verges Vidal, Pedro L. *Biografía del General Héctor B. Trujillo M.* (Ciudad Trujillo: Editora del Caribe, 1957).

———— *Dos biografías: Duarte y Trujillo* (Ciudad Trujillo: Impresora Dominicana, 1954).

————. *Hitos de la carrera militar del Generalísimo Trujillo* (Ciudad Trujillo: Editora del Caribe, 1957).

————. *Trujillo: procer anticomunista* (Ciudad Trujillo: Editora del Caribe, 1958).

von der Mehden, Fred R. *Politics of the Developing Nations* (Englewood Cliffs, New Jersey: Prentice-Hall, 1964).

Walker, Stanley. *Journey Toward the Sunlight: A Story of the Dominican Republic and Its People* (New York: Caribbean Library, 1947).

Wallich, Henry C., and Robert Tiffin. *Monetary and Banking Legislation of the Dominican Republic* (New York: Federal Reserve Bank, 1953).

Welles, Sumner. *Naboth's Vineyard: The Dominican Republic, 1844-1924.* 2 vols. (New York: Payson & Clarke, Ltd., 1928).

White, John W. *The Dominican Republic of Today* (Ciudad Trujillo: La Nación, 1945).

————. *The Land Columbus Loved* (Ciudad Trujillo: Editora Montalvo, 1945).

White Book of Communism in the Dominican Republic (Ciudad Trujillo: Editora del Caribe, 1958).

Wiarda, Howard J. *The Aftermath of the Trujillo Dictatorship: The Emergence of a Pluralist Political System in the Dominican Republic* (Ann Arbor: University Microfilms, 1967).

————. (ed.) *Dominican Republic: Election Factbook* (Washington: Institute for the Comparative Study of Political Systems, 1966).

Wipfler, William Louis. *The Churches of the Dominican Republic in the Light of History* (Cuernavaca, Mexico: Centro Intercultural de Documentación, 1966).

Wise, George S. *Caudillo: A Portrait of Antonio Guzmán Blanco* (New York: Columbia University Press, 1951).

Wittfogel, Karl. *Oriental Despotism* (New Haven: Yale University Press, 1957).

World Horizon Reports. *Basic Ecclesiastical Statistics for Latin America,* 1960.

Zinsser, Hans. *Rats, Lice, and History* (New York: Blue Ribbon Books, Inc., 1935).

Book Reviews

Alexander, Robert J. Review of Juan Bosch, *Trujillo: Causas de una tiranía sin ejemplo* in *Journal of Inter-American Studies*, III (April, 1961), 292.
Hallett, Robert M. Review of Germán Ornes, *Trujillo: Little Caesar of the Caribbean* in *Christian Science Monitor* (July 1, 1958), p. 9.
Kantor, Harry. Review of Rafael Trujillo, *The Basic Policies of a Regime* in *Hispanic American Historical Review*, XLII (May, 1962), 281-82.
Wiarda, Howard J. Review of Bruce Palmer, *Hecatomb* in *Palm Beach Post Times* (July 25, 1965), p. F-9.

Unpublished Studies

Atkins, George P. "The United States and the Dominican Republic During the Era of Trujillo," dissertation, American University, 1966.
Bautista y de Oleo, Narciso Elio. "La protección de la clase obrera en la era de Trujillo," dissertation, University of Santo Domingo, 1961.
Bernholz, Herman. "Survey of the Dominican Administration," study, United States Agency for International Development, 1963.
Bosch, Juan. "Un Camino para el Pueblo Dominicano," San José, Costa Rica, mimeographed, June 1, 1961.
"Informe sobre la República Dominicana," unsigned typed carbon copy, University of Puerto Rico, 1959.
Kantor, Harry. "The Destruction of Trujillo's Empire," mimeographed copy of lecture delivered to Peace Corps, Seattle, Washington, 1962.
MacMichael, David C. "The United States and the Dominican Republic, 1871-1940: A Cycle in Caribbean Diplomacy," dissertation, University of Oregon, 1964.
Martínez Hiciano, Rafael. "La creación de las fuerzas armadas y la policía nacional: Obra de Trujillo," dissertation, University of Santo Domingo, 1961.
Nyomarkay, Joseph. "Classes and Totalitarian Movements: A Critique of S. M. Lipset's Class Interpretation of the German National Socialist Movement." Paper delivered at the American Political Science Association Convention, Washington, D.C., 1962.
Pimental Castro, Lázaro Euclides. "Evolución de los sindicatos en la República," dissertation, University of Santo Domingo, 1961.

Periodicals

El Caribe, 1948-61
El 1J4, 1961-62
Department of State Bulletin, selectively
Fides, 1961-64
Foreign Commerce Weekly, selectively
Gaceta Oficial, selectively
Hispanic American Report, 1948-61
Inter-American Labor Bulletin, 1950-64
La Información, selectively
Listín Diario, selectively

A Look at the Dominican Republic, 1935-61
Miami Herald, selectively
La Nación, selectively
New York Times, 1930-61
Official Bulletin of the Partido Revolucionario Dominicano, selectively
Renovación, 1953-61
La República [Puerto Rico], selectively
Unión Cívica, 1961-62
United Nations *Monthly Bulletin of Statistics*, selectively

Index

215